Praise for *Pure*

"Eye-opening . . . compelling . . . For those who seek spiritual community without gender bias, Klein offers empathy and new choices."

—*BookPage*

"Linda Kay Klein's *Pure* is an important book for this moment in history, as women come to the collective understanding that the institutions we spend our lives serving are not created to serve us. Women are canaries in religious coal mines—and *Pure* emboldens us to escape toxic misogyny and experience a fresh breath of freedom."

—Glennon Doyle, #1 *New York Times* bestselling author of
Love Warrior and founder of Together Rising

"Riveting and important . . . The relevance for this both inside and outside of the Christian community is immense, and this is a book that should stir intense thought about the way we all live."

—*Santa Barbara News-Press*

"A potent account of purity culture that deserves our attention."

—*Library Journal* (starred review)

"*Pure* is above all for those who came out of the purity movement—a guidebook for survivors. . . . Its final message is healing through the movements that have arisen to combat purity culture."

—*Women's Review of Books*

"An important book from an important new voice."

—Rev. Brian D. McLaren, author of *The Great Spiritual Migration*

"To those outside the church, Klein offers a well-researched insider's point of view. To those affected by the purity movement, Klein offers a healing balm through personal testimony. To both she offers an invitation to further discourse as we seek to make our culture a safer place for all people."

—*Chapter 16*

PURE

Inside the Evangelical Movement
That Shamed a Generation of Young Women
and How I Broke Free

LINDA KAY KLEIN

ATRIA PAPERBACK

New York London Toronto Sydney New Delhi

ATRIA
PAPERBACK

An Imprint of Simon & Schuster, Inc.
1230 Avenue of the Americas
New York, NY 10020

Copyright © 2018 by Linda Kay Klein

Pages 323–25, Permissions, constitute an extension of the copyright page.

First Atria Paperback edition July 2019

ATRIA PAPERBACK and colophon are registered trademarks of Simon & Schuster, Inc.

For information about special discounts for bulk purchases, please contact Simon & Schuster Special Sales at 1-866-506-1949 or business@simonandschuster.com.

The Simon & Schuster Speakers Bureau can bring authors to your live event. For more information, or to book an event, contact the Simon & Schuster Speakers Bureau at 866-248-3049 or visit our website at www.simonspeakers.com.

Interior design by Jill Putorti

Manufactured in the United States of America

10 9 8 7 6

Library of Congress Cataloging-in-Publication Data

Names: Klein, Linda Kay, author.
Title: Pure : inside the evangelical movement that shamed a generation of
   young women and how I broke free / Linda Kay Klein.
Description: First Touchstone hardcover edition. | New York : Touchstone,
   2018. | Includes bibliographical references and index. |
Identifiers: LCCN 2018005457 (print) | LCCN 2018028718 (ebook) |
   ISBN 9781501124839 (eBook) | ISBN 9781501124815 (hardcover) |
   ISBN 9781501124822 (pbk.)
Subjects: LCSH: Women in Christianity. | Evangelicalism. | Christian
   women—Sexual behavior. | Sex—Religious aspects—Christianity. |
   Women's rights—Religious aspects—Christianity.
Classification: LCC BV639.W7 (ebook) | LCC BV639.W7 K556 2018 (print) |
   DDC 261.8/357—dc23
LC record available at https://lccn.loc.gov/2018005457

ISBN 978-1-5011-2481-5
ISBN 978-1-5011-2482-2 (pbk)
ISBN 978-1-5011-2483-9 (ebook)

This book is dedicated to all those who so bravely told their stories to me,
and all those whose stories have not yet been told.

Contents

CONTENTS

PURE

Introduction

As a teenager, I went to the sandbox in the empty playground beside my church when I wanted to be alone. I dug my bare feet down deep, cooling them in the damp sand.

"God, I would do anything for you," I remember saying there one afternoon.

"Anything?" I imagined God's reply.

"Anything," I promised.

"Would you become a missionary in a foreign land?" God tested me. "Giving up the lavish life of an actress that you dream about?"

I squeezed my eyes shut and pictured myself a poor missionary living in a small, rural village somewhere on the other side of the world. In my imagination, I wore a thin, cotton dress and my long brown hair whipped around my face in a way that could only be described as romantic.

No, I shook my head abruptly. *Not like that. God is asking if I'm willing to make a* sacrifice *for him,** I reminded myself. *I could become deathly ill from serving the sick; I might not have access to clean drinking or bathing water; I might spend days working in the hot sun without any protection.* I imagined my dress dirty and the skin under it covered in burns and

---

* Though I now see God as having no gender, I use masculine pronouns to refer to God in this book when the people themselves would have done so—as I certainly would have at this point in my life.

1

unidentifiable wounds. Satisfied with this new image, I opened my eyes and looked back into the sun.

"Yes God," I promised. "I would do that for you."

"Would you give up your parents?" God continued.

"Yes," I said quickly.

"Would you give up . . . your boyfriend?"

I winced.

"Who you think about all day and every night?" God continued. "Who makes you feel so utterly alive every time he touches you? Who you are sure is sin incarnate, even if he is a born-again Christian and thus 'technically' safe to date, and sure, all you've ever done is kiss, but the way he makes you feel . . . the way he makes you *feel*, you *know* must be wrong?"

"Yes," I whimpered. "Yes, God. I would."

Later that afternoon, I called my girlfriends for an emergency concert of prayer.*

"I think that God wants me to break up with Dean," I told them, trembling. Not one of them asked me why. They didn't have to. After all, we'd learned together that there were two types of girls—those who were pure and those who were impure, those who were marriage material and those who were lucky if any good Christian man ever loved them, those who were Christian and those who . . . we're not so sure about. So, God wanting me to break up with a high school boyfriend who made my whole body scream every time he looked at me?

Yeah.

Sure.

That made sense.

It's only now, more than twenty years later, that I can see another story beneath the only one my friends and I were able to see then. It's the

---

* The definition of this term depends on who you ask. Though historically a concert of prayer refers to a major prayer movement, in everyday Christian life it is often used in reference to group prayer organized around a specific purpose.

story of me—a sixteen-year-old girl in her first real relationship. Willing, no, *wanting* to be tested so she could prove to her God, her community, and *herself* that she was good.

After all, my sexual energy, sometimes off-color humor, and the '50s pinup *va-va-voom* of the hips I'd recently acquired were already worrying some in my community. If I wasn't careful, they warned me, I might just become a stumbling block. And maybe I already was one.

In the Bible, the term *stumbling block* is used to reference a variety of obstructions that can be placed before a Christian. The concept is used in reference to sexuality just once: "You have heard that it was said, 'You shall not commit adultery'; but I say to you that everyone who looks at a woman with lust for her has already committed adultery with her in his heart. If your right eye makes you stumble, tear it out and throw it from you; for it is better for you to lose one of the parts of your body, than for your whole body to be thrown into hell."[1]

Yet, in the years I spent as an evangelical Christian, I never once heard anyone use the term the way it's used here—in reference to the onlooker's lustful eye. Instead, I heard it used time and time again to describe girls and women who somehow "elicit" men's lust.* As I have heard it said, sometimes our interpretations of the Bible say more about *us* than they do about the Bible itself.

In junior high, the term *stumbling block* annoyed me. The implication that my friends and I were nothing more than *things* over which men and boys could trip was not lost on me. When half the guys stripped their shirts off and began a water fight at the youth group carwash outside of the Piggly Wiggly, I thought it was unfair that it was *me* who got

---

* In *Totem and Taboo*, Freud suggests that sometimes "a person may become permanently or temporarily taboo without having violated any taboos, for the simple reason that he is in a condition which has the property of inciting the forbidden desires of others and of awakening the ambivalent conflict in them."[2] This is what I experienced as an adolescent evangelical. I was taboo—guarded, and guarded against—long before I had ever done anything "wrong," lest I awaken someone's ambivalent conflict.

reprimanded for having my shirt sprayed by their hoses. But even as I bristled, I obeyed. I went home and changed into a dry shirt, longer shorts, longer skirts, higher backed dresses, and higher necked tops. By the time I was in high school and had my first boyfriend, I had been "talked to" about how I dressed and acted so many times that my annoyance was beginning to turn into anxiety. It began to feel like it didn't matter what I did or wore; it was *me* that was bad.

In the evangelical community, an "impure" girl or woman isn't just seen as damaged; she's considered *dangerous*. Not only to the men we were told we must protect by covering up our bodies, but to our entire community. For if our men—the heads of our households and the leaders of our churches—fell, we *all* fell.

Imagine growing up in a castle and hearing fables about how dragons destroy villages and kill good people all your life. Then, one day, you wake up and see scales on your arms and legs and realize, "Oh my God. *I* am a dragon." For me, it was a little like that. I was raised hearing horror stories about harlots (a nice, Christian term for a manipulative whore) who destroy good, God-fearing men. And then one day, my body began to change and I felt sexual stirrings within me and I thought, "Oh no. Is that me? Am *I* a manipulative whore?"

My Diary—May 1995:

My senses are never so alive as they are when I'm with Dean. I don't deserve this happiness. We sit across from one another, and we are so close that our cheeks rub up against each other. If he shaves in the morning, he is already ruff by evening. I rub his back. He rubs mine. It is sweet. It is innocent. But can we be moving too quickly even in the midst of our innocence?

"I think you have gotten prettier since I first met you," Dean said to me.

"I don't think so."

"I do. You used to be pretty, but now . . ." He took a deep breath and gazed at me.

"You are so beautiful," Dean mused, as he rubbed my face tenderly. He is always touching my face. It makes me feel precious.

"What do you think it means to fall in love?" I asked him.

"I don't know," he answered me.

"Do you think it's possible that I could be falling in love with you? Puppy love?"

He kissed me.

"Do you think it's possible," I spoke the words between kisses, "that you," a long kiss, "could be falling in love with me . . . puppy love?"

"Puppy love," he answered me.

I am in the middle of reading Passion and Purity: Learning to Bring Your Love Life Under Christ's Control *by Elisabeth Elliot in my small group right now. In it she says that her husband Jim touched her for the first time by rubbing his finger across her cheek. AFTER he was already her fiancé.*

So what does that mean? Once again, I worry that Dean and I are moving too quickly. We have already French kissed. You know, with tongue and all. Yeah, that's too fast.

Dear Jesus, Dean is a sweet gift from You. Please don't allow me to destroy this gift that You have given me with foolish passion. Dean doesn't want to push me. He respects me. How far we go is in my hands. But I don't want it there, because I don't know where exactly You do and don't approve of my hands being . . . Father, please show me what is "too far."

*　　*　　*

This is going to sound disgusting, but when Dean rubs his face in my hair or breathes into my ear, my groin kind of flips. I don't know how else to put it. Is that what it means to be "turned on"? I don't know.

Have I turned into a slut? I feel dirty and worthless. How can respect exist when I am such a slut?

A slut.

What is one?

Who is one?

I am not a slut.

Nobody is a slut.

That is a despicable word.

But how dare I call myself a Christian? I spent my morning primping. I spent my afternoon making out with my boyfriend. Then I spent my evening leading a Bible study!

My girlfriends rushed over to my parents' house for the concert of prayer. We sat in a circle on the floor of my parents' basement, bowed our heads, and together asked for God to help me fulfill his command: To break up with Dean.

When the last of them later filed out of the front door, I walked to my bedroom, called Dean, and told him we needed to talk.

Dean cried.

He said he didn't understand.

I said I didn't either. But I was sure. It was what I had to do.

Five years after I broke up with Dean, I was still calling myself a slut—though it was no longer high school kisses that spurred my shame, but college attempts to have sex with my long-term boyfriend. Now twenty-one, I had left my religious community, having determined that I was incapable of being the woman they made it clear I needed to be in order to belong. I had changed my mind about attending Bible college and begun attending a secular liberal arts college outside of New York City.

Yet, when the lights were turned low, it was as though nothing had changed. The closer I got to losing my virginity, the more likely it was that the word *slut* would run through my mind on ticker tape. Eventually, I'd find myself in a tearful heap in the corner of my boyfriend's dorm room bed, tormented by the same fear and anxiety that had driven me to break up with Dean when I was sixteen.

I had left the evangelical church but its messages about sex and gender still whirred within my body. Even after I calmed myself down and apologetically kissed my boyfriend goodbye, I couldn't let go of the lingering fear that we had gotten too close to having sex this time, that I had gotten pregnant, and that my sexual sins would soon be exposed to the religious community I'd left but still desperately wanted to approve of me. Eventually, I'd walk to the local drugstore and buy a pregnancy test. I was still a virgin, but taking the test was the only way I could steady my breathing.

Until the next time.

I searched for books, articles, and online communities that might help me understand what I was experiencing. And when I was unable to find any, I called up first one, then two, then several of my childhood girlfriends from my former church youth group. I told them what was happening to me, and then, I sat in stunned silence as they told me they were experiencing many of the same things. The relief I felt knowing I was not alone sustained me, but my struggles continued. Until, at the age of twenty-six, I quit my job, drove across the country to my midwestern hometown, and set out to find the others.

I sat down at my parents' kitchen table and paged through old church directories. One by one, I called the families of girls who I thought might still live in town: *Hi, I don't know if you remember me but I went to youth group with your daughter . . . Linda Kay Klein . . . Right, right! . . . It's nice to hear your voice too . . . Yeah absolutely . . . You know, I haven't talked with your daughter in so long, do you think I could get her number or email address from you?*

I spent a year meeting with childhood friends. Some were single; others were married; some had had sex before marriage; others had waited to have their first kiss at the altar; some were still evangelical; others were decidedly *not*. Yet in many of their whispered stories, I heard themes I recognized from my own life—fear, anxiety, shame.

That year, I began to piece together an epidemic that I have not been able to turn away from since: evangelical Christianity's sexual purity movement is traumatizing many girls and maturing women haunted by sexual and gender-based anxiety, fear, and physical experiences that sometimes mimic the symptoms of post-traumatic stress disorder (PTSD). Based on our nightmares, panic attacks, and paranoia, one might think that my childhood friends and I had been to war. And in fact, we had. We went to war with ourselves, our own bodies, and our own sexual natures, all under the strict commandment of the church.

This was the beginning of a twelve-year journey. In these years, I earned an interdisciplinary master's degree for which I wrote a thesis focused on white American evangelicalism's gender and sexuality messaging for girls; I worked alongside inspiring gender justice warriors to create change within the world's major religions; and I connected with hundreds of evangelicals and former evangelicals from across the country and talked with them about the impact that the purity movement had on their adult lives.

"So, freshman year of high school, sex ed. The PE coach decides to do abstinence education," Renee told me, sitting cross-legged on the couch in her college apartment, where she was telling me about her upbringing in the South. I moved my recorder closer to her to be sure I was capturing her voice. "She said, 'Who wants this Oreo?'" Renee continued. "Everybody raised their hand. Then she passed it around the class and had everyone spit on it, or drop it on the ground, and when it got back to the front of class it was disgusting.

"Then she said, 'Okay. *Now*, who wants this Oreo?' No one raised their hand.

"It was an analogy for: 'If you're sexually promiscuous, no one will want you.'"

I have heard many stories about object lessons like this one being taught in churches, community-based organizations, and public schools like Renee's. One object lesson uses a car metaphor: virgins are described as a shiny new car that everyone wants to buy, and all those who have had sex are described as used cars that nobody wants (having gotten stained, rusty, and more and more broken down with every "ride").* Another uses a tape metaphor: virgins are described as a new piece of tape that can easily bind to things (a virgin woman capable of emotionally binding with her husband), but that picks up more dust and dirt each time that it is stuck to something new until it is too dirty to stick to anything (or anyone) anymore. Then there is the unused tissue versus the "used" tissue full of snot, mucus, and phlegm, which is said to represent a girl or woman who has had sex; the clear glass of water versus the one to which food coloring has been added (the tiniest drop changing it forever); and the seemingly endless iterations on food: the untouched cookie or candy bar versus the one that has been chomped into; the unwrapped lollipop versus one that decreases in size and desirability after being licked for the first time, just once, and then licked again by anyone who is willing to put somebody else's saliva in

---

* This object lesson also comes in a bicycle variety.

their mouth; the new piece of gum versus the one that has been chewed; and so on.

Though shaming language is embedded into sexuality messaging for both boys and girls, it is especially intense and embodied when delivered to girls. In fact, the only one of the aforementioned metaphors that I have personally heard applied to both males and females is the tape metaphor.

Though Renee was "relatively innocent" sexually, in her words, she told me the lesson made even her limited sexual experience feel life-defining. "'Well I'm spoiled now,'" she reasoned, looking at the disgusting Oreo no one wanted. "'So I may as well do whatever.' It was really damaging to my development."

"It's interesting," I replied to Renee. "The emphasis on being devoured, right? This message that we should look at our sexuality as food—"

"For someone else," Renee finished my sentence.

I nodded. "As though it's all about how well we are able to feed others," I continued. "Like, 'If I let this person eat, then this other person won't be properly fed. Or won't want to devour me—'"

"Or 'I just won't be any good anymore,'" Renee added, frowning.

The purity message nestles neatly into the larger "us" versus "them" messaging I was raised with in the church. Those on the "positive" side of the binary are said to have access to God, Heaven, the community, and a happy life as one of "us." Those on the "negative" side of the binary are said to be isolated from God, alone, and headed for Hell, a place of suffering reserved explicitly for "them." Though one's place on that binary is technically supposed to be determined by one's belief system, let's face it—you can't see into another person's heart and know whether she really believes these things or has just memorized a bunch of talking points. So if you want to assess who's really a Christian and who's not—and *lots* of people do—you need a proxy, some externally measurable quality that is deemed representative of the person's internal commitment. Among single people in the church, one of the most popular proxies is sex. The celibacy represented by a purity ring*—real or metaphorical—identifies evangelicals as one of "us." This may never be spoken, but as a girl in the subculture, I can assure you, it is *felt*.

Growing up, I heard a lot of talk about how evangelical Christians were better people than secular or other religious people (funnily enough, I now hear the exact same self-congratulatory messages from secular liberal people). But the truth was, I couldn't always tell the difference between a Christian and a non-Christian. I saw both lie, both steal, both love, and both unselfishly give to others. But one tangible thing we could point to as evangelicals was that we didn't have sex before marriage. There was that. There was *always* that. Which is why, I believe, the threat of losing that so-called sexual purity seemed so grave. Were we to have sex outside of marriage, could we even call ourselves Christians anymore? What if we made out? Kissed? Held hands? Had a crush? How close to sex could we come before we were no longer Christians?

"Sex is the big issue that for some reason marks your spiritual standing with God," Renee illustrated. "Like Jessica Simpson. People considered her a Christian because she waited to have sex until marriage. That was her whole marker of faith in God. And every testimony† you hear from someone, they have to mention the sexual sins of their past. They might not mention the fact that they . . . I don't know . . . got rid of their shopping addiction, but they mention the fact that they got rid of their addiction to porn. It's like, '. . . and then I stopped sleeping around. I became a Christian and I stopped sleeping around.'"

After all, what other sin is said to fundamentally change you forever? You can be born again and have your slate wiped clean of lying, stealing, even murder. And if you do these things again later but honestly apolo-

---

* A purity ring is a ring that a single person wears, often on their wedding finger, to remind themselves of, and communicate to others, their commitment to not having sex before marriage.

† One's testimony is the story of how they became a born-again Christian.

gize to God, your sin is again forgiven. But sex outside of marriage is the only "sin" that I have ever heard described as changing *you*. Before sex, you are a virgin. After sex, well . . .*

> I remember there was this girl's high school retreat where the leader was talking about purity and how important it was and how she felt disgusting. Basically, she started breaking down crying because she hadn't stayed pure, and this happened all the time in my church. My youth pastor's wife, she had walked down the aisle pregnant and now they are married and she has two boys, but she would still weep about it. Not that the *youth pastor* who she had the baby with is weeping about it! But his wife still weeps about it and says how she feels ashamed, disgusting, and wrong twelve years later. (Muriel)

Sometimes one doesn't even need to have *sex* to feel this way. The purity movement teaches that *every* sexual activity—from masturbation to kissing if it elicits that special feeling—can make one less pure.

> What does it even mean to be "pure"? The lines were so blurred, and there was so much tragedy tied up with it: "Don't do this, because if you do this you're ruining your relationship with your future spouse . . ." "Don't just be pure in body; you need to be pure in spirit . . ." Everything was just so intertwined with each other. It almost seemed like if you weren't being physically impure, you were being spiritually and emotionally impure. Being "pure" became this

---

* It should be noted that revirgination ceremonies (which I have personally only heard of being offered to and attended by women) are hosted by some churches. Though the idea of revirgination reflects the purity ethic that implies virgins are somehow "better" than non-virgins, and brings with it all the complications that come with that, I have heard these ceremonies described as healing experiences for some, particularly for those who have been raped or sexually abused.

really heavy, heavy weight to bear all the time. It almost made me go crazy questioning, "Well, is this impure? . . . Is this wrong? . . . Is this okay? . . . Is this going on?" (Holly)

Some purity movement advocates even teach that sexual thoughts and feelings can make one impure.

I sort of thought of being naked with a guy. I didn't picture him naked. I didn't picture me naked. I just sort of imagined, "I could marry him and be naked with him one day." And I felt terribly guilty over that for a long time. (Rosemary)

And it is implied that the sexual thoughts, feelings, and actions of others can be signs of your impurity as well (because surely you did *some*thing to make them think, feel, or do what they did).

I had one half-kiss at the age of sixteen that made me brush my teeth for ten minutes afterward.* It wasn't even a kiss. He kissed me but I did not kiss him back. I think I mostly just stood there, kind of horrified and fascinated at the same time. But I felt guilty, ashamed, dirty for years. How screwed up is that? I thought I was dirty and ruined, a soiled package. But you know how it is. They say, "Make sure you don't have to tell your husband the high number of people you've kissed someday. Your first kiss should come from your husband." And I had just ruined it. I ruined it by letting this happen. *[But didn't you say you didn't kiss him back?]* Yes, but I felt I let it happen. I didn't

---

* There is no definition for "half-kiss," though it is a term I hear often in evangelical circles. One person might use it to refer to a peck or an otherwise short kiss, another to a kiss that she turned away from, etc. For many, the intention is to keep at least as many purity points as she deserves by not claiming a whole kiss when, for whatever reason, it didn't really feel whole.

read the signals. I wasn't on my guard. We jump through hoops to make it about our shamefulness. (Jo)

The purity message is not about sex. Rather, it is about *us*: who we are, who we are expected to be, and who it is said we will become if we fail to meet those expectations.

This is the language of shame.

Shame is the feeling "I *am*—or somebody else will *think* I am—bad" (as opposed to *guilt*, for example, which is associated with the feeling "I *did* something bad"). The religious purity messages many of us received as girls were not about what we might do, but about what we would *be*, or be seen as. Of course, we are all different and therefore respond to shaming of this kind differently. Our family dynamics, the affirmation we receive (or don't receive) for other aspects of ourselves, the intersecting messages we are given about who we are based on our race, our ethnicity, our socioeconomic status, our physical and mental health, and so on all have roles to play. But the conversations that I have been having over the past twelve years make it clear that the influence of the consistent shaming embedded into the religious purity message, particularly during stages of extreme neural plasticity such as adolescence is for sexual development, can be extreme for many.

After all, researchers have found that our brains bend toward whatever it is that our attention is directed to.[3] It follows that if an adolescent is regularly given shaming messages—like the purity message that a girl or woman is utterly and fundamentally pure or impure, good or bad, pleasing or displeasing, desirable or undesirable, et cetera, based on her sexual expressions or lack thereof—she will become more likely to experience shame in association with sex than she otherwise may have been. As psychiatrist Dr. Curt Thompson explains in his book *The Soul of Shame: Retelling the Stories We Believe About Ourselves*, "With repeated exposure to events [in which we feel shame], we pay attention to and, via our early neuroplastic flexibility, more permanently encode these shame networks. Thus, they become more easily able to fire later on, even when activated by the most minor or even unrelated stimuli."[4]

This is not good news for the shamed individual, or their potential partners. Shame tends to make people feel powerless and even worthless. It creates a fear of abandonment that, ironically, makes us push others away. We want to hide those aspects of ourselves we are ashamed of, so we may emotionally withdraw from those close to us, lash out at them to keep them at bay, or isolate ourselves in self-blame. Whatever it takes to keep the world (including ourselves) away from those parts of us that we have come to believe make us bad.

Over the years, shame adds up, but it can happen so slowly we don't even notice it. We may look at each shaming incident one at a time and tell ourselves that what was said or done to us wasn't that bad. In time, we become less and less sure that we can, or *should*, heal. Rather than seek help, we bury our shaming experiences deep in our bodies, where they are held similarly to trauma.

Shame researcher Dr. Brené Brown explains this phenomenon in her book *I Thought It Was Just Me (But It Isn't): Making the Journey from "What Will People Think" to "I Am Enough."* She references the work of Harvard-trained psychiatrist Dr. Shelley Uram, who calls attention to the importance of recognizing "small, quiet traumas" which she has found "often trigger the same brain-survival reaction" as larger traumas, such as a car crash. In *I Thought It Was Just Me (But It Isn't)*, she writes:

After studying Dr. Uram's work, I believe it's possible that many of our early shame experiences, especially with our parents and caregivers, were stored in our brains as traumas. This is why we often have such painful bodily reactions when we feel criticized, ridiculed, rejected, and shamed. Dr. Uram explains that the brain does not differentiate between overt or big trauma and covert or small, quiet trauma—it just registers the event as "a threat we can't control."[5]

Perhaps this explains why I have heard so many stories of PTSD-like experiences in association with people's sexuality, their bodies, and the church.

Today when I go into a church, I can't stop panicking. I feel like I am going into a place in which I was raped, though I wasn't. It is light-years easier for me to talk about being sexually abused as a child—I could give a public lecture about that—than it is for me to talk about what that religious community did to me. Sexual abuse is something that happened to me, but this was at the core of my identity. I participated in the community's messaging about who I was, and allowed it to define me for years. The fear, the obsessing, the anxiety. It's torment. It is Hell. It felt like torture. (Nicoletta)

And yet, the impact that shaming can have on people's lives generally goes unacknowledged and sometimes even unnoticed within the communities in which it most regularly occurs. In some cases, shaming is so common it is coiled around core beliefs, laced through theology, and twisted into doctrine, making it nearly impossible to see.

I'm trained as a therapist, and I didn't even recognize the trauma that I had in my life around religion until a few years ago. I've never spoken about these things with anyone else, not even with my closest friends. I have been through years of therapy and I've never once mentioned it to a therapist. (Nicoletta)

Shame can become like the smell of our own homes. The hum of an air conditioner. The feel of a wedding ring. It's just . . . there. Which is when it is *most* dangerous. Because it is then that we are most likely to dismiss, rather than deal with, its dangerous effects.

I can't tell you how many people are experiencing the kinds of things that my interviewees and I have and do. But the regularity with which I am approached and asked if I will talk to someone, or someone's friend, or someone's partner about the way in which religiously rooted sexual shame is impacting their lives makes one thing clear: It's enough people that we need to be talking about it.

"So, what exactly is an evangelical?" I'm asked by non-evangelicals and evangelicals alike. After all, most evangelicals simply call themselves Christians. By which they mean *real* Christians (as opposed to those who think they are Christians but have got it all wrong, like non-evangelical Catholics and mainline Protestants).

Evangelical Christianity is a very new religious expression, though it has roots in older forms of Christian faith. It was just 1948 when a group of largely conservative individuals calling themselves the new evangelicals branched away from various Protestant groups* to form the National Association of Evangelicals (NAE).[6] And it wasn't until the 1990s that evangelical Christianity became the political and cultural force we know it as today.

Some say the word *evangelical* comes from the Greek *euangelion*, which translates to "good news." Evangelicals define the Good News as Jesus's death and resurrection, which allows sinful people to enter Heaven. Most believe a person must be "born again" to receive this salvation (so many, in fact, that the Pew Research Center considers people evangelical if they report either being "evangelical" *or* "born

---

* Fundamentalist Christianity was chief among these groups.

again").* An individual's born-again experience can happen during a group altar call,† or sitting alone in one's living room the day one decides to give up trying to do things one's own way and start trying to do them God's way. However one is born again, afterward, he or she is expected to spread the Good News to others—that is, to evangelize. Evangelicals are often further distinguished by their theological and moral conservatism, biblical literalism, emphasis on personal piety, conservative political positions, and engagement with technology, popular culture, and capitalism. But I can personally think of exceptions to every single one of these definitional rules.

Even the core tenets of evangelicalism around believing in, and evangelizing about, the Good News are often defined, and engaged with, differently by various individual evangelicals. As an illustration of the diversity among evangelicals, one evangelical woman recently told me that an evangelical must have three things: "First, intimacy with Jesus, which looks different for everyone. For example, my brother can have a beer with Jesus, whereas I wrestle and beg and devote time to biblical study. Second, trying to be like Jesus, which leads some people to vote Republican and others to vote Democrat depending on how they read who Jesus is and what he stands for and against. And third, promoting the Good News, which, when I was young, I understood to mean getting born-again decisions for Jesus, but today I consider to be about spreading loving, forgiveness, and acceptance."

In 1995, former president of Auburn Theological Seminary Barbara Wheeler said the best definition of an evangelical may be "someone who understands its argot, knows where to buy posters with Bible verses on

---

* However, a growing number of evangelicals are moving away from this emphasis on the born-again experience.

† An altar call is an invitation for individuals to gather as a group and be led through a collective conversion or "born-again" experience. Generally (though not always), it takes place at the altar of a church.

them, and recognizes names like James Dobson* and Frank Peretti."†7 Her references are a bit dated, but her point is right on: evangelicalism is best thought of as a subculture. By this definition, a churchgoing Catholic who reads a lot of evangelical books, listens to an evangelical Christian radio station, and has a close circle of evangelical friends is more "evangelical" than the unengaged individual who occasionally attends an evangelical church, but is otherwise disconnected from the community. After all, you only get the real stuff of evangelicalism—the feelings, the fervor—by being in the room.

The evangelical subculture is diverse, decentralized, and constantly changing. After all, evangelical Christianity is the single largest religious grouping in the United States. More than a quarter of Americans belong to it, and more than a third of American adolescents do.[8] Within the United States, some evangelical communities are predominantly white, some African American, some Asian American, some Hispanic, some more mixed, and so on. Some evangelical communities are charismatic, some fundamentalist, and some Pentecostal. Some are conservative, some moderate, and a smaller number progressive. When I use the term *evangelical* in this book, I am, unless otherwise noted, referring to the largest evangelical grouping—the white, conservative, American evangelical Christian subculture within which I was raised.

Within evangelicalism there are several denominations, like the Assemblies of God and the Southern Baptist Convention, but Mennonites, Holiness groups, and Dutch Reformed groups are also generally considered evangelical, as are many nondenominational church groups, such as the Christian and Missionary Alliance and the Acts 29 Network. Most nondenominational evangelical (and an increasing number of other) churches brand themselves independently, taking on inspiring names

---

* The founder of Focus on the Family.
† A contemporary evangelical author.

like New Life Church, or naming themselves plainly—for example, taking the name of the city or neighborhood in which they are based and adding the word *church* to it. There are also many evangelical house churches, missional communities, and experimental church groups, not to mention Catholic and mainline Protestant churches and groups that self-identify as evangelical.

Unlike other forms of Christianity, evangelicalism lacks a traditional hierarchy, but that doesn't mean there aren't rules within it. The rules are simply translated—as they are in any subculture—through a culture of cool (or "moral" or "pure" or "Bible-believing") and disseminated through pop culture: celebrities, books, music, events, speakers, et cetera. Still, evangelical institutions—by which I mean colleges, publishing houses, music production houses, and so on—and organizing bodies like the NAE are anything but obsolete. When the subculture expands, evolves, or in some other way threatens to transform itself, as it has many times in its short history, these institutional forces often step in—declaring a former evangelical rock star who is pushing the boundaries of the belief system to be a heretic, or firing evangelical professors who too boldly challenge its conservative core. And because every kind of evangelical belief (spiritual, religious, political, and cultural) goes by the same name—*Christian*, a loaded term that defines whether or not you are going to Heaven—people's beliefs about your salvation sometimes depends on institutional leaders' assessments of your opinions on things that many would argue should have nothing to do with religion, like who you vote for. Those are high stakes for an evangelical who is considering going against the subculture's dominant stance.

Within all of this diversity, the sexual purity message is one of the most consistent elements of the evangelical subculture. Among my interviewees, a remarkably similar language and set of stories about gender and sexuality surfaced. The same adages, metaphors, and stories from books, speakers, and events were described to me over and over again, though those I spoke with grew up around the country and in some cases the world.

As Donna Freitas writes in her study of college students' spiritual and sexual lives, *Sex and the Soul: Juggling Sexuality, Spirituality, Romance, and Religion on America's College Campuses,* this creates a very consistent set of sexual attitudes among young adults who grew up in the purity movement.

Though the evangelical students I interviewed broke almost every liberal preconception about them, proving to be diverse in their politics, nuanced in their expressions and beliefs about Christianity, and perfectly willing to swim in a sea of doubt and life's gray areas, their pursuit of purity is the one area where almost all of them could see only black and white. Falling short of ideal purity can jeopardize not only a young adult's standing among her peers but also, as these young adults are taught through purity culture, her relationship with God.[9]

Overtly shaming messages, like the object lessons that I mentioned earlier, are easiest to identify. But the more powerful, and far more prevalent, messages are *covert:* shaming attitudes embedded into everyday language, shaming lessons slipped into stories, shaming treatment felt by those who are being shamed and observed by those who fear they will be shamed *next.* Sometimes, you can be in the room when these covert messages are relayed and not even hear them. They are *that* commonplace. If the messages don't hurt you, you are less likely to hear them (for instance, a straight person is less likely to hear a covert homophobic message than a queer person is). And if the messages *benefit* you, you are even *less* likely to hear them (for instance, a husband whose pastor turns to him and asks if he can hug the man's wife may not "hear" the pastor subtly referring to his wife as his property . . . but *she* might).[10]

Purity preaching is not new, nor is it exclusive to evangelical Christianity, but evangelicals have played—and continue to play—an important role in bringing this message to the mainstream. After the sexual revolution, Americans were scared. AIDS was killing people by the thousands, there were growing concerns about other sexually transmitted infections (STIs), and many conservatives believed a return to traditional values, including chastity, was the only solution. Spurred by this perspective, federal money for abstinence-only-until-marriage education began to flow—first under Reagan,* then more under Clinton,† then still more under Bush.‡[11] This influx of government money catalyzed the purity industry.

According to the Sexuality Information and Education Council of the United States (SIECUS), over $2 billion in federal funding has been allocated for abstinence-only programs in the United States since 1981.[12] Much of this funding came through the Title V abstinence-only-until-marriage program, which is still in place today. This program requires states to match every four federal dollars they receive with three state-raised dollars, presumably increasing the state-level contributions made toward abstinence-only programming in the process as well. The money is then redistributed to community-based organizations, faith-based organizations, local and/or state health departments, and schools. Every state but one (California) has at one time accepted Title V federal funding for abstinence-only-until-marriage programming.[13]

With money like this just waiting to be spent, purity purveyors previously focused on small religious audiences moved into the mainstream marketplace, selling events, speakers, and curricula. This is when we

---

* The Adolescent Family Life Act (FY 1982–FY 2010) was passed in 1981. Overall, AFLA received $209 million, a portion of which went to abstinence-only-until-marriage programs.
† The Title V abstinence-only-until-marriage program (FY 1998–present) allocated $50 million per year in federal funds to states until FY 2015, at which point it went up to $75 million per year.
‡ The Community Based Abstinence Education (FY 2001–FY 2009) funding stream has allocated $733 million in federal funds for abstinence-only-until-marriage programming.

began to see purity-themed rings,* bracelets, necklaces, shirts, hats, underwear, books, journals, devotionals, magazines, Bible studies, trainings, guides, DVDs, planners, and other products. I have come across purity-themed, posters, coffee mugs, key chains, buttons, stickers, water bottles, mints (on which the words "sex is mint for marriage" are printed), and have even read references to purity-themed lollipops (which I assume are sold to remind people of the lollipop object lesson in which every sexual experience is compared to a lick on the lollipop of one's life, making them less and less attractive to potential suitors who would prefer an unlicked and unwrapped lollipop for their sole consumption). It is nearly impossible to assess who purchased each of these products and with what money, but the government certainly wasn't the only buyer. Many of these products were ultimately bought by the audience for whom they were originally intended—evangelical Christians. As Doug Pagitt, pastor of the progressive evangelical church Solomon's Porch, explained: "When it came to sex, churches had gotten quiet. *Too* quiet. We wanted resources. We *needed* resources. So when someone made them, we used them."[14]

Within the evangelical Christian subculture, the purity industry gave many adolescents the impression that sexual abstinence before marriage was *the* way for them to live out their faith. This is perhaps best illustrated by the production of purity-themed Bibles. The *Abstinence Study Bible* produced by the Christian group Silver Ring Thing, for example, includes sixty pages of non-biblical material such as dating advice like "avoid the horizontal" and "keep your clothes on, in, zipped and buttoned."[15] When about one-sixth of an adolescent's Bible is marketing about the importance of abstinence, how could she *not* reach the con-

---

* Rings range in cost and quality and are often engraved with a Bible verse or personalized message. They are marketed to adolescents, parents, and groups that may be interested in bulk orders. Parents can even buy special purity rings for themselves, which are intended to remind them to pray for and daily encourage their kids' sexual abstinence.

clusion that her sexual thoughts, feelings, and choices determine her spiritual standing?

Products like these integrate purity messaging into a young person's daily life. Imagine a seventh-grade girl arriving at her middle school on a snowy day. She takes her mittens off and her attention is caught by the sparkling ring that she has promised to wear until the day she gives the gift of her virginity to her husband. *This, she recalls being told, will ensure your husband will never leave you. But if you ever break your promise . . .* An eighth-grade girl kisses a boy for the first time. Skipping home on a high, she is sure the sky has never been so blue or the light quite so clear. Approaching her front door, she pulls out her keys, noticing her purity-themed key chain. She stops in her tracks. *Will my husband be upset when he finds out my first kiss wasn't with him?* she asks herself, her anxiety rising. A ninth-grade girl brushes her teeth in front of the bathroom mirror where she has taped her copy of the purity pledge she signed at a rally. (The other copy of the contract was sent to the True Love Waits headquarters.) Her youth pastor had suggested she put the contract somewhere she would see it every day, especially since she started dating Mike.

When products are purchased using government money, the teachings are supposed to be non-religious, but sometimes, things get messy. The group called the Silver Ring Thing, launched in 1993, offers an example. They received $1.4 million in federal funding.[16] In 2005, the American Civil Liberties Union filed a lawsuit contending that the Silver Ring Thing was evangelizing at its government-funded events. A settlement was reached and the government stopped funding the Silver Ring Thing in its current form.[17] Now solely supported by private money, the Silver Ring Thing's events, which continue to be offered to this day, culminate in an invitation for adolescents to sign a purity pledge and give their life to Christ at essentially the same time, again connecting the concepts of salvation and sexual purity.[18] The Silver Ring Thing reports having hosted nearly 1,300 of these events and having reached more than 684,000 people.[19]

Also launched in 1993, this time by the Southern Baptist Convention, True Love Waits is generally considered the most powerful player in the purity industry. True Love Waits never received federal funding, but its relationship with the government was robust nonetheless. True Love Waits actively campaigned the government to allocate money to abstinence-only-until-marriage programming and, a year after its launch, startled the country by bringing 20,000 adolescents to the National Mall, where they staked 211,156 signed purity pledges on the lawn. Afterward, 150 purity activists had a special session with President Bill Clinton.* Two years later, Congress allocated $50 million a year for the aforementioned Title V abstinence-only programming.

It's hard to estimate just how many young people have been impacted by the purity industry, but one purity curriculum provider approved for federal financial support boasts on its website of having reached over 4 million students in forty-seven states.[20] That's about 10 percent of the total number of ten- to nineteen-year-olds living in the United States and its territories today!† If that many young people have been reached by just this *one* curriculum, we can only begin to imagine how many have been reached by the vast array of other products.

In 2008, federal funding for abstinence-only-until-marriage programming was curbed under the Obama administration after a congressionally mandated, comprehensive nine-year study showed that students who experienced abstinence-only education in public schools were "no more likely than control group youth to have abstained from sex and, among those who reported having had sex, they had similar numbers of partners and had initiated sex at the same mean age."[22]

---

* This effort was organized in conjunction with Youth for Christ's DC '94.

† According to US Census Bureau estimates, in 2015 there were over 41 million ten- to nineteen-year-olds in the United States and Puerto Rico Commonwealth and Municipios. It should be considered, however, that this curriculum's reported numbers likely span the curriculum's over-twenty-year lifespan, whereas the census estimates represent only one year.[21]

But the purity industry may be making a comeback.

Dedicated federal abstinence-only-until-marriage funding meaningfully increased again in 2016, bringing the total federal funding to $90 million for 2017.[23]

But this time, even evangelicals don't seem so excited about that, at least not those that are working on the ground.

"It made youth workers feel like they were doing good work because they were talking about these taboo issues like sex that the church never talked about before and that needed to be talked about," said Pastor Doug Pagitt—who I cited previously—about the purity messaging. "Then, after a few decades, people were like, 'Oh. This stuff is bad.'"

"Progressive evangelicals realized that?" I clarified. "Or mainstream evangelicals?"

"Across evangelicalism. Not just progressives."

"So where is mainstream evangelical sexuality education today?" I asked him.

"It's in huge flux. It's a changing landscape. Everyone is confused."

"So, it's a moment of 'not that . . . but now what?'"

"Yes," he answered definitively.[24]

Not every adolescent who consumes purity messaging will have the same experience. It's one thing to receive a shaming message at a public school assembly while your friends snicker, and quite another to receive it from inside a closed community where the messages are deeply revered by all. As Dr. Curt Thompson writes: "When I perceive that I am receiving the shame from a community of voices, the pain can become unbearable. When the collection of the voices of an entire community shames us, it is more unwieldy due to our inability to locate it centrally in any one place. And so when I feel shame in my family or my church, addressing it feels quite overwhelming."[25]

Perhaps this explains why the National Longitudinal Study of Adolescent Health found that evangelical adolescents are more likely than their peers to expect that if they have sex, it will both upset their mother and cost them the respect of their partner. Evangelical adolescents are also among the least likely to expect sex to be pleasurable, and among the most likely to expect that having sex will make them feel guilty.[26] Yet one's level of religiosity (there is a 30 percentage point gap in anticipated sexual guilt between the least and the most religious youth)[27] and one's gender (girls are a whopping 92 percent more likely to experience sexual guilt than boys)[28] have even greater impacts on one's likelihood to experience sexual shame than one's denominational affiliation. Considering my interviewees and I were all at one time 1) highly religious, 2) evangelical, 3) girls, it is likely that our reactions to the purity movement's messaging is in some cases more extreme than those of individuals outside our demographic might be. Yet our stories illustrate intensified versions of experiences I believe almost all women and many others have had.

Right now, groundbreaking research is being performed among young adults raised in three conservative Christian communities—Baptist, Catholic, and Latter-day Saints. This research that reiterates many of the previously mentioned findings and posits several new ones that can help us better understand just how and why purity messaging is impacting girls. The researchers write in their brief:

> There is little support indicating that the mechanisms currently used in our society (abstinence education, chastity pledges, and religious grounding) to curb teenage sexual activity actually work. The question remains, "Is our focus on sexual abstinence doing anything?"
>
> It turns out that those who are sexually active and have experienced abstinence education and/or have stronger beliefs that the Bible should be literally translated [a core tenet of evangelicalism],

have more sexual guilt.* ... females report significantly higher sex guilt than males (and) sex guilt from the first sexual experience is predictive of higher sex anxiety, lower sexual efficacy, and lower sexual satisfaction. So, females, in particular, who have strong religious beliefs and are engaging in premarital sex, are having unsatisfactory sex, they have high anxiety about it, and don't feel that they are capable of changing their situation.

Lastly, the relationship between sex guilt and sex anxiety, sexual efficacy, and sexual satisfaction, doesn't diminish over time; it gets stronger.† ... This is not a recipe for young women to embark on a fulfilling relationship with their partner and we predict could be an indicator of further sexual problems and relationship issues.[29]

To summarize, first, the researchers are finding that purity teachings do *not* meaningfully delay sex. Second, they are finding that they *do* increase shame, especially among females. And third, they report that this increased shame is leading to higher levels of sexual anxiety, lower levels of sexual pleasure, and the feeling among those experiencing shame that they are stuck feeling this way forever. Oh, and it doesn't get better with time ... it gets worse!

Yep. Sounds about right.

I have seen the Bible used against people many times. For some of those I've spoken with, it is the literature of their trauma and I feel no need to

---

* I was able to confirm with the lead researcher that what the research team calls sex guilt is the same as what I am in this book calling shame.

† The researchers later clarified that this doesn't mean that the guilt gets more intense over time, but that the relationship between guilt and sexual anxiety, sexual efficacy, and sexual satisfaction is stronger for guilt more recently felt than guilt remembered from the first sexual experience. In this study, participants reflected on past feelings; longitudinal data was not collected.

redeem it for these individuals. But I take comfort in knowing that when I read the Bible today, I find more liberation in its pages than I was taught to see in it growing up. Take stumbling blocks. Interestingly, the verse most purity preachers point to when accusing girls and women of being stumbling blocks isn't the one about sexuality that I referenced earlier. It's a verse about food. In Romans 14, Paul suggests that his readers not eat unclean food in front of those they think it will distress: "Let us then pursue what makes for peace and for mutual upbuilding. Do not, for the sake of food, destroy the work of God. Everything is indeed clean, but it is wrong for you to make others fall by what you eat; it is good not to eat meat or drink wine or do anything that makes your brother or sister stumble."[30]

Those who call women and girls stumbling blocks interpret Romans 14 as a metaphor: Girls and women are technically free to dress how they want, just as we are all free to eat what we want, but if girls and women care for their brothers, they should dress and behave modestly so they don't become stumbling blocks to them.

But look a little earlier in the chapter and it becomes clear that Paul's larger point is that we should spend less time judging others' choices as right or wrong—arguing that a multiplicity of choices can honor the Lord depending on the heart of the individual—and that we should spend more time loving one another:

> Those who eat must not despise those who abstain, and those who abstain must not pass judgment on those who eat; for God has welcomed them. Who are you to pass judgment on servants of another? It is before their own lord that they stand or fall. And they will be upheld, for the Lord is able to make them stand. Some judge one day to be better than another, while others judge all days alike. Let all be fully convinced in their own minds. Those who observe the day, observe it in honor of the Lord. Also those who eat, eat in honor of the Lord, since they give thanks to God; while those who abstain, abstain

in the honor of the Lord and give thanks to God.[31] . . . Why do you pass judgment on your brother or sister? Or you, why do you despise your brother or sister? For we will all stand before the judgment seat of God.[32] . . . So then, each of us will be accountable to God. Let us therefore no longer pass judgment on one another, but resolve instead never to put a stumbling block or hindrance in the way of another.[33]

I don't know about you, but within the larger context of the chapter, it seems to me that *judgmentalism* is the stumbling block Paul is most concerned with here, not modesty. Reading these verses as an adult I cannot help but shake my head—the whole time my childhood friends and I were being told that *we* were stumbling blocks, our accusers were, even then, placing the *real* stumbling blocks before us: purity-based shaming and judgmentalism that pushed many of us right out of the church.

This book is divided into four sections. The first section describes four purity culture stumbling blocks for girls. These stumbling blocks are: 1) the accusation that if purity culture doesn't work for you, it's *you* (not its teachings) that are the problem; 2) the requirement that all girls and women must perform a stereotypical gender role to be acceptable; 3) the expectation that all unmarried girls and women must maintain a sexless body, mind, and heart to be "pure"; and 4) the systematic mishandling of sexual abuse cases and survivors.* The second and third sections of the book delve into the challenges these stumbling blocks pose to girls as they become adults inside, and outside, of the church, respectively, and the ways they find to break free from the purity message in both places. The fourth section of the book explores how individuals raised in the

* Please be aware that stories of rape, intimate partner violence, and incest do appear in this book.

purity movement are personally hurdling these stumbling blocks and charting new pathways for those who come after them. Each of these four sections opens with a chapter highlighting a story from my own life. Chapters that follow feature the stories of my interviewees.

The individuals whose stories are shared in this book are between their early twenties and their early forties, having been raised as evangelical Christian girls sometime between the late 1980s and the early 2000s. Many, but not all, grew up in my hometown, where my interviews began. Most are using pseudonyms and, unless otherwise noted, all are white Americans.

When I started interviewing people twelve years ago, it felt important not to muddle all of the racially and ethnically distinct evangelical subcultures together in an attempt to "speak for all" when—as a white woman aware that her race and ethnicity protects her from other forms of oppression that intersect with the purity message—I can really only speak for one. So, I stuck to collecting the stories of white American evangelical girls, like me, as they grew up. Yet over the years, I have faced the reality that the purity industry has impacted many more people's lives. I have heard stories similar to mine and those of my interviewees from many outside of our demographic. From Catholics, mainline Protestants, Jews, Muslims, and many with no religion at all. From African Americans, Hispanic Americans, Asian Americans, and other Americans of color. From people around the world. And from men. Lots and lots of men.

As recent conversations spurred by #MeToo* and #ChurchToo† have

---

* The Me Too movement was founded in 2006 by Tarana Burke to support and unify sexual violence survivors, particularly women of color in underprivileged communities. In 2017, actor Alyssa Milano encouraged her Twitter followers to use the hashtag #MeToo if they had personally experienced sexual harassment and/or assault. The hashtag went viral.[34]

† #ChurchToo was founded by poet Emily Joy and writer and religious trauma researcher Hannah Paasch. Many women—and men—used the #ChurchToo hashtag to document personal stories about the church's contribution to sexism and violence against women on Twitter.[35]

made plain, the evangelical Christian church is not alone in shaming and silencing women and others. As such, I expect the stories in this book will be unfortunately familiar to many.

For more information about the individuals featured in this book, please see page 291.

Some of my critics will say, "I grew up in purity culture, and had a great experience." I wouldn't want those for whom this is true to change a thing about their lives. Except, that is, the belief some hold that because purity culture worked for *them*, it ought to work for *everyone*.

Other of my critics will point to people raised in the purity movement who do not represent its messaging in adulthood, arguing that the movement obviously didn't impact them. "I can think of half-a-dozen women off the top of my head who are evangelical, but whose lives do not fit the purity model," one evangelical man informed me, for example. "I can't imagine that these women are experiencing or ever have experienced the things you are talking about," he added with finality. I wonder if this man has ever taken the time to *ask* these half-a-dozen women about the impact the purity movement did or did not have on their development. I urge us all to consider that everyone around us is dealing with things they are not showing to us. Some may have never been asked about their shame; some may be making the choice not to share about it even when they are asked about it; and others may experience shame so regularly that they don't even notice it . . . but that doesn't mean it isn't there.

Still more of my critics will say, "You turned out alright. You're happily married with a great family. You're a strong Christian (even if you're not an evangelical). Whether or not you liked the purity message, it appears to have been good for you." Though evangelicalism offered me many gifts—a deep spiritual life, mentors I could rely on, leadership opportunities that boosted my confidence, and more—the purity message was *not* one of them. Intended to make me more "pure," all this message did was make me more ashamed of my inevitable "impurities."

When I was young, I thought God was in the hand that scooped me up when I joined the evangelical church. The hand cradled me, and I felt safe and protected. I believed that God lived here, in this one religious expression with all of its interpretations, rules, and regulations, including those that felt wrong to me even then, like the purity ethic.

But as I grew older, the hand began to squeeze me, and I became uncomfortable. I tried to make myself smaller, squishing myself down so I could fit inside of it, but all of the ways in which I was not the "right" kind of Christian woman squeezed through between the hand's fingers and I was exposed. I tried cutting parts of me off, the appendages that made it more difficult to fit, but I didn't have the guts to really cut them off. I just hid them under my clothing, like a character in a B movie hiding an arm inside her shirt and pretending the dangling sleeve means it isn't there. Finally, I decided I'd try to stretch out, make myself some room. *Maybe*, I thought, *the hand will loosen a little in response*. But instead, the hand tightened its grip. More and more of me came oozing out between its fingers until one day I came bulging out between its thumb and its pointer finger like a giant bubble, and with a plop, I dropped. Fell from grace. And landed flat on my face.

I remember how I felt. Scared and alone. Lying there trembling on the floor while looking up at the hand that once held me. I had lost so much—my community, my purpose in life, and worst of all, God, whom I missed so badly my body ached. I looked up at the hand sometimes, and wished that I was there so I could touch God again. But I didn't feel I was allowed to.

Eventually, I gathered up my broken body. There on the floor, with no one paying attention to me, I uncovered those parts of me that I had tried to hide or make small. And I watched, amazed, as these parts of me unfurled—some gorgeous, some terrifying, and others plain. From time to time, I felt something I thought I had lost—a holy presence, the feeling someone was watching out for me. In time, I came to trust, to know, that God was still with me. That God was in the hand, yes. But also here . . . and here . . . and here. That no hand can confine something so great.

Today, I am a Christian, but I stand outside of the hand I grew up in. Waving to those in it and saying, "It is good in the hand. God is there. And s/he is also here. So let's come together to end the shame that hurts all of us. For there is much work to be done."

The Stumbling Blocks

1

Sin, Psychosis, or System

I yanked my T-shirt up, exposed my twenty-year-old belly, and strained to lift my head from the bed so I could survey the damage. A nearly foot-long open wound, freshly stuffed with gauze, ran the length of my abdomen. Bandages of various shapes and sizes papered areas around it. And in the lower right-hand corner of my stomach a plastic ileostomy bag was attached to a nub of small intestine that protruded from my side. The bag would catch my waste and gas for a year until my surgeon would one day bend a piece of my small intestines into a makeshift colon to replace the one I'd lost.

I closed my eyes, and I whispered, "I take it back, God."

Growing up, my mom and I were an evangelical Christian community of two. Though we were technically Episcopalian, everything Mom learned about evangelical Christianity from her friends or the Christian radio station, she shared with her fellow congregant: me. When she told me about "praying your way through the day" (being in a constant state of prayer), I did my best to master the art of studying for a grade school spelling test and praying at the same time. And when she told me that demons were always lurking around me trying to lure me away from God, and that to get rid of them I had to command them to leave in Jesus's name, I spent whole nights sitting up in my bed repeating the phrase: *Be gone all evil by the blood of Jesus Christ; be gone all evil by the blood of Jesus Christ.* In the process, I formed a very real, albeit roughly made, relationship with God, and a deep love for the Christian faith.

Then one day I was crying, gulping in air, my head spinning, my heart on fire. I was thirteen years old, responding to a flashy altar call that, in a moment, altered the course of my life. That day, I left my intimate church of two and joined what I would soon come to recognize as a powerful religious network.

My brother had also been born again as a teenager, though he and my sister—who are much older than me—now lived across the country. So when I was also born again, it tipped the familial scale and my parents and I started attending a nondenominational evangelical church. My parents watched proudly as I joined a titanic community of teens from around the country dedicated to advancing our faith. Teeming with youthful energy and abandon, my new friends and I craved depth. We craved profundity. We craved intensity. We craved the truth of Jesus Christ in our lives at every moment, without exception.

The eight years I spent as an evangelical didn't seem like a phase, like adolescent experimentation, or an outlet for teenage passions or emotions. They seemed like a beginning, *the* beginning. Being a Christian became my life's purpose, the embodiment of my entire identity.

I began to eye even my own parents' teachings with increasing suspicion, putting my total trust in what a new set of teachers had to say—Christian pop stars, authors, pastors, and my peers' more church-involved parents who, despite what I can only imagine must have been a multiplicity of perspectives among them, presented what is in retrospect an astoundingly consistent set of messages. I went to church, Sunday school, and youth group weekly; to Bible studies, retreats, mission trips, conferences, trainings, and concerts regularly; and to youth group-organized parties, movie nights, sleepovers, concerts of prayer, and church lock-ins whenever they were offered (and they were offered a lot). I sang and played guitar in the youth group praise band; started and led a very well-attended Bible study at my public junior high school; launched a girls' Bible study for anyone in the city, which I led out of my parents' basement; and made it a habit to talk to everyone I could about how they could ask Christ into their hearts and experience the spiritual awakening I had experienced. I got up early every morning to do daily devotionals before school, read the Bible before bed each night so its wisdom would settle into my subconscious as I slept, and continued my childhood practice of trying to pray my way through each day.

And it may have stayed that way.

Had I not been a girl.

The need I felt to prove that I was good despite my developing body was never quite so strong as when the cast list for a play was released. I would run eagerly up to the list in hopes that maybe this time I had been cast as the romantic lead only to see my name, yet again, next to the role of a demon or a Jezebel. And it didn't just happen in church plays either. Even in school and community plays, I somehow always seemed to be cast as the same kind of character. Once, in a mime I performed for a church mission trip, I was even cast as *sex* itself. My role was to silently seduce *Christian* with my body. Christian would refuse me and then slam a Bible in my face, after which I would jump back and wither onto the floor as Christian moved on to his next temptation: *money*.

After one performance, one of the actors, a pastor's son, pulled me aside.

"You're good at that part," he told me.

"Thanks," I replied. I had actually worked really hard at it, practicing my seductive moves and dramatic wilting until it was just right. This was what I wanted to do when I grew up after all! Find a beautiful, evangelical, actor husband and start a Christian theater troupe that would travel around the world changing hearts and minds for Jesus Christ through missionary mimes . . . *sigh*.

The guy smiled. "Maybe *too* good at it," he raised his eyebrows.

"What do you mean?" I asked him, my face burning.

"Nothing," he said. Then he turned away, repeating in a singsong, "Nothing at all."

But I knew exactly what he meant. I wanted to make my leaders, my friends, my*self* believe I was good, but my stupid, floppy, breasty body was always getting in the way.

Later on the same mission trip, one of the girls handed me a piece of notebook paper. "Rob [the guy I'd had the conversation with] drew this," she said. "He told some of the other boys it's you."

"What's it supposed to be?" I asked, studying the long, thin pencil-drawn line with jagged teeth at the bottom of it.

"He said it's a hoe," she answered, scrunching her face up in sympathy. My eyes hardened. *A hoe?* I had been around the public school block enough to know exactly what *that* meant.

I found Rob and gave him a lecture about why it was wrong to call me, or anybody, a *whore* that was so long and passionate he almost cried. But the lecture itself, that wasn't what mattered. Not to me anyway. What has always mattered to me is what happened next.

Minutes after Rob limped away, a group of other guys on the mission trip formed a circle around me.

Finally, one stepped forward.

"That. Was. Amazing," he said.

"I thought he was going to cry!" another hollered, laughing.

"Oh man! He will never do that again!"

"Don't mess with Linda, y'all. She will *destroy* you!" said Dean, the boy who would later become my boyfriend. (Until, of course, I broke up with him for God.)

It was one of those moments, those rare moments in which you learn something about yourself by seeing yourself through others' eyes. That day, I learned that I was tough. And that that was cool. But I would've given anything to be the kind of good girl that the pastor's son never would have said those things about in the first place.

And so I prayed: "Don't just give me the milk, Lord. Give me the meat."

I was referring to 1 Corinthians 3:1–2.

And so, brothers and sisters, I could not speak to you as spiritual people, but rather as people of the flesh, as infants in Christ. I fed you with milk, not solid food, for you were not yet ready for it. Even now, you are still not ready.

I had heard a sermon in which the milk was interpreted as easy living, and meat was interpreted as suffering. The message that suffering is somehow "good for us" is repeated often among some Christians, particularly Christian women. Our reward for suffering "with joy"—smiling and not complaining—is being told we are "good."

Even outside of the church, everyone loves the good suffering woman: the pretty spinster who never admits her unending love for her sister's husband (who secretly loves her too, of course); the single mother who gives up her dream so she can make enough money for her kids to pursue theirs; the pregnant woman who forgoes treatment for her terminal illness because she fears it could endanger her unborn baby and dies in childbirth. In books, movies, and just about everywhere else, girls get the message that the more selflessly and painfully a woman suffers, the more we love her. But nowhere is this message quite so clear as it is in religion.

As an example, in her book, *A Year of Biblical Womanhood: How a Liberated Woman Found Herself Sitting on Her Roof, Covering Her Head, and Calling Her Husband "Master,"* progressive evangelical author

Rachel Held Evans highlights a subcategory of female martyrs that we especially love—"like Agatha (scourged, burnt, torn with meat hooks for refusing to marry the pagan governor of Sicily), Agnes (beheaded for refusing suitors and consecrating herself to Christ alone), Lucy (executed for distributing her wealth among the poor rather than marrying), and Blandina (a young slave thrown to wild beasts in the arena for professing Christianity)."[1]

Having been raised on stories like these, I lay across my daybed praying for the opportunity to prove that I was not a "woman of the flesh." To prove that I too could be an Agatha, an Agnes, a Lucy, or a Blandina. If I was just given the chance.

My senior year of high school, I studied abroad in Australia. For the first time in five years, I was living apart from my religious subculture. When I began to experience a mysterious abdominal pain and blood loss from my anus while living there, the first thing I did was thank God for the opportunity to grow spiritually. But the second thing I did was schedule an appointment with a doctor. Because come on, suffering was all well and good, but God liked to work miracles from time to time, right?

The Australian doctor I saw took one look at me and said my real problem wasn't blood loss; it was acne. I hid my face in my hair. I had been working hard to embrace my acne, which had gotten worse in recent months, even silently cheering on a self-assured classmate rising through the ranks of popularity at my school despite her own outbreaks. *That's right*, I would say to myself as she ignored me in the hallway. *Our physical appearance shouldn't dictate our level of confidence! After all, we are creatures of the spirit, not of the flesh alone!* The pain and blood loss worsened, but I didn't go back to the doctor. *If he didn't take it seriously*, I thought, *it must not be that serious.* Instead, I popped a few ibuprofens.

My last month in Australia, a thick envelope arrived in the mail with my parents' return address. Inside were articles in which I learned that my church youth pastor had been charged (and was later convicted) of child enticement with the intent to have sexual contact with a twelve-year-old girl from my youth group. He was caught after having lured the girl into a closet in a darkened part of the church basement during a youth meeting, an article read. A friend of the girl opened the door to the closet; she turned the light on; he stopped touching the girl; the girl called her friend's name; he grabbed the girl from behind and tried to pick her up, before finally putting her back down.

Though the girl told the police of earlier incidents, my youth pastor was charged with only one felony. Later, my youth pastor told a detective he had been dismissed from two other Christian staff jobs for "improper behavior" with similarly aged girls, which had somehow never come up in his reference checks.[2]

Throbbing with rage, I tucked the articles in my back pocket and walked to the rocky beach near my host parents' home. There I sat alone overlooking the water and read and reread the articles, crumpling their edges in anger.

"Two Christian institutions before ours?" I appealed to God as I looked out over the ocean. "Two boards of leadership that could have prevented him from doing this to her . . . and *didn't*?" Though it would take me many more years to come to terms with it, I know that the fire I feel in my belly for reforming the church went from smoldering coals to a flame that day, as it was the first time I saw the systemic nature of injustice in the church. Sitting on that rocky beach burning with anger at my youth pastor and, moreover, at the two other supposedly Christian institutions that had sent him to our community *knowing* what he might do—apparently more interested in protecting their reputations than the safety of children—I couldn't stop thinking about the twelve-year-old girl in my church. How must she have felt sitting through those True Love Waits lessons in which we learned that good girls were not sexual stumbling blocks to men and boys? Did she wonder if what our youth pastor was doing to her meant she was not one of the good girls after all?

I gripped one article so tightly in my hands that it tore. I balled it up and threw it down the rocks. Then I climbed down to the beach, picked it back up, and read it again.

When I returned home from Australia, a newly minted high school graduate, I was glad to have aged out of youth group. My mom had already made an appointment for me to see a gastroenterologist. The doctor did a short scope and diagnosed me with Irritable Bowel Syndrome, but before I left his office I remember him telling me that if my symptoms were as severe as I claimed they were, I wouldn't be smiling so much.

Clearly, he had no experience with good Christian girls and our truly outstanding capacity for smiling. My girlfriends and I knew it was our responsibility to represent Jesus to the non-Christian world. The word *Christian*, after all, meant "Christ-like." So if we were a drag, people would assume that Jesus was a drag. But if we were fun, we might entice someone to join the church and save them from eternal damnation. And so, even while we suffered, *especially* while we suffered, we smiled. We laughed. We wrote people encouragement cards. I even made Christmas cookies and dropped them off at every storefront open on Christmas Eve one year. And when my friends and I got home from a long day of smiling goodness, our smiles got even bigger, because we knew it was also our role to be what my pastor called "cheerleaders" for the "football players" in our lives—our fathers, brothers, and husbands. You never saw a group of teenage girls so . . . happy.

One of the most common themes that arose in my interviews was the pain that those I spoke with felt at not being allowed to express their true feelings.

When I was a teenager, I wasn't allowed to experience anger or sadness because that was just evidence that you're giving in to the Devil and him wanting you to feel that way—not having joy in the Lord, and all that stuff. When I would go to my friends' houses, I went from my home environment of almost no emotion to an environment where families were screaming at each other all the time and just having these horrible fights and throwing stuff. It was crazy. But it was refreshing. Because it was like, "This is what normal humans are like when you're not forced to behave a certain way all the time." It was just nice. (Holly)

Some of those I've spoken with said they eventually got so good at denying their feelings that they could no longer access them, even when they wanted to. They couldn't touch their anger, their sadness, their pain; they couldn't even feel happiness.

I didn't even know what happiness was. Happiness was a sign that you're on the wrong path, because if you're happy, then things were too easy, and things are only too easy when you're really giving in to your sinful nature. If we wanted to be holy, it was going to have to be a struggle. So, you have to be struggling and suffering constantly. There is no happiness. There is no peace. It's as though I'm only comfortable operating in chaos. When the chaos and pain are gone, I feel off-centered and somewhat guilty. I was taught I should always be in a state of suffering and don't deserve to be happy. Things have been going really well for both me and my husband lately, which has filled me with a sense of dread. (Holly)

I think that if you're trained to be subservient, if you're trained to submit, then the logic is that your happiness probably means you haven't done enough to submit because there's part of you that's still getting satisfied. And if you are really submitting, then actually none of you is supposed to be satisfied. I am happy. It's depressing that that's hard to admit. I have to be unhappy about my unwillingness to admit my happiness, right? (Piper)

And yet, we were expected to be "joyful."

I was so sad and so alone. I was living in this world where I was supposed to be "joyful," right? We're taught joy is different from happiness, it's innately blah, blah, blah. So I was acting. It was like, fake it until you make it because you want other people to be attracted to Christ, so you're joyful. But I was so sad and alone. (Meagan)

It's said that you have joy in suffering because God's getting you through your suffering well, and because you know you're going to Heaven because you're suffering on earth. So you have that joy deep within you because you know what's coming and because you're doing a great job at suffering. (Holly)

Some readers who have attended evangelical churches—particularly more Charismatic ones where congregants may throw up their arms, break into tongues, and fall onto the altar with weeping—may find themselves perplexed by my interviewees' disconnection from their emotions. Surely, they may suppose, evangelicals are more connected to their emotions than just about anyone else!

On many subjects, they're right.

As an adolescent, evangelicalism's emphasis on feelings was one of the most compelling parts of the faith for me. Here, all my wonderful, terrible, unavoidable, feelings were encouraged and intensified by a religion in which every decision was not only a matter of life or death, but a matter of *eternal* life or *eternal* death. The dark swell of my own disgrace; the overwhelming terror of the abyss that lay awaiting all un-forgiven sinners; the ensuing relief that I had been saved from it; the life-giving elation of singing praises to God; the intimacy of tear-filled prayers with my peers; the gripping of one another's warm hands when we admitted our most painful truths, wordlessly saying to one another: *I am listening.*

In 1912, Émile Durkheim identified the emotional high individuals get from being part of religious group experiences and the effects that high has upon the group itself. He called it "collective effervescence." In *The Elementary Forms of Religious Life* he argues that by creating positive feelings among participants, collective effervescence enables a group to overcome divisions. Today, scholars like Dr. David Chidester see forms of collective effervescence in everything from singing the "Star-Spangled Banner" to attending Tupperware parties.[3] However, I have never seen collective effervescence as intense as when a bunch of evangelical adolescents, fired up on hormones, get together. Here, the adolescent's most extreme emotions are called forth time and time again. In 1923, the theologian and philosopher Rudolf Otto said that there is a kind of heat in religion—"vitality, passion, emotional temper, will, force, movement, excitement, energy, activity, impetus," all coming together to create a "consuming fire."[4] Still today, I yearn for it. There are few places in this world that we can go to feel like this.*

But in the church, not all emotions are equal.

At certain times and concerning certain topics, admitting that you have feelings, particularly the "wrong" feelings, is tantamount to admit-ting the Devil has got a hold of you. Yet at another time and concerning

---

* "The only time it really sucks," my interviewee Biz said, "and is really complicated, is when that feeling is coupled with certain ideas. When your body senses . . ." She strug-gled to find the words. "When your body is having such a euphoric experience and then you hear, like, that gay people and feminists and women who have sex before marriage are going to Hell. That kind of euphoria becomes associated with those things."

another topic, you may be accused of not being godly enough if you *don't* express emotions (by which I mean, of course, the "right" emotions for a Christian, for the particular moment, and for your gender). It can be tough for a newcomer to get the hang of the rules, particularly rules like these that are never spoken outright. But if you spend enough time in the subculture, and experience a few shamings to help show you the way, you eventually figure it out: Express lots of emotions here, perhaps even falsifying emotions if you don't have them, and put on your "joy" mask the rest of the time—disconnecting from or hiding feelings that don't fit.

> In order to survive in the church, you have to live on the surface. Every action is filtered and judged as good or bad and the depth of the reality is lost in the process. If you are vulnerable, you will have hands laid on you. People saying, "I'll put you in my prayers," because there is something wrong with you. There is something wrong with feeling that way. There is something wrong with you having those thoughts. There is something wrong with you being real with yourself. This forms a hard-surfaced layer, the only layer you can show. And you learn to live from it. (Johnnie)

When the gastroenterologist told me I couldn't be in as much pain as I claimed to be if I was smiling so much, it triggered something deep in me. The implication that I was a "bad girl" performing sickness for—what?—attention?—(when I was actually a "good girl" performing health)—was enough to shut me up for another year or so. I put less energy into *getting* better, and more energy into *suffering* better.

In their book, *Proverbs of Ashes: Violence, Redemptive Suffering, and the Search for What Saves Us*, Rita Nakashima Brock and Rebecca Ann Parker write:

I've heard stories of abuse and rape that break my heart—from ordinary kids. I counsel some of the religious kids, and the more attached they are to traditional ideas about Jesus, the more likely they are to think of their abuse as "good" for them, as a trial designed for a reason, as pain that makes them like Jesus. They are often in denial about the amount of pain they live with. It amazes me that they survive and appear so "normal."[5]

I am quite certain that almost anybody who knew me in those years would have called me normal. I don't think that anyone had the slightest suspicion of just how much pain I was in, including my parents. Though my mom was concerned, and pushed me to continue seeing doctors, even she didn't know that—two years after seeing the doctor in Australia—the pain had grown so bad that I was taking up to five ibuprofen before my first-year college classes. Or that by the start of spring break that first year of college, I was bleeding what I remember to be a quarter-cup of blood and intestinal lining at a time into the toilet. Or that in the middle of spring break, I had lost so much blood that I tumbled off of the toilet and onto my college dorm's bathroom floor. I managed to pull my pants up but I was too weak to stand or even get back onto the toilet to continue bleeding into it. I heard my friend Sebastian's voice in the hall and called out to him. When he entered, he discovered me curled in a ball in front of the toilet. Helping me to my feet, he called a cab and together we went to the emergency room.

Crohn's disease—which was my ultimate diagnosis—is the immune system's failure to recognize the presence of food and stool in the intestines as normal. The disease tricks the immune system into thinking these essential entities are bad. Attempting to protect the person from the food and stool the body must process in order to survive, the immune system attacks the intestines, making itself the thing that the person *really* needs protection from (in the same way that those who use shame to "protect" people from natural aspects of themselves, such as their sexuality, can inadvertently become the thing from which the person actually needs protection).

So while my mind told my guts to shut up, to not be such a bother, my immune system attacked them physically. Neither my mind nor my immune system understood at the time that every part of us is a part of us. That we cannot separate our bodies from our spirits from our minds from our hearts. We are one entity.

The gastroenterologist at the hospital the day that Sebastian took me to the emergency room took one look at me and said, "You're really sick, aren't you?"

I nodded.

"You're white as a sheet, your eyes are dark, and if you're losing as much blood as you say you are, we have to get you in the hospital right now," he continued.

I was so relieved I started to cry on the spot. For the first time, somebody *saw* me. And somebody gave me permission to see *myself*. Permission to admit I was suffering. Permission to ask for help. Permission I was not yet able to give to myself.

After several weeks in two hospitals, another gastroenterologist determined the medications the first gastroenterologist gave me weren't working. In a very frank discussion, he told my mother and me that they could continue to try medication but that the disease had gotten so out of control that my intestine could perforate at any moment, which could kill me.

"Before you decide to do surgery, though," he told me, "I want you to know you'll have a long, ugly scar. For a young woman, I know this can be difficult."

A scar? I thought. *Who cares about that? What? I'm going to die because of vanity? Please. I am a woman of the spirit, not of the flesh alone.*

"Let's do the surgery," I said flatly.

We did it the next morning.

Afterward, my surgeon told me that my large intestine had been so ravaged by my immune system that it had nearly fallen apart in his hands. It was as though someone had scraped the entrails with a Brillo pad, he said. None of it could be saved. My surgeon was one of the best in the country, but there was so much disease in my belly during the time of the surgery that infection had spread. In the weeks afterward, the pain grew worse, at some points becoming so severe that I would shake uncontrollably, my teeth banging against one another as I pressed a button to release painkillers into my bloodstream again and again. One surgery became two, became three. Each night, I bled the bed the way children pee theirs, blood from my unhealed intestine pouring out of my anus. I would wake and press a button for my nurse, who would come in with a sad look on his or her face and say, "Did it happen again?" before lifting me out of the pool of blood in my bed, changing my sheets, my blankets, and my hospital gown, and placing me lightly back in. One nurse tried placing a bedpan beneath me while I slept to catch the blood but lying on it bent my body back, tearing at my wounds. Another tried dressing me in diapers, but the blood ran out the edges, pooling beneath me again. Finally, the Kegel exercises they had taught me began to work and my anal muscles grew strong enough to hold the blood in, even while I slept. And after nearly a month in the hospital, they sent me home.

The first stumbling block those raised as girls in the purity movement must overcome is the message that if you are suffering, it's your fault: *It may be your sin; it may be your psychosis; but it is certainly not the shaming system you find yourself in.* When taken to heart, this message can make us miss—or, when we do see it, *dismiss*—our suffering, until one day, it's too late.

Christianity has a long history of glorifying gore and gorifying God.

At the center of the Christian religion is the story of a bodily anguish so terrible that it saved the world. After all, according to most evangelicals, even Jesus, who lived a perfect life, did less good with his life than he did with his death. It was Christ's torment, not his joy, that set us free. It was his death, not his life, that allowed us to enter Heaven. So when our bodies are beaten and our hearts broken, it is sometimes thought we reflect the perfect life of Christ, whose pain and death is the hinge upon which God's plan for the world turns. The more God allows us to suffer, the more opportunity he gives us to be like him and prove our unshakable devotion to him.

When I eventually returned to college after my fourth and final surgery, I was fascinated by tales of Christian mystics, monks, and nuns sleeping with spiked clamps on their legs or wearing an item of clothing that pierced them under their habits. They caused themselves physical harm, one professor explained, in order to feel the pain of the God with whom they had entered into marriage.

The stories captivated me because I knew from personal experience that the ideas behind them were not as outdated as my professor made them sound. I knew that even those of us who do not live cloistered lives, those of us who shop at the Mall of America and take our kids to see Disney on Ice, sometimes silently endure incredible levels of preventable pain for some of the very same reasons.

And when we stop, when we complain, when we expose that whatever isn't "supposed" to be happening in our church, our school, or our home *is* happening, too often the response is that whatever's happening is our "fault." Be it from a doctor who says your real problem is your acne or your complaining, not your pain, or from a church board who decides to let the pastor who admitted to touching you go, but then quietly moves him on to another church, implying that they don't think he will do it again there, which means, of course, *he* isn't the problem. *You* are.

*   *   *

When I got home from the hospital, I was forty pounds lighter. I felt hollowed out, empty like a drum. My body was flat like that of a child again, and yet too big for the girlish daybed I returned home to. My feet stuck out between its footboard's white wooden slats making me feel more like Alice in Wonderland after having gobbled a piece of "eat me" cake than a grown-up. Looking down at them it suddenly occurred to me, my feet had been sticking out that way for years, all throughout my teens, and yet somehow, I hadn't noticed until now.

My former youth pastor had been sentenced to nine months in jail, placed on probation for twenty years, and forbidden to work with youths again.

And I was questioning *everything.*

"Linda?" my mom called from outside my bedroom door.

I quickly pulled my T-shirt back down over my belly.

"Yes?" I called back.

The door opened and my mom's face appeared through the crack. "Can I come in?"

"Sure," I said.

"I wasn't sure if you were sleeping." She opened the door the rest of the way.

"No," I said. "I changed my dressing," nodding toward my stomach.

"Pastor called," she said softly.

I turned onto my side and planted my palms firmly on the mattress, releasing my weight onto them to ease the strain on my stomach, and tried to push myself upright. She watched me, her forehead furrowed with concern, before putting her arms on my shoulders and helping me the rest of the way.

"Thank you," I grimaced.

"He told me they're going to have live animals in the nativity scene this year," she continued, helping me straighten my body. "Donkeys, cows, chickens. They've even got llamas."

"Cool," I said, lowering my head and closing my eyes. I still got dizzy every time I went from lying down to sitting, because I was easily dehydrated after having lost my entire colon and much of my small intestine in the surgeries.

My mom ducked down so she could make eye contact with me. "Linda, in this year's nativity scene . . . they want you to play Mary."

"Me?" I said, lifting my head.

"You would even get to hold a real little baby." She beamed.

Were I not in so much pain, I might have laughed. There was no way I could hold a baby. I couldn't even hold my*self* up.

"Mom," I said, shaking my head. "I can't do that."

"I know," she sighed, taking my hand. "I know honey. I told him you were still too sick." I raised my eyebrows in an implied, *yeah*. "But I thought you would want to know, they chose you."

"Mary . . ." I said quietly.

Mom smiled at me. "Mm-hmm."

I closed my eyes again. Desperate to be counted among the praiseworthy women, I had once been like the foolish king who wished that everything he touched would turn to gold and wound up killing all he loved in the process, as even his daughter turned into a golden statue. I had made a foolish wish, the wish of a child. I had prayed that God would allow me to suffer, and suffer he had allowed me to do.

But that prayer, foolish though it was, was not misinformed. Suffering *had* transformed me in my community's eyes. For the first time, I was "good." Between surgeries, when I gathered up enough energy to go to church, I was no longer chastised for looking too sexual. I was complimented for looking so beautiful. I was given hugs; I was prayed for with tremendous earnestness; I was asked what presents I might like congregants to drop by the house to cheer me up; our head pastor asked me to read Scripture in church; the youth pastor asked me to lead a first-year high school girls' group; and now this . . . the Virgin Mary! Whereas my sexuality had once hidden my goodness from their view, my suffering seemed to *expose* it.

And yet, I knew I was the same person now as I had been then. Just as selfish, just as selfless, just as caring, just as careless, and wearing the same little dresses and skirts I'd always worn. My sorrow made me purer in their eyes—stripping me of my sexy vitality, and allowing them to forget my body. But as for me? I was more aware of my body than ever— of how much I missed it. And as I lay in bed I would have traded in the church's newfound perception of me as good to be able to run and jump and play in a minute.

There were several factors that I imagine went into my illness getting as out of control as it did—the limited medical understanding of diseases like Crohn's at the time, the healthcare industry and the lack of time doctors are given to assess situations, and gender dynamics that often result in the suffering of women being overlooked. Yet I too must take some responsibility. My need for approval and my fear of being blamed shut me up when I should have been standing and shouting for people to pay attention.

Looking back at the day my mom told me I had been cast as the Virgin Mary, it seems to me to be a kind of strange nativity scene. Only in this birth story, I wasn't playing Mary, or any mother at all. I was playing a baby—too big for her daybed crib already, and yet just being born. Unformed. Unsure of so many things, but completely sure of one: I was done trying to be who they wanted me to be.

2

The Lie

When I met Piper at my first evangelical Christian church retreat, I was thirteen years old. It had been months since I'd been born again at the church altar call and, so far, my life hadn't changed at all. When my dad suggested that I attend a weekend spring retreat with the youth group that met in the church at the end of our block, I told him it would probably suck. He told me not to say that word. And I asked him what word. Suck?

When my dad's friend pulled into the church parking lot in a minivan, Dad walked over and shook his hand through the window. I sat in our car protesting being there and watched the man's daughter emerge from the car yawning. From the second I saw her, I knew Piper was cool. She dropped her backpack onto the pavement and dragged it over to the youth pastor who was loading the bus, cutting through crowds of junior high schoolers hugging and laughing without making eye contact with any of the kids who yelled out to say "Hi!" When my dad finally pulled me out of the car and introduced us, Piper didn't even smile. She just looked up and said, "I'm not awake yet."

I laughed. "Me neither!" I said a little too loudly.

Though obviously, I was.

When I walked down the center aisle of the bus later, Piper called out to me.

56

I sauntered over trying to look like I didn't care.

"Sorry I was so out of it before," she apologized. "I hadn't had my coffee yet." Piper lifted a plastic-capped mug into the air. Then she patted the back of the seat in front of her.

"Sit here," she said.

"Okay," I shrugged. I shoved my backpack under the seat in front of me and sat down. Piper introduced me to her friends, Ann and Jessica, before pulling a bag of lime-flavored Tostitos out of her backpack.

"Want some?" she asked.

"Sure," I said, a little taken aback. It couldn't have been much after seven AM.

The youth pastor stood at the front of the bus. "Ausssh ausssh," he said, his version of a hushing sound.

"Ausssh ausssh" a couple of the kids repeated back to him good-naturedly.

I smiled.

"We're going to head out in a minute, so make sure you have everything with you," the youth pastor said as we quieted down. I turned and looked out the window. My dad waved. I smiled at him, but I didn't wave back. I didn't want my new friends to see me do something like that.

I turned back to Piper. "Let's open those chips." Piper ripped the bag's edges as the bus lurched forward and lime-flavored Tostitos flew down the aisle. She immediately fell into uncontrollable laughter. Ann asked me if I'd seen that.

"Yeah," I said, smiling.

"You saw that?" Ann said again, laughing harder.

"Yeah!" I exclaimed this time, and doubled over. Piper hit me with her hat.

"You try to open these things!" she shouted over the rumble of the bus, now pulling out of the parking lot.

"Next time, I will!" I shouted back. I reached into the bag, grabbed my first-ever lime-flavored Tostito, and loved it. As we pulled out of the parking lot, it was just us. Just us in all the world. No parents. No teachers. I turned and looked out the window at my dad, still waving, as he grew smaller in the distance before asking Piper for another chip. She handed me the bag.

This is my testimony, the moment I became an evangelical Christian—a member of the subculture that would come to shape my adolescent and teenage years. It wasn't in the church crying and praying with a team of volunteers during the altar call months earlier. Perhaps it was then that I answered *God*'s call. But the day I answered the church's call, I was sitting in the back of a bus with a group of awkward junior high girls eating my first lime-flavored Tostito.

That weekend was one of the best of my life. I was high on Jesus. At least that's what the youth pastor said during his evening sermon, adding: "Hold on to that high, guys. Take it back home with you to your family; take it back to school on Monday; shine the light of Jesus wherever you go." I nodded with the fervor of a convert.

At my public school, cruelty was currency, but here, it didn't matter if you sat in the back of the retreat's rugged sanctuary with your hair hanging over your face in hopes that no one would notice you or if you were the star of the local soccer team and magically maintained a tan through the winter—everyone was welcome, worthy of time, attention, and love. I had never been somewhere where all I had to do to be accepted was walk into the room. Where my mere existence was enough. It was everything that I had thought the world should be up until this point, and nothing of what I had found it actually was. But for the first time in my life, I felt like I could change all that. Here. With these people. Sitting around the campfire with my new friends our last night there, tears came running down my cheeks just as they had when I was born again months ago, and I claimed this faith to be my faith and these people to be my people.

*   *   *

The last day of the retreat Piper, Ann, Jessica, and I were leaving the cabin at the beginning of our few hours of coveted "free time" when our cabin leader, one of the other girls' moms, made the abrupt announcement that everyone in our cabin was to find another place to be except thirteen-year-old Piper and me. Sensing anger in her voice, my mind skidded through everything that had happened since we'd arrived at the campground two days ago, searching for something we might have done wrong. I tried to catch Piper's eye to see if she knew what was up but she was staring at the concrete floor.

As the screen door fluttered shut and the sound of our friends squealing grew distant as they ran toward the lake, the cabin mom turned to me. She smiled. I smiled nervously back. Then she walked over to an empty bunk. She sat on the edge of the plastic-lined mattress and patted the place next to her. I moved slowly toward her and sat.

"Linda," she said softly. Piper walked across the room, still staring down, and sat down beside me. "Are you happy here?"

"Oh," I said haltingly. "Yes."

"Good. Because I want you to be comfortable in our youth group. I want you to be happy here," she said softly. "Do you understand?"

"Yeah. Yeah, I, uh, thanks," I stammered.

"And I want to make sure that the other girls are making you feel comfortable."

"Oh, they are," I said.

"Are you sure?"

"Yeah."

"Good."

She turned away from me and I exhaled deeply.

Then the cabin mom leaned forward. She rested her elbows on her knees and stared quietly at the cabin door for what seemed like minutes. I started to get uncomfortable again. Suddenly she turned. She looked past me to Piper. Then she said, "Why do you need so much attention?" My eyes bulged. Piper was silent. "You raise your hand every time the pastor asks the group a question," the cabin mom continued. "Why?"

I glanced quickly over at Piper. Her eyes were on her hands, which sat in her lap. She didn't look up.

Piper finally broke the silence. "I actually don't think I raise my hand all the—"

"You do," the cabin mom interrupted. She paused to allow Piper to take this in before continuing. "Is it insecurity?"

I looked straight up, focused on the wooden planks of the top bunk, tried counting things—knots, lines in the wood. The cabin mom leaned toward me to get closer to Piper. I pulled my chin in and leaned back to make room.

"Is that what makes you feel like you have to be the center of attention? Insecurity?"

"I don't know," Piper mumbled at her lap.

"Do you think that the boys like it when you show off like that?"

Piper shrugged.

"Well they don't," the mom answered her own question. "And I can tell you right now, they won't in the future either."

I don't remember how the conversation ended. What I do remember is that when the cabin mom finally dismissed us, it was with a hug and a smile for me, and a stern suggestion that Piper reflect on the root of her insecurity. But Piper, reflecting back on it twenty-five years later, remembers more. She remembers the cabin mom telling her she was obnoxious, loud, and couldn't stand not being the center of attention. She remembers it was all she could do to will herself not to cry so as not to validate the mom's power over her. She remembers wanting to fight back, but not being able to. She remembers feeling frozen, as though she got the wind knocked out of her, unable to think, talk, or move.

Afterward, Piper and I both remember walking to the lake in silence. We remember finding Jessica and Ann in a cabin that looked out over the water. We remember telling them the story of what had happened, and their listening in stunned silence. And then, we both remember Piper beginning to cry. First softly and then in heaving sobs as Jessica, Ann, and I gathered around her, holding her tightly around the shoulders and telling her that she was awesome—smart, funny, cool, nice, loving. And the thing is, Piper really was all of those things. She was the epitome of the radical acceptance that made me want to be a part of this group. And so, I chalked up what had happened in the cabin as an anomaly. That cabin mom just didn't get it, I decided. She didn't understand what we were all trying to do here.

But in the years to come, I would encounter some version of this scenario again and again. My friends and I were told in one breath we were loved unconditionally, accepted just as we were, and headed for Heaven, and in the next we were warned of the evils of feminists, homosexuals, women who had sex outside of marriage, and other Hell-bound individuals. It didn't even occur to me then that some people in youth group might already see themselves as fitting into some of these categories that I wouldn't see myself in for years, and how that must have felt to them then, but what did occur to me was this: That unconditional love that I had fallen for in my early days in the church? It was conditional.

If the first stumbling block those raised as girls in the purity movement must overcome is the message that if purity culture doesn't work for you it's because there is something wrong with you, the second stumbling block is its strict gender role expectations. At a time when many in our society are rejecting the importance of gender distinctions altogether, the religious purity movement is doubling down on them, teaching what is called complementarianism—the idea that there are two distinct genders that have equal worth in God's eyes, but very different roles, responsibilities, and expectations here on earth: The man is to be undeniably masculine, even as he practices patience and understanding as a leader, whereas the woman is to be irrefutably feminine and to lovingly consent to and support the leadership of the man. They *complement* one another—hence the name complementarianism—creating the perfect whole. But if either gender strays from his or her designated role, the balance upon which it is said the stability of the family, church, and society rests is in jeopardy.

Growing up, I had learned to loathe the power-hungry women that we were told ruined families, tore apart churches, hated men and children, and wore big, boxy shoulder pads—the kind that went by the f-word: feminist.

I remember the day the pastor announced that our church was seeking a volunteer to fill the recently relinquished role of head usher. The new head usher, he explained, would write the schedule for all of the ushers and sometimes usher himself. A friend whose dad was on the church board leaned over to me during the announcement: "You know, a woman volunteered and they turned her down. They said it was inappropriate for a woman to schedule a man's time, so she couldn't take on the role."

For some reason, this information shocked me. I had been tacitly accepting that women were banned from certain roles in the church for years. But the absurdity of a woman not being allowed to say, *Randy, you've got the fifth; Isaiah, you're the twelfth; Oh, you've got a wedding out of state that day? Okay, Randy can you swap with Isaiah? Great*, made all of the rules about what women were and were not allowed to be and do seem suddenly crazy to me.

Week after week, the pastor stood at the pulpit pleading for someone to volunteer for the position, and I burned inside knowing that someone had. Still, if someone were to have called me a feminist in high school, I would have recoiled.*

There is a lesson in the 2004 version of the popular sex education curriculum Choosing the Best, which I mentioned in the opening (it's the one that claims to have reached over 4 million students in forty-seven states), called "Knight in Shining Armor" that illustrates complementarianism well. The lesson features the story of a knight in shining armor and a princess. This princess happens to know a thing or two about how to slay dragons. So when a dragon threatens them, she suggests the knight in shining armor use a noose on the dragon. He does, and it works. But the knight, the lesson tells us, would have rather used his sword. When the next dragon comes, the princess suggests the knight use poison. Again, he follows her advice. And again, it works. But again, the knight is unhappy, because it wasn't the weapon *he* wanted to use. One day, the lesson continues, the knight hears another maiden calling for help. The maiden doesn't have any advice for the knight, so he uses his sword to protect her. Afterward, the knight leaves the princess for the maiden, and—as the story goes—they live happily ever. The moral of the story, as shared in the curriculum? "Occasional suggestions and assistance may be all right, but too much of it will lessen a man's confidence or even turn him away from his princess."†1

How was Piper, who wanted to be the president of the United States since she could remember, to function within the complementarian context? Piper who asked her mom what the Anti-Christ was when she

---

* It is important to acknowledge that some evangelical churches are much more embracing of women's leadership than others. In these churches, you can sometimes even find head pastors who are women. However, I have been assured by many of these pastors, this does *not* mean they do not experience gender discrimination in the church.

† It appears this lesson was replaced by a different lesson in the latest version of the curriculum. In the new lesson, the princess is engaged to a prince who prefers jousting with the other knights and buying the princess gifts to talking with her about their future life together. The princess proceeds to fall in love with a blacksmith, who *does* talk with her, and leaves the prince for him.

was in the third grade and, when her mom responded that the Anti-Christ would be the leader of the world before Jesus came back, thought that sounded like a pretty good gig?

"I can think of several times when I was very explicitly told, 'No man will want you if you're like this,'" Piper said sitting on the edge of my couch in New York City when we were both in our late thirties. Piper was wearing a chic, gray tailored dress, a far cry from the kinds of baggy clothes I had grown accustomed to her wearing when we were growing up. Her hair, bleached and dyed a pale blue, was slicked back in a way that gave her more class than edge. She was visiting New York City for her high-powered job.

"The common thread was always that I was vocal and opinionated," she continued, holding the cup of espresso I had just made her on my stovetop. "I was essentially told, 'Don't disagree with the men around you. They don't want you to be smarter than them. They don't want you to have opinions. You'll make them intellectually uncomfortable. No one will want you if you're like this.' But being sexually fulfilled in a context that would lessen me intellectually? I didn't want that," Piper said definitively.

No matter how many warnings she received from people like our cabin mom, she wasn't willing to give up her ambition or her desire to prove she was the smartest person in the room. So instead, she gave up guys. Piper interpreted the story that all of us girls were told about who we could and must be if we wanted to be loved in a way that allowed her to live. At a young age, she accepted that she would never be attractive, never date, never kiss, never marry, never have sex, and if any man was ever fool enough to love her, she would warn him that she would likely destroy his life. But she *would*—dammit—become president.

As I listened to Piper, I thought back to the experiences of others I'd spoken with. Two other women had told me almost the same story—that they didn't want to give up their intelligence so they shut off their sexuality, wishing they were boys so they could be fully free of it. One even thought deep down she *was* a boy for the sole reason that she really liked books. When she got her period, she was disappointed to see she was a girl after all.

"I think we joked about my prolonged grunge phase," Piper said to me, raising her eyebrows as though challenging me to tease her. "But I wouldn't say that I repressed my sexuality. I just sort of nothinged it," she explained. "I said, 'This doesn't matter.'" At least it didn't matter to Piper. Making it not matter to everyone else, on the other hand, was more of a challenge.

"We had a square dance during my college's freshman orientation," Piper said, setting her cup of espresso down on the coffee table. "There was this guy on the basketball team who was 6'8" who was my square dance partner. We would talk about basketball. And it was kind of funny because he was so much taller than me, and we were like *do-si-do* and he would put his hand on my head because he couldn't reach my arm. And I remember coming back from that—this was my third day at college—and a taller girl who lived in my dorm, I mean she was probably 5'11", came up to me and said, 'Why do all the short girls always take all of the tall guys?'" Piper gave her a great Valley girl accent, and she and I both laughed.

"I was like, 'This is a fucking square dance,'" she continued.

"You said that?" I gasped, knowing her Christian college well enough to know how people would have reacted.

Piper nodded. "And I definitely used the f-bomb, which also freaked her out. I think I started using that word in particular once I got to college. It became an easy way for me to signal to people, 'I'm not like the rest of the girls here.' I felt like a misfit. Almost like in *Rudolph the Red-Nosed Reindeer and the Island of Misfit Toys*? Where you're half teddy bear but there're all these weird things there?"

Eventually, Piper explained, the feeling that "there's no place for me here" can lead to the belief that "there is no place for me with Jesus. And the flip side of that coin is eternal damnation," Piper said dropping her voice. "And that's terrifying. The hatred of self that comes from that lack of place in the community."

Within the various complementarian communities she found herself in over the years, Piper remembers two types of standouts: a handful of women vehemently chastising her for her subversion of the gender expectations—from the cabin mom to some of her best college girlfriends—and a handful of men subverting the expectations and affirming her just as she was.

"Senior year of college, I went on a Student Activities Council retreat led by the assistant dean of student life or whatever, I don't even know," Piper detailed. "We were playing Trivial Pursuit and the last question that our team had to answer to win the game was a question about who played for the Cleveland Browns, held all these NFL records, and is in the Pro Football Hall of Fame. The two guys on my team looked at each other and they kind of shrugged their shoulders. And I said, "Guys! It's Jim Brown!" I was right. We won and our advisor looked at me and he said in a very non-gross way, 'Gilbert'—my nickname was Gilbert because my last name is Sullivan. He said, 'Gilbert, you're going to make some guy so happy someday.'

"I'll never forget that moment. We were on this retreat and . . ." Tears gathered in Piper's eyes. "I haven't thought about this in a really long time . . . but it was so affirming. We were on this retreat and we had decided, for whatever ungodly reason, we weren't going to shower and so, we were just all gross. We'd been camping in the woods, so I looked like hell. It was totally asexual. But, it was the first time the smart, sports-loving part of me was explicitly affirmed and that it was in such a hardcore evangelical setting . . . it was really awesome."

Research shows that people tend to shame others for what they are ashamed of, which might explain Piper's experiences with women's judgmentalism. But sharing shame doesn't have to pit us against one another, making us enemies; it can go the other way around.

Within months of her experience on the Student Activities retreat, Piper became very close to a female friend. "My last semester of college, my friend Lucy and I realized that each of us had latched onto what we called 'The Lie,'" Piper said, her voice beginning to tremble again. She paused and took a deep breath. "I'm really emotional about this," she tried to explain. "Because I realize how lucky I am that I had people in my life that I could engage with on this. I'm—I'm absolutely terrified of what would've happened to me if I didn't have those outlets." I nodded as she wiped her eyes. "Lucy's version of The Lie was almost the exact opposite of mine," she continued. "Mine was 'no one will want you if you're smart and opinionated,' and hers was 'I have to put up with everything in my relationship because my opinions don't matter and what I want doesn't matter.'"

"I don't know that those *are* opposites," I suggested. "You were both reacting to the same gender-based lie: Be submissive and be loved, or be a leader and be alone forever. It's the same story, the same lie. You just made different choices within it. Lucy chose submission for the sake of having a relationship; you chose being alone forever so you didn't have to submit."

"Yes, yes, yes," Piper said. "And we were well-positioned to see one another's stuff. I saw what happened to Lucy when she clung to The Lie—she stayed in a very abusive relationship. And Lucy pushed me to see that my acceptance of The Lie had consequences too."

The shared root of Piper's and Lucy's challenges is important to recognize. Research shows that complementarianism upholds abusive dynamics among conservative, evangelical women whose religious lives are integral to their sense of identity. The women in one study, "The Process of Recovery and Rebuilding Among Abused Women in the Conservative Evangelical Subculture," reported facing many challenges to their healing post-abuse, but said that the challenge that posed the greatest threat to their recovery was the church's emphasis on traditional gender roles. And yet, this is often the last thing the church looks at when addressing intimate partner violence.

The authors of the study write: "The contrast between the church's ideal of the family and the reality of the abusive situation created problems for both the church and these women. The church's idealized conception of a dutiful wife in submission to a loving husband under the authority of God was threatened. . . . As in other family systems, the church family system sought to maintain its own equilibrium and belief system through denial, minimization, and spiritualization of the abusive situation. The women experienced isolation and alienation as the church denied or minimized the severity of the family violence problem. When counseling was provided, the church often suggested the problem would be alleviated if the abused woman followed what the church believed was the Divine pattern of loving obedient submission to her husband."*2

As an illustration, one woman who came to her pastor about the abuse was advised: "Pray more. Submit more." After being given this advice, the woman reports she "was feeling sad and hurt, and I felt like the Lord was telling me, 'don't feel sorry for yourself: you have to forgive this guy.' . . . God doesn't feel sorry for me because I have to forgive him . . . and carry on, so I said, 'okay, I'll get strong and suck in my guts and when he comes home I'll tell him that I'm sorry' . . . and I did. I went and apologized to him for [his] being abusive to me."3

And yet, the study's researchers report that when these women stopped listening to the black-and-white gender-based analysis of their religious leaders, and developed a healthier spiritual life in which they allowed themselves to reframe their understanding of how God saw abuse, their faith was transformed from a dangerous influence that maintained their abuse into "a powerful source of comfort, hope, and insight" that al-

---

* As an example of what happens when this thinking is taken to its extreme, more than one of my interviewees report having been told (sometimes by men and women in leadership) that the most Christ-like thing a woman can do is submit to being raped.

lowed them to heal from that same abuse.[4] The researchers explain: "The women's faith functioned as a meaning-making framework that could either engender shame and guilt or inspire hope and empower transformative change. The church functioned as an extended family system that could minimize, deny, and enable abuse or provide much-needed social support, spiritual encouragement, and practical assistance."[5]

Like the women in this study, Piper and Lucy healed themselves and each other by developing greater spiritual autonomy, unleashing themselves from religious leaders who hurt them with their analysis of what was right and what was wrong—which they called "the truth"—and doing their *own* spiritual analysis, which included naming some of that "truth" as lies.

"One of my most poignant memories is laying on the bedroom floor of Lucy's apartment and just crying," Piper told me. "I knew something in how I was perceiving and acting in the world was just horribly askew. I just couldn't reconcile it. I couldn't manage it. And I remember Lucy put her hand on my head, and she prayed to let me release The Lie. She prayed that God would let me realize how I was made and that I was loved. It was really powerful. It felt—I started to be able to put the pieces together. I stopped fighting with God because I thought he made me in a way that set me up to fail, and started thinking about how I could better reflect what he had made me to be, and accept it as a gift."*

A little more than a year after she graduated from college, Piper moved to Washington, DC. Save the occasional pity date with some poor sap who Piper saw as foolhardy enough to like her despite the dangers she still believed she posed to him as an intelligent woman, Piper had lived entirely without romance up to this point in her life. Listening to her tell her

---

* Piper contacted Lucy after our interview and asked if Lucy would feel comfortable with her story being shared in this book. Lucy enthusiastically agreed, expressing her belief that it was important for others to hear her story.

story, I couldn't help but smile at my memory of seeing her at a wedding when we were both in our early twenties. All of the unmarried women were called into the center of the reception hall to try to catch the bride's bouquet. As Piper and I walked forward, I remember her uncharacteristically clinging to my arm with discomfort, whispering into my ear: "I hate this, I hate this, I hate this." When the bride threw the bouquet, she abruptly let go of me and ran. I remember watching the mass of huddled women heave toward the bouquet in one direction, and then Piper, running the opposite direction as though the bouquet was a bomb.

But in DC, "it was just weird," she said. "All of a sudden I was going to receptions and getting hit on by important people." For the first time, she went on a few real dates and even had two "half-kisses." Then she began hanging out with a group of friends from her Christian college who had also moved to DC, including a young man named Michael who she hadn't really known well in college. "Our relationship was very DC," she said. "We would go to embassy parties and receptions together. We would work the room and not talk to each other, but we were falling in love across the room.

"I remember three days before our wedding having a meltdown in the church parking lot," Piper said. "Just saying to him, 'Everybody's coming here. Are you sure that you really want to do this?'" The Lie had reared its ugly head, and Piper was afraid she would ruin Michael's life, just as the complementarian message she had been raised with promised. "Then after we got married, I remember one of Michael's friends had a wedding close to the presidential election in 2004. It was a fun wedding. People got along well. I was chatting about politics, and Michael and I got into it like we usually do." (Michael is a Republican. Piper is a Democrat. They actually spent their first wedding anniversary volunteering for opposing presidential campaigns.) "And a couple of people just dropped their jaws like, 'You don't agree on this?' Multiple weddings, multiple times people have come up to him and said, 'Wow, your wife is really opinionated.' Or,

'Your wife doesn't always agree with you.' And without missing a beat, he's always like, 'Yes, and I love it. I wouldn't want it any other way.' "

But twelve years into their marriage, The Lie still makes it hard for her to believe what Michael says.

"Even now, we laugh about it. That I have to work to remind myself that I know he loves me. It's no shortcoming of his whatsoever. When I sit back and let myself be objective about my relationship with Michael, I know that the things about me that he loves are the same things that I fear are the nuggets of destruction. But there have been times where I have not fully allowed myself to experience everything with Michael because I just . . . it's a pinch-yourself moment. It's like, 'This can't be real.' He would say, 'I love you,' and I would say, 'I know.' And then I would try to *make* myself know. It's ridiculous to even hear myself say it. I'm a smart girl. I have fancy degrees. But the circuits still don't fire for me on this."

"On feeling loved?" I asked.

"On feeling romantically loved," she answered. "We've had several conversations in which I've said, 'I think you should break up with me because I think I'm going to ruin your life.' He is always so steady, saying I don't get to make that choice for him. I get to make that choice for myself in terms of whether or not I wanted to be with him, but I can't decide for him whether or not he wants to be with me."

"How do you fear you might ruin his life?" I asked.

"It's a vague notion. I was taught smart, strong women destroy men. So it's like, 'Someday, somewhere you'll regret that you were with me. You're probably not going to want me. One of these days you're going to wake up and realize you don't want me. So let me save you from that experience.' There was a time when I was like, 'I have to be as horrible to him as possible, to make sure that he knows the absolute worst of me.' Every once in a while, I just need to punch him in the face," she said metaphorically. "I've never framed it in those terms, but that's a lot what it's like.

"I haven't ever cheated on Michael, but I've come close twice. I'm really glad that in both of those cases I had enough of my senses to be like, 'I'm sorry; I need to get out of here.' I always picture people cheating because of something they feel like they're not getting. It was very much not that. It didn't happen because I was looking for something better than him. Certainly not because I was looking for something better than him.

"In both of those cases, I told Michael about it," Piper continued. "I remember Michael saying I was aiming for some sort of climactic end to things, right? That somehow, somewhere I thought we're just going to have to break up and it's going to have to be terrible. I'm looking for the melodramatic end, and by God, I'm going to make that melodramatic end."

Piper picked up her espresso, took a sip thoughtfully, and set it back down.

"There's absolutely no way that I would have been able to be a healthy person without all of the amazing people in my life. My parents weren't raised in the church," she said, though they both identified as evangelicals by the time they raised her. "I don't think they realized how much of a struggle it was for me, so I don't think they knew how much I needed it to be actively counteracted.

"But still, I was engaging intellectually with my father on the gender topic from an extremely young age, and the fact that he took an eight-year-old seriously is pretty ridiculous. And what I observed from my mother was someone who was so perfectly confident and sure of herself. She would say that she needs to submit to my father, but then she would laugh and make a joke about it being really easy to submit to someone who does whatever you tell them. Something like that. And I had other strong women in my life during the right periods to help me work through things. I had absolutely every opportunity to be fully okay. I had *every* opportunity. And it's still something that, every once in a while, leaves me at the doorstep of destruction. That causes me to behave in such a way that makes me feel that I want to cheat on my husband, right? I don't know how people who don't have great parents even survive."

Another interviewee seemed to agree with Piper on this count. During our interview, she brought up Piper's name, saying Piper was the one person from our youth group who she could think of who she assumed was unaffected by purity culture.

So much for that.

"So, how has all of this affected your relationship with God?" I asked Piper, who now loosely identifies as Episcopalian.

"It's hard," she said. "Until I could really affirm the way that God had created me, both as a physical being and an intellectual being, I was basically saying that God messed up. And theologically, what does that mean for God as a good creator?"

"Mm-hmm. I think what I'm hearing you say is, if you believe all the 'shoulds' that purity culture taught us, then . . . God is not cool if he has instilled in you deep parts of your personality that feel unchangeable—such as your strong opinions and your sense of competition—things that the church says aren't in a good woman . . . but are in you."

Piper began nodding vigorously.

"So either you're bad, or God is," I continued. Piper was still nodding. "Or . . ." I smiled, "the 'shoulds' are the problem. The shame is the problem."

"Yes," she said with a final nod. "Exactly!" She threw her hands up in the air. "This is energizing! Putting it in a context—this is what it looks like—I feel like, I don't know, I'm not totally fucked. It's a the-emperor-has-no-clothes moment. Somebody has got to stand up and say, 'actually wait a second,' and then all of a sudden you realize that there's a lot of people out there that were just waiting for you to say it!" Her smile widened.

"That's the idea," I smiled back.

3

Pure Destruction

The sun was setting when Chloe suggested we move from the outdoor table where I had been oohing and aahing over her wedding book to the restaurant's dimly lit basement bar heavy with the dank scent of a microbrewery. I watched as Chloe, now in her midtwenties, lifted her floor-length floral skirt to reveal a pair of stocky brown boots as she headed toward the winding stairwell. She looked just the way I remembered her from youth group: thin and petite with a pixie-like turned-up nose, the same stick-straight strawberry blonde hair falling all the way to her behind, and her arms and legs thick with freckles that thinned on her face, where they scattered across her nose and cheeks like a warm blush.

"I'm so glad that you want to talk to people about sex," Chloe said looking back at me as she descended the stairs. I paused on the edge of a step. I had never heard Chloe say the word *sex* before and, knowing she was still an active member of the evangelical church, I wasn't sure how comfortable she would be talking about it tonight.

"Why's that?" I asked before continuing behind her.

"We never talked about it enough," she said.

Chloe was right. We talked about sexual *purity* all the time, but sex? Never.

"We need to be better equipped to function in the world, you know?" Chloe continued as she approached a small bar table at the bottom of the stairwell. "Did you know that I didn't even know what testicles were until I was in my twenties?"

"Really?" I asked, taking my jacket off and hanging it over the back of my chair.

"I once asked my mom what they were. I must've been sixteen or seventeen at the time. I'd heard them mentioned in a movie. She said, 'I don't know.'"

"Do you think that was true?"

"Well, when I asked her again when I was twenty-four, she said she knew. I told her, 'You said you didn't know what they were when I was seventeen, and I needed to know *then*.' These days, when people make sex jokes, I ask them to explain them to me so I can learn something," she laughed. "Linda, I didn't even know what *sex* was until I was in my twenties. I mean, I thought I understood what it was, but I didn't figure out that the penis goes in and out of the vagina and doesn't just go in and, sort of . . . sit there, until I was a senior in college."

"Believe it or not," I told her, "you are not the first person to tell me that."

"And the whole time, I was having oral sex with girls," she shook her head.

"Wait. What?" I asked.

Chloe nodded. "Since I was eight."

"Hold on," I said.

I hadn't heard *this one* before.

The waitress approached our table and stood over us impatiently until we both ordered a beer.

"Um, before you go," I stopped the waitress as she started to walk away, "do you have a notebook I could use? And a pen?"

I hadn't planned to interview Chloe that night, as it was our first time seeing one another in a few years, but I've learned that you never know when someone is going to open up.

The waitress raised her pen into the air. "I need this," she announced. But she handed me an empty order pad from the half apron tied around her waist before hurrying to the next table.

"Thank you!" I called after her. "I'm sorry," I said, turning to Chloe then. "I know we haven't seen each other in a while and we hadn't really talked about this being an interview, but do you mind if I write this down?"

"That's why I'm telling you," Chloe said, handing me a pen out of her bag. "I want you to know. What you said on the phone, you're right. We need to start talking about these things."

The third stumbling block those raised as girls in the purity movement must overcome is the destruction of what author and cofounder of the popular online community Feministing, Jessica Valenti, refers to as "the purity myth." In her book, *The Purity Myth: How America's Obsession with Virginity Is Hurting Young Women*, Valenti defines this term as the myth that girls' "only real worth is their virginity and ability to remain 'pure.'" Valenti argues this myth is as present in religious sexual shaming as it is in secular sexual exploitation:

> Abstinence-only education during the day and *Girls Gone Wild* commercials at night! Whether its delivered through a virginity pledge or by a barely dressed tween pop singer writhing across the television screen, the message is the same: A woman's worth lies in her ability—or her refusal—to be sexual. And we're teaching American girls that, one way or another, their bodies and their sexuality are what make them valuable.[1]

Valenti goes on to describe the cultural, legislative, and other ramifications of this "virginity fetishism," saying: "It's time to teach our daughters that their ability to be good people depends on their *being good people*, not on whether or not they're sexually active."[2]

The cornerstone of the purity myth is the expectation that girls and women, in particular, will be utterly and absolutely nonsexual until the day they marry a man, at which point they will naturally and easily become his sexual satisfier, ensuring the couple will have children and never divorce: one man, one woman, in marriage, forever.

For this formula to work, my girlfriends and I knew we had to follow a slew of rules. Unfortunately, none of us knew what they were. Sex was such a shameful topic that we never got real talk on what we were and were not allowed to do. It was assumed that if no one ever talked to us about sex, it would just sort of go away until we needed it. So our "sex talks" were all generic metaphors and warnings about what would happen to us if we crossed a line, which was defined differently by so many people that we were left guessing all the same. Meanwhile, we knew we would be shamed if we asked sexual questions; shamed if we discussed sexual decisions; shamed if we shared our confusing sexual feelings and thoughts; and shamed worst of all if we admitted we had already done anything sexual. So each of us guessed at what the rules might be, hoped we were right, and didn't tell anyone about our sexual lives just in case we weren't.

For her book, *Sex and the Soul: Juggling Sexuality, Spirituality, Romance, and Religion on America's College Campuses*, Donna Freitas tracked evangelical college students' understanding of just how far one could go and still be sexually pure. Unsurprisingly, she found a great deal of variation among them. They defined purity as:

- Waiting till the wedding ceremony for the first kiss.
- Waiting till the engagement for the first kiss.
- Trying to avoid all lustful thoughts or feelings of sexual desire prior to marriage.

- Dressing modestly (especially for women).
- Restricting kissing to public places as a way of preventing further sexual intimacy.
- Kissing only while standing up.
- Kissing while lying down but avoiding any other "sexual contact."
- Kissing and touching but never achieving orgasm.
- Engaging in "everything but" intercourse, including oral and anal sex.[3]

You get the picture.

It is worth remembering that "purity" is a proxy for "sameness." Whether we are talking about sexual purity, gender purity, racial purity, ethnic purity, or religious purity, we use the term *purity* to refer to "keeping out" or even "cleansing" humanity of diversity. To be "pure" in someone else's eyes is to be like them—absent of the elements that make you difficult for them to understand or accept. Of course, the reality is there is no such thing as purity, as we are all different! And so, when we try to be the same, or "pure" as defined by one person's or group's concept of normality, we are set up for failure.

The lack of sexual knowledge and wisdom among young people extends beyond evangelicalism as well. As Mark Regnerus* writes in his book *Forbidden Fruit: Sex & Religion in the Lives of American Teenagers*: "It is widely believed that today's adolescents typically know more about sex than their parents did at their age. When researchers probe their knowledge, however, what is often uncovered is a hodgepodge of facts and fictions, myths and truths."[4] Regnerus references the National Longitudinal Study of Adolescent Health, a nationally representative study of seventh–twelfth graders with four waves of research beginning in 1995 and ending

---

* As I feature some of his work in this book, it is important for me to note that Mark Regnerus's research on same-sex parenting—which is not included here—has been quite rightly critiqued as highly problematic.

in 2008. It is considered "the largest, most comprehensive longitudinal survey of adolescents ever undertaken."[5] The study asks five questions about sex and pregnancy risk. Adolescents' scores are around 50 percent. Yet as Regnerus points out: "Unfortunately scoring 50 percent on a true/false quiz does *not* indicate that teens know the correct answer to half of the questions. Flipping a coin would produce the *same* score, on average. Until a category of adolescents scores reliably better than 50 percent, we cannot have confidence that they know any of the correct answers." Meanwhile, adolescents who attended church weekly and said that "religion was 'very important' to them" score even *lower* than the unchurched kids, despite the purity movement's surplus of vague "sex" talks.[6]

And so we wander into the forest of sexuality without a compass, grabbing hold of whatever trinkets we can find to guide us. Yet if our natural curiosity leads us into an off-limits section of that forest, we are told we should have known—or worse yet, we *did* know—just what we were doing.

As we waited for our beers to arrive, Chloe told me it was a girl she knew from a church program who'd first introduced her to oral sex.

"She and I prayed about it afterward," Chloe explained. "'What does God think about this?'" she said, turning her head to the right, miming a conversation between her eight-year-old self and the other little girl. "'I don't know. Let's ask,'" she said turning to the left. "In the Bible, Gideon put a sheepskin out when he was seeking God. So I said, 'I have a rabbit skin,' a tourist thing. I thought I'd put the rabbit skin out in the yard for God. But then I pulled it back because I didn't want to wreck the rabbit skin in case it got wet. I decided instead to ask God, 'If there's dew outside in the morning, you're okay with this. If not, you're not.'"

"You wanted a sign," I suggested as the waitress dropped off our beers.

"Right," she said. "There was dew. So I thought, 'What a great thing to share with my friends!' And I did—with a neighbor, some of my homeschooling friends, about three, one of whom, we did it constantly. Another, we took baths together and there were sexual overtones to all of our conversations. Another I told about it and we did it once.

"When I was turning ten, I had a party with five or six people, two of whom I'd shown it to," Chloe continued. "I told everyone, but there was one homeschooler who wouldn't participate." Chloe had begun to speak faster and I was having trouble keeping up on the waitress pad.

"Pause for a second," I said. "I want to get all this down."

Chloe took a long swig of beer before continuing.

"She told her mom. And her mom told my mom.

"Mom asked me if this was true.

"I said 'yes.'

"She told Dad. I knew I was in big trouble. Dad cried," Chloe continued without pausing. "He said, 'Get down on your knees and ask God for forgiveness.'

"'I didn't know what I was doing,' I told him.

"'Yes you did,' he told me.

"But I didn't," Chloe looked right at me and stopped speaking, her light brown eyes pleading with me to believe her.

"I got down on my knees in front of them and asked for forgiveness," she went on. "It was horrible. So humiliating. Then every morning for five or six days, I went into my mom's room and told her bit by bit every sexual exploration I'd ever done. She made me listen to Frog and Toad books on tape. There was one on self-control and Mom said, 'You need to listen to that one.' It made me feel bad, like I was bad."

I flipped past page after page in the waitress's order pad, trying to get down each word Chloe said, but by now she was talking so fast I was missing whole paragraphs.

"Let me just catch up," I said again, and for a moment, the music blared overhead as I wrote and our table was silent. When I looked up, I saw Chloe had torn the paper coaster her beer had arrived on into nervous scraps.

"After the little girl tattled on me," Chloe continued more slowly now, "my mom divulged the whole oral sex thing to twenty-five or thirty moms at once at a homeschoolers meeting," Chloe said, explaining that she and her mom had been attending support groups for Christian homeschooling moms since she could remember. The mothers exchanged ideas for teaching math, science, and English from a religious perspective while the kids played together.

"None of them were even mothers of girls I'd been with," she continued. "The kids were off on the other side that day, but I was hanging out near the moms, I think, because I heard her blabber it to everyone. One of the ladies was a social worker. She went and talked to the little girl who taught me—they pulled her out of class at school—but she denied everything. So they thought I must have learned it from my parents. And meanwhile, my parents were getting counseling for their marriage, which didn't look good. So the social worker said it was her job to 'report it' to Child Protective Services, that she was legally bound to report suspicious acts like this in case adults were involved.

"After that, when the phone rang during school hours, we were never allowed to answer it. And when the doorbell rang, we had to run to the basement. My parents didn't want anyone to know that we were homeschooled. They told us that Child Services was anti-Christian and took four kids away from their parents because they were homeschooling."

Though "adult-like" sexual experimentation among children can be a sign that a child is a victim of sexual abuse and so should be taken seriously, sexual experimentation among children and adolescents of the same gender and age can also be quite normal.[7] And yet, Chloe was immediately shamed by her parents for it, and her parents were immediately shamed by the larger community.

"Did anyone know any of this was happening?" I asked Chloe with concern.

"The pastor once called and I accidentally answered. Mom screamed at me and, I remember, the pastor reprimanded her. That was the closest anyone ever got to coming inside our home and seeing what was really going on. Being homeschooled, being in this environment constantly, was very damaging. Mom was volatile and depressed. My job was to save my family—protect everyone from Mom. I remember I used to look at Scott Ryan, the epitome of cool," she said referring to the coolest kid in our youth group. "He and I had a normal conversation once and I was terrified the whole time because I was so uncomfortable with myself. I didn't know how to talk to anyone. I felt so stupid all the time. I was lonely. I needed intimacy so badly. Every paper I ever wrote was about loneliness. Youth group was my only outlet because I was homeschooled. My whole socialization was youth group. Can you imagine that?"

"No," I said, shaking my head, closing the now full waitress pad and grabbing a stack of napkins from the plastic container on the table so I could continue writing.

"I remember I thought, 'If people in youth group knew what all went on in my life, I'd at least get kudos for having a great testimony.' I pictured myself sitting on the stool that the singers and speakers sat on in youth group and telling everyone what had gone on so they'd get me, notice me, give me attention. I imagined them saying, 'Wow! God really worked through your life!'

"But I couldn't actually tell anyone about this stuff. It was too bad . . . or not bad enough. I wasn't going through the 'right' kind of hard times. It wasn't drugs or any of the other 'right' struggles. I couldn't get up in front of youth group and say, 'Hey, I had oral sex with a lot of my girlfriends. You don't want to hear about that? You don't want to talk about that? I think we should talk about it!'

"I was ten . . . nine. . . eight when I first started thinking I was a lesbian," Chloe continued. "I remember thinking that the ultimate rebellion would be to move in with my girlfriend and become a fabulous, haunting, piano-playing artist."

I smiled.

"Going to a liberal evangelical college later was great because I had only ever known conservative Christians. There were signs up that said 'Gay and Lesbian Discussion Group' and I had some good conversations with my hall director. My freshman year I really began to question my own sexual orientation." But in the end, Chloe married a man, as evidenced by the ornate wedding book still sticking out from her bag.

"When I got out of college, I worked at a local bookstore. All of a sudden, it occurred to me that my coworkers weren't Christians and were going to Hell according to my beliefs. I always thought that if people just got Christianity, then they would believe. But my coworkers *did* get it, and they didn't believe. It made me think . . . what do *I* believe? All of a sudden I wondered if God even existed. And since then . . . I've never been able to get that belief in him back. I don't have the peace I once had. It scares me. I've struggled with meaning in life ever since I first doubted God's existence. I've plotted out my suicide to every detail. Suicide makes sense in a Christian framework, because isn't Heaven better than earth?" she looked at me.

I looked up from the napkin I was writing on, my eyebrows furrowed.

"Honestly, I believe what I believe because I'm unwilling to part with the assurances that the faith gives me," Chloe continued. "Even though my faith is nothing like it used to be, I can't *not* believe these things. But I don't really believe them anymore either. I mean, my beliefs make me crazy because they don't all make sense, but I *can't not believe them*," she repeated. "I'm scared, Linda. I'm scared. I'm like, 'Okay, Christianity is true enough. Do we have to harp on it? Can't we just stop talking about it? Can't I just say I believe and we leave well enough alone?!'"

Then she went silent.

I finished writing the sentence she had said, and then I put my pen down.

"I've come to believe in predestination though, because of all the times God has brought me back to Christianity," she offered.

"I get it," I answered her. "I mean, I'm still here too, right? I let go of everything. And yet, here I still am."

"Here we still are," Chloe repeated.

4

Sexual Violence, Classified

"Do you mind if he stays?" Laura gestured toward her boyfriend as she opened the front door to her small Washington, DC, studio apartment. "Everything that happened to me," she explained uncomfortably, "shows up in our relationship. And he and I were thinking, maybe it would help if he heard the whole story."

This isn't usually something I recommend. My interviewees tend to talk about sensitive matters, and the pressure that an extended audience puts on them can be difficult. But looking into Laura's pleading eyes I thought, *What do I really know about what Laura*—whose story I was already aware was more sensitive than most—*needs at the end of the day?*

"I can offer Concord grapes," her boyfriend said sheepishly.

I laughed. "I do love Concord grapes."

Laura sat down on the edge of a folded futon in sweatpants and an oversized T-shirt; I sat facing her on the other end of the futon; and her boyfriend, whom Laura had instructed to be as unobtrusive as possible, sat across from us on a kitchen chair.

Laura, one of the few people who chose to use her real name—Laura L. Dunn, Esq.—is the youngest daughter of a midwestern preacher. She remembers watching older siblings face consequences around the issue of sexuality and determining early on that she would avoid a similar fate by remaining "pure" until the day she married. "I have this memory of playing in the playground when I was eleven and being like, 'If I die, I want to be this age in Heaven' . . ." Laura took a deep breath as her voice began to crack. "Somehow I knew, even as a child, that everything would get a lot harder with puberty."

And it did.

"My mother constantly implied to me that my body was inherently sinful," Laura said of her adolescent years. "She would describe me to people as a Barbie doll because of my figure. I had big breasts and was otherwise really thin. When I was a freshman in high school, my mom said, 'The way that you're dressing—your clothes are too tight, and you're making all your brothers-in-law uncomfortable.' It disgusted me. It made me feel sick. If that's what they're thinking, isn't that *their* problem? I was just wearing the clothes that I had, clothing that my parents bought me. If I was developing and they didn't fit anymore, she could have just helped buy me clothes, rather than shame me.

"I got the idea that I was inherently sexual so it mattered even more that I committed my virginity to God. It was going to be this beautiful gift that I would give to my husband, to connect over. I would become my husband's sexual fantasy.

"When I was eleven or twelve, my middle sister won a radio competition and got five golden rings for Christmas. She gave them to us sisters. I got a sapphire one, which was my birthstone. I remember knowing it was under the tree and looking forward to opening it on Christmas Day. Everyone was in bed one night and I was sitting under the tree and promised my virginity to God. I did it privately. It wasn't anything my parents asked me to do, though I knew it was 'a thing' in the Christian community. That some people had purity rings and stuff—but I just did it privately and personally with God."

Laura began to cry. "I had that ring," she continued, tears streaming down her face. "I used to wear it every day. Not everyone knew what it was. But *I* knew what it was."

"Do you want to talk about why this feels emotional?" I asked gently. "Because," she confided, "I actually *meant* all of it."

Rolling Stone magazine, June 19, 2014:

April 4th, 2004, is a date Laura Dunn has never forgotten. That was the day the Midwestern preacher's daughter who didn't believe in sex before marriage says she lost her virginity to not one but two University of Wisconsin–Madison athletes. Dunn was a freshman member of the crew team, attending a boozy frat bash, and she lost count of her intake after seven raspberry-vodka shots. She remembers two older teammates led her out, guys she knew. She was stumbling drunk, but one of them helped her walk, and they headed, she thought, toward another campus party. Instead, they led her to one of their apartments, where she found herself on a bed with both of them on top of her, as she drifted in and out of consciousness. When she started to get sick, one of them led her to the bathroom, where he penetrated her from behind while she was throwing up.

The next morning, she went back to her apartment, tossed her bloody underwear in the hamper and took a shower. "It was awful. I was trying to get it off my skin." In the afternoon, one of the teammates called. "He said, 'I felt bad for you, are you OK?'" recalls the petite brunette, a recently graduated law student. "I was like, 'Why did I find blood in my underwear?' He was like, 'Do you want to talk about it?'" They agreed to meet later, off campus. Both young men showed up. "I said, 'What did you do?' And then one said, 'I raped you.' But the other teammate was like, 'No, it was a threesome. It was great.'"

It took Dunn more than a year to come to terms with the truth of the first assessment.[1]

*   *   *

Laura pushed her body against the arm of the futon as though hoping she could disappear into it. Tears streamed freely down her face as they had been for nearly an hour as she told her story. And they would continue to fall that way for the entirety of our time together.

"Do you want a hand to hold?" I asked at one point, reaching toward her.

She shook her head vigorously.

"I'm not very emotional," she said. Her words didn't match her face, but I thought I understood what she meant: She wanted to push through, to let the tears come, fine, but not to give into them, not allow them to stop her. I looked over at her boyfriend. He was watching Laura intently but didn't make a move. I pulled my hand back.

"Afterward, I remember being in my parents' kitchen," Laura continued. "I have an image of Mom behind the cupboards. I remember preparing for it, because I knew telling my parents was going to be horrible. I already knew. I was like, 'Mom, I need to tell you something.' I said, 'I've been raped.' The minute I said it, my mom gasped then walked out of the house. There's a sliding door there, and she just left. Then I have just flashes of memories. At some point, she was back and my father was there. Again, I don't really have linear memories of this. But the first thing my father said to me was, 'What were you wearing?' I just screamed, 'Does it matter?!' I was very angry that he did that. That was the second time I ever yelled at my father in my life.

"I left a few days later and went on a road trip with a girlfriend. When I came back, the first thing my parents did was sit me down. My dad said, 'You have an option. You can either come home and submit to us'—meaning leave the university, move home, and go to a smaller campus nearby—'or go on a mission trip.' I just had to 'submit.' Come home and live by their rules and whatever they decided for my future. I was supposed to do that, or they would cut me off because I had sinned by drinking and brought shame on my father. My parents said that my father's a pastor and, according to the Bible, a pastor is judged by his children, and so my having done this reflected badly on him, which . . . I don't think I can do justice to the feeling I had then in that moment . . . but obviously, it was horrible.

"I was crying, but I didn't protest.

"I just said, 'You're right. I did drink. That was wrong. But I'm not coming home. If you want to cut me off, you can cut me off.'

"And I left.

"I think that was more hurtful than anything else," she said, her voice barely audible through the tears. "It's the only thing that I just can't wrap my brain around, trauma-wise.

"I was hysterical by the time I got to my college apartment. My parents owned my car and my work required me to have a car. If I couldn't get to my job, I didn't know how I was going to pay for my apartment, how I was going to pay for school. I didn't know how I was going to pay for anything. I was hysterically crying.

"Then I got a call on my cell phone from a number I didn't recognize. I answered and it was my father. He had left the house and walked all the way to the Christian school where he taught when he wasn't pastoring. He called me from that phone and said that he was proud of me, 'You handled yourself well and I'm going to make sure that you get financial support' or something to that effect. Apparently, my accepting their criticism of my drinking and still standing up for myself without fighting against their judgment saved me," Laura told me, shaking her head.

Still, Laura said, "my mom decided I was responsible for the rape. I worked at Victoria's Secret at the time, so she thought I got drawn into that kind of culture that's sexualizing women and celebrating sexual beauty and things like that. I was drinking so I was sinning. I was breaking the law. I was giving in to drunkenness. And the night that it happened, I was being more sexual than—" she caught herself mid-sentence, stopped, and corrected herself. "I was being a normal fucking college student. But according to the old framework, I was being 'too sexual.' Like many other victims, I still struggle with self-blame. I don't have everything figured out. I still hurt a lot. And I guess I've sometimes wondered . . . if me promising my virginity to God is not . . . 'why' it happened, but . . ." Laura trailed off.

"I don't understand," I told her.

"It was something my mom said: 'You bragged about your virginity.' I don't think that's true. I know a lot of people assumed that I wasn't a virgin because I dated someone much older than me in high school and because I had a certain type of body. So a lot of people suggested I was sexually evolved and I would have to defend myself—'I really *am* a virgin.' I even bought a shirt from the Virgin record store that said 'Virgin' on it during a mission trip. I thought it was kind of funny. It was one of those things my mom threw in my face after the rape."

"Because you were too prideful about your virginity?"

"Yes," Laura said. "You can't win. That's why I want to try to talk about the religious stuff and the family stuff that still haunts me. I don't know what to do with that. I don't know what anyone does with that. The shame that religion puts on it, just religion's general hostility toward sex, sexuality, the human body in its sexual form—it created the environment for me to be mistreated by my family."

"Are you—?" I began as Laura's crying intensified again.

"I'm okay," she answered quickly. "I felt like I needed to get the truth out for a minute."

"Do you want to keep going? We could pause—"

"Yes," she finally gave in. "Sure."

And I turned the recorder off.

*   *   *

The fourth stumbling block girls raised in the purity movement must overcome is the wrongful classification of rape and other forms of sexual violence. By this I mean both that the purity movement *classifies* sexual violence by systematically silencing and hiding it, and that if and when it is exposed, the purity movement then *mis*classifies sexual violence as "sex" rather than "violence." Long-indoctrinated in this illegitimate logic, Laura's parents did not consider her solely a survivor, but also a sinner, and were more focused on their daughter's sins and how they led to the loss of her "purity" than on the violence that was perpetrated against her. And they followed through on that logic when she told them she was raped—by controlling Laura to protect her from her own sinfulness rather than comforting and defending Laura to protect her from the sins of others. Equating survivors' actions, such as drinking in Laura's case, and perpetrators' actions, such as assault, is called sin-leveling, and is often categorized as a form of spiritual abuse.

Having been raised with this messaging herself, Laura began having anxiety about the effect her body would have on people long before college. "One time, I remember just trying on clothes over and over and feeling that all of them were really tight on all my curves and I was getting really upset," she told me. "I remember my high school boyfriend getting really mad at me because we were going to be late to a graduation party, but I was so upset that I couldn't find an outfit that didn't make me look really curvy. I just started crying at some point. Another time when it happened, I explained to my boyfriend why I was getting upset. He kind of laughed, 'You're supposed to be curvy, there's nothing wrong with that.' I said, 'No, my mom will say something to me. You just wait.'"

This kind of body shame came up often in my interviews.

I actually really hate a lot of things on my body that I feel are sexual, like my chest. So, I just wear baggy clothes. I never show cleavage. I'm just like, "Don't look at them; don't look at me." Hiding it. I wanted to bind or get a reduction or something like that because I just don't want to be viewed as sexual. (Jasmine)

I remember a couple of times very vividly in college standing in front of a mirror and just being, "Why do I look this way? Why did you make me like this?" I mean, I came very close to spending $10,000 on a breast reduction for no apparent reason. (Piper)

At first glance, the modesty doctrine may appear harmless—perhaps even healthy—but the logic of victim-blaming that we too often see in rape cases begins here. When we demand that an individual dress in just the right way so as not to inspire sexual feelings in others, we set a precedent of blaming individuals for the thoughts, feelings, and actions of other people that can play out in dangerous ways in rape and abuse cases.

Why didn't you do that? Why didn't you cover up? You shouldn't have been wearing a skirt that was that short. You caused him to stumble. You lured him. You caused him to lust. It's your fault. You don't want to be a stumbling block. Why would you make it harder for the people who you care about and your friends and your brothers in Christ? It completely perpetuates rape culture! (Emily)

In Laura's story, we see what can happen when one experiences sexual trauma within a community that has wholeheartedly embraced shaming theologies such as the modesty doctrine. The community's understanding that women and girls are responsible for men's and boys' sexual thoughts, feelings, and actions toward them can halt a survivor's own internal healing and, if she seeks support from within this community, can even lead to further traumatic experiences, such as having the first question your father asks after you tell him you were raped be: "What were you wearing?"

*   *   *

In recent years, *The Boston Globe's* work, highlighted in the Oscar-winning film *Spotlight*, has forced us to face the concealment of sexual abuse in the Catholic church. *The Boston Globe's* journalists challenged the assumption that religious sexual abuse cases are outliers when they exposed the "extensive and almost systemic abuse by clergy."

Boston Globe journalist Michael Rezendes spoke with *The New Yorker* about the ten thousand pages of Church documents the journalists reviewed that ultimately revealed the extent of the abuse the Church had been covering up: "What was not in the documents was any indication anywhere of concern for the children who had been harmed. Not anywhere. It was all about protecting the reputation of the Church, and then, in parens, keeping it secret. It was always about the secrecy."[2]

Yet the classification of sexual violence is not limited to the Catholic church. Whether we are looking at religious institutions, colleges and universities, our armed services, or any number of other places, we are consistently faced with the painful reality that sexual violence survivors who choose to speak up are likely to be silenced by the institutions and communities to whom they go for support if the violence could be in any way associated with that institution or community. Many survivors are told not to press charges or alert the authorities, as the institutions will deal with the perpetrator themselves—often by quietly moving the perpetrator on to a new community, as we saw happen with my own church youth pastor. And some survivors have it even worse—being actively shamed, blamed, and disbelieved by those to whom they turn for help and healing.

For more than a year, Laura remained silent. But when she heard a professor say that most survivors do not report the sexual crimes committed against them, she decided she no longer wanted to be part of the silent majority. Coming forward brought its own challenges. The University of Wisconsin determined that "since both parties were drinking, consent was 'moot' "; Laura filed a Title IX complaint against the university; the Department of Education ruled against her; and the police never brought charges.[3]

"I was so desperate to be believed," Laura said when we turned the recorder back on. "I had a very twisted thought that if I killed myself, then they would know that it really happened. And the whole time I struggled for justice, I had these overwhelming desires to go into churches and seek solace, but I had a really messed up relationship with religion after the rape. Because the church says nothing to survivors; people say nothing to survivors. It's one of the worst forms of suffering. And there's nothing for you. I've never seen a sermon crafted for people who suffered from sexual trauma. What? They don't know this happens? They don't know this is damaging? The only messages that come close to addressing it are the worst ever. We need healing. We need support."

Silence—not just the silencing of survivors, but the absence of any mention of this incredibly common form of trauma from the pulpit or (in many churches) from anywhere else—is another way that sexual violence is classified. That is to say, it literally becomes classified information. Although 90 percent of female teenagers who are active in their faith communities say that they would like programs to help them avoid rape, sexual harassment, and sexual abuse, many of their churches will never directly discuss these issues.[4]

"I guess it's playing into the idea that there is a certain type of person that gets raped," Laura said. "There's a certain type of woman who's asking for it, or who is looser or whatever the victim-blaming stereotype is. There's a certain type of person that deserves it, or is vulnerable to it, or finds herself in those settings. Within religious communities that stereotype makes people think that 'other' people get raped, not Christian women, not people within the church. It's prostitutes; it's drunks; it's party girls; it's something else.

"My sister actually got her pastor to come talk to me two months ago. My family used it as an opportunity to preach to me, to call me back. This pastor knew nothing about what to say to me. He admitted it a lot: 'I'm not a psychologist. I'm not trained.' That was part of what he was saying. 'I don't know what to say to you.' I was like, 'Okay. Everything I ever thought about no message existing is still true.'"

Then Laura paused.

"There was *one* sermon from another pastor," she said thoughtfully. "He was talking about ministering to this young woman who believed that there was something wrong with her because she was raped, like she was at fault or she was evil. He said that was a lie, a lie from the Devil to keep her down. That's part of the message I would like to hear from the church. Because I don't think people see rape victims as innocent. I think that most people view them as having some responsibility.

"And then, another time," she now recalled, "there was a chaplain who cried when she heard my story. I felt bad that she was crying. But I also was kind of touched. Showing emotion, crying . . . she wasn't afraid to do that. It made an impression. My story is sad; it *should* be cried over."

Laura didn't find justice on campus or in court, so—while in law school—she started an organization to help others find it. For eight years she ran SurvJustice, a nonprofit organization that provides survivors of sexual violence with legal assistance for administrative complaints, campus hearings, civil lawsuits, and criminal cases. Having recently stepped down from the executive director role so SurvJustice can continue to grow under a more experienced executive director's leadership, Laura is proud of the work she was able to accomplish while at the organization, including lobbying for and then advising the White House Task Force to Protect Students Against Sexual Assault established by the Obama administration, and helping to ensure the passage of the 2013 Violence Against Women Reauthorization Act.

"I feel like a big part of what I do is try to give a narrative to survivors that you don't have to be broken or ashamed," Laura said. "You can be strong. You can change the world.

"I didn't celebrate graduating college because it wasn't a celebratory moment for me. It felt like I had survived. However, graduating law school, I wanted to celebrate. I felt like I had overcome. I asked my parents to come up for the graduation ceremony. My siblings bought me a necklace for graduation since they could not attend. It's a heart with a cross in it. On the front is 'April 4th, 2011,' which is seven years to the day I was raped—the day my story changed civil rights law under Title IX in this country. On the back, it says, 'Redeemed.' I'm not quite sure what they meant by that, but I feel like maybe the idea is that I was sinful and this is God redeeming me, taking something that was ugly and evil and maybe sinful, I don't know, and using it for good? If that is what they meant, it reinforces what I always suspected—the reason why my family left me alone after the rape is they really viewed me as part of a sin that occurred, that I had caused it or had drawn it, or somehow had left myself vulnerable to it, which is apparently just as bad.

"And yet," Laura added, "when my mother tried to shame me in order to prevent me from using my real name when I talked to the media, it was my sisters who called me up and told me, 'There is no reason to feel shame about this.' In fact, they told me I needed to do it to show others there was no shame. They helped give me the strength to reject the stigma.

"And I think things are changing. It always surprises me, in a good way, when I see parents fighting for their child. In a case I was working on recently, a rape case, the victim's family was all around her. They were all there, every single day. Grandparents sitting next to parents, sitting next to uncles, sitting next to family friends. They were *all there*. That's what it should be. You should have whole churches sitting there. Maybe if there were messages in the church . . ." she trailed off.

At the time of our conversation, Laura was working on a case at

Catholic University, "a really prominent college here that's under Title IX investigation," she explained. Reading through the university's old president-approved Code of Student Conduct,* she told me she observed something unsettling.

"They had a list of misconducts," she told me. "The first category of misconduct has to do with doing physical violence to someone, causing bodily injury," she said, holding her hand high in the air. "You would think that would be where you might find sexual assault," she said. "It's not.

"The second category of misconduct is about harassment and the hurt that that causes," she continued, moving her hand down an inch. "You'd think sexual harassment would be there. But it's not.

"Then, aaaaall the way near the bottom," she says, moving her hand down several more inches, "there's another category called 'Sexual Offenses.' Even that section doesn't start with sexual assault; it doesn't start with sexual harassment; it actually starts with consensual sex and how God intended it to be for a man and a wife." And there in the Sexual Offenses section, alongside consensual sex outside of marriage, you find sexual assault.[5]

Laura shook her head. "I think that's the whole thing about the church. I read it and the absurdity is so obvious to me, but it's also like, 'Yes, it makes sense that you're more worried about sex outside of marriage than you are about rape.' People think rape doesn't happen to people in the church, but we need to protect against pre-marital sex. I just feel like I fell through a crack in the church."

"Not even a crack," I said. "A category. You fell into the Sexual Misconduct category. It's not that the purity movement has nothing to say about sexual assault; it's that it has *something* to say about it and that something is—"

---

* The Code of Student Conduct referred to here, which was last updated in October of 2014, is not the school's current policy.

"Worse," Laura completed my sentence. "I'm on national television speaking publicly as a survivor and I've never gotten justice in a court, even once. To me, that's God. That's not me. Having a national organization, having some stability with that, each thing is a gift from God that helps stabilize me in my path.

"I founded my organization before I graduated law school. I did it for all of 2014 without charging any fees for advocacy services. I just went all in. In 2015, I became a lawyer and I was struggling. At some point, I was just like, 'Why did you do this? What is wrong with you that you didn't think this was going to be really hard and that you might fall flat on your face and be absolutely broke? How did that thought never come up?' It was this really intense moment of panic right before I got a big grant through Echoing Green. I viewed that grant as God saying, 'You're on the right path; let me help you out. You're starting to have doubts.'

"Yes, it's an odd degree of certainty. I look back and I think, 'How? Why? What were you—?' I guess I just try to follow because I think the path is being laid out. Every day that I wake up and go to work, I believe it's God's will that I'm alive."

As I walked toward the door to leave Laura's apartment that day, I watched Laura's boyfriend stand and come toward her, awkward yet attentive. As he did, it occurred to me that Laura's boyfriend had done for her that day what she had wished her parents would have so many years ago. He listened. Silently, as she had asked him to, for hours. He didn't tell Laura what she should think or feel or what she should have done then or should do now. He just listened to what she *did* think, feel, and do.

As I saw Laura turn to her boyfriend, I closed the door quietly behind me and moved quickly down the hallway. It was their time now.

Stumbling Through Church

5

Man-Made Girls

"Come in," I heard Blue say.

I opened the door slowly. Blue Jones, the musician I was studying with my sophomore year of college, almost never called me into her office when I knocked. She preferred to open the door wide and present herself to me. She'd look me up and down. Then finally, she'd invite me in.

"Is everything okay?" I asked, peeking into Blue's office.

Blue sat silently at her desk, her jaw set as though to say, *I don't take any shit*. She wore a slick black suit jacket, an emerald silk shirt, and hoop earrings the size of a fist. Blue gestured for me to sit on the small stool in the corner of her office, and I set my acoustic guitar down against her office wall. I fumbled with the zipper of my JanSport backpack, removed a pen and a pad of notebook paper, and sat down on the high stool. Blue waited. I poised my pen over the pad in my lap and looked up at her.

"Are you settled?" she asked.

"Yes," I said.

"Are you sure?" she pushed.

I nodded.

Then, she leaned dramatically across the desk toward her answering machine, and pressed play.

"Hi Blue," squeaked a small, thin, high-pitched voice. "Um, I'm calling because, I'm sorry but, um, I'm just feeling really sick this morning and, uh (cough, cough), I was just wondering if maybe we could, um, reschedule our independent study?"

It was a message I had left Blue the week before.

"I'm just feeling, like, really, really terrible, and um, well, just, well I guess just call me and we'll find another time to meet this week if that's okay with you? Or if you can't do later this week just let me know and I'll come in today anyway. But I don't want to get you sick and . . . anyway, thank you. I'm really sorry. Okay. Sorry. Bye."

The tape stopped.

"What was that?" Blue looked up and asked me.

"Um . . ." I stammered.

"More to the point," she corrected herself, "*who* was that?"

As usual, I had no idea what she was up to.

"Me?" I looked at her to see if I had gotten the right answer. Blue looked away with exasperation.

Clearly, I had not.

"You," she repeated. "That was *you*?"

"I mean—" I began.

"That squeaky little I'm-so-sorry-somebody, that was you?" she continued.

I opened my mouth to respond and then shut it again. I wasn't sure where Blue was going with this. Was she mad at me for calling in sick last week?

"I'm sorry I—" I finally tried.

"I'm disappointed to hear that," Blue cut me off again. "I'm disappointed to hear that that was you." She let her words linger in the air for a moment before going on. "Because if that's all there is in there . . ." She shook her head.

I looked down at my notebook, ashamed of myself without really knowing why. My pen still stood readied on the page. What was this? Some kind of lesson? What did she want me to say? Finally, I set my pen down on the paper and looked up at her, pleading with my eyes for her to explain.

"You're not fooling me!" Blue finally hollered. She walked around the desk and threw herself down on the chair opposite my stool. "You may be fooling you, but you're not fooling me." She slammed the rewind button on the answering machine. The tape spun backward, screaming its high-pitched zip of words in reverse. Finally, the rewind button snapped back. I jumped.

"Nobody's voice is that high," Blue said, leaning toward me. "And I've heard you sing, Linda. So I know. That little girl on the answering machine? She isn't you. Stop. Trying. To. Pretend. She. Is."

With that, she pressed play again.

And again.

And again.

We listened to that recording until I had every pause, every lift, and every dip of my own voice memorized. And then, Blue told me to go home and think about what I had heard.

"You don't want to hear the song I wrote this week?" I asked, nodding toward my guitar.

"Don't you understand what we're doing here yet?" she replied incredulously. "You will never be able to write a song that matters if you don't believe that you matter. First things first. Go home."

I walked back to my dorm room fuming. Did she have any idea how much I was paying for this class? For this school? My family wasn't made of money. I actually wanted to learn something in my classes! I opened my dorm room door and threw my guitar down onto my bed. I had been writing songs on my acoustic guitar for years, but it was while recovering between surgeries that I began writing a song a week and playing in coffee shops around my hometown, as my health allowed. And so when I was finally well enough to return to school, I had approached Blue and asked her to do an independent study on songwriting and performance

103

with me. But it wasn't what I thought it would be. Last week, Blue and I had spent fifteen minutes going through a Mary J. Blige album jacket, discussing what the artistic director was going for in each photo, and what my own style choices—or lack thereof—said about me.

"You know what your jeans and T-shirt tell me?" she had asked. "Nothing. They say, 'I've got nothing to say. No unique point of view.'"

I had been wearing a bright orange T-shirt that read: *Support Wisconsin. Eat Cheese.*

"What does she know?" I said, pulling the shirt out of the back of my drawer where I had stuffed it after class last week and putting it on. "This shirt is awesome."

I wound up at Sarah Lawrence College—one of the most liberal and experimental colleges in the nation, the kind of place where someone like Blue Jones taught—entirely by accident. My senior year of high school I had applied early decision to Biola—which is an acronym for Bible Institute of Los Angeles—where I had planned to train to be a missionary, in preparation for my career as a traveling missionary actress. When I left to spend the second half of my senior year studying abroad in Australia, everything was set. I would return from Australia in August. Two weeks later I would start school at Biola.

But the night I returned from Australia, I was still burning with anger at what my youth pastor had done, and gotten away with doing, to young girls in too many churches. Talking with my parents in the living room the night that I returned from Australia, I admitted that I no longer wanted to be a missionary. I still loved our faith, but I couldn't be its spokesperson anymore. I told them I would probably transfer to a secular college where I could major in theater, something I couldn't do in any Bible college I'd found, after my first year of school.

"Why go to Bible college at all then?" my dad replied.

My eyes widened.

"Sounds like a waste of money we don't have to me. Your mom and I haven't seen you in six months. We'd rather you not leave again in two weeks. Definitely not to go to a school you don't want to attend."

I looked over at my mom. Her eyes were even wider than mine.

"Take a year off. Work. Go to community college. Figure out what the right school is and apply there," Dad continued. My mom sat frozen beside him, a look of terror on her face. But, as a staunch complementarian believer in male authority, she wasn't about to challenge my father. And, for once in my life, that worked out for me. The following morning, I called Biola and told them I wouldn't be coming after all.

A year later, I found myself at Sarah Lawrence College, just outside New York City, knowing almost nothing about the school besides its brochure promises.

"You're different," the brochure cover read.

I folded the flap back.

"So are we," it continued.

Oh.

That was good.

"At Sarah Lawrence, you don't learn what to think; you learn *how* to think." I had to stop and set it down for a moment. Such a place existed? For the first time, I felt as though I had found a place in which a misfit like me might just fit.

As it turned out, however, being "different" in your midwestern evangelical Christian community isn't the same as being different in . . . wherever my new classmates were from. My fellow Sarah Lawrence classmates had constructed beautiful dresses entirely out of tampons for their high school proms. They performed secret brass band concerts in campus elevators, shocking me with a tuba in my face when the doors opened on the third floor. They worked through bad breakups by spending entire nights alone in their dorm rooms making ocean-themed piñatas that they hung from the ceiling, replacing their usual lightbulb with a blue one and imagining themselves living under the ocean—far, far away from their ex-boyfriends.

Here, this lifelong misfit felt like a painfully average, fanny pack–toting tourist visiting a foreign land. I quickly became known as the gosh-darn-sweetest girl on campus, a real salt-of-the-earth type, sugar and spice and everything *ugh*. People often stopped me on campus and asked why I was smiling at them.

"Do I know you?" they'd press when I told them that I was just being friendly.

"No. I'm just being nice."

"Oh. Okay," they'd say, narrowing their eyes.

"I'm from the Midwest," I'd explain.

"Ohhhh," they'd respond with understanding.

Within weeks of starting school, I had earned the following nicknames: "The Milk Maid," "The Token Straight Girl," and "The Gap Girl," a title bestowed upon me when I made the grave mistake of admitting that I shopped at the Gap, apparently an embarrassingly mainstream choice.

I didn't tell many of my new classmates when I started losing a lot of blood, or when the pain from the undiagnosed Crohn's disease got worse. I just smiled, popped a handful of ibuprofen, and carried on. When everyone came back at the end of spring break the first year of college and I wasn't in class—because I was on the other side of the country undergoing surgery—I imagine most people never would have guessed why I, the most smiley girl on campus, wasn't there.

While my classmates finished their first and second years of college, I underwent four surgeries and lived at my parents' house. When I was well enough in the months between my third and fourth surgeries, my church asked me to become a youth group leader for ninth-grade girls. Though I was still healing and couldn't leave the house more than a few times a week, I said yes. I was more clear-eyed about the church's challenges than I had ever been, and I thought my presence there could make a difference. I imagined myself giving that group of girls the *truly* unconditional love and support that I had yearned for when I was their age—providing all the best evangelicalism had to offer and none of the worst. But when the girls started coming to me with stories about being called stumbling blocks and asking me what I thought of what other leaders said about the gender and sexuality expectations they were required to meet, I didn't know what to say.

Okay, I'd tell one girl while sitting beside her on a park bench during one of my weekly one-on-ones. *So, another youth group leader told you that if you masturbate you will ruin your sex drive, emasculate your future husband, and destroy your eventual marriage.* The girl nodded. *Well, what do you think of that?* I'd listen, urging the girl to look at the issue from multiple angles and not immediately assume that the other leader was right, though I never contradicted the leader either. Or, *Alright*, I'd say during a small group. *One of the leaders said that if you call a boy, he will see you as unfeminine and won't want to date you. Let's assume that's true—which it may or may not be. If it is true, is he the kind of guy you would want to date? Someone who would judge you like that just for calling him?* I closed almost every one of these conversations with a phrase that became a mantra for me in those months: *Take it with a grain of salt. Take what this leader said with a grain of salt; take what that leader said with a grain of salt; take what I say with a grain of salt; take it all with a grain of salt.* It was the only advice I felt I could offer with integrity.

After about six months, I retired from the role. I told the girls it was because I was still too sick. But really, it was because I was still growing up. Still being the "good girl"—the one on the answering machine with the high-pitched voice hoping not to upset her teacher, the one too afraid of how the church would react if she were to admit to a ninth-grade girl what she *really* thought about her being called a stumbling block, to open her mouth and say it. Those girls needed a grown woman to mentor them, and I wasn't one.

A study published in *Youth & Society* surveyed thirty girls and women between the ages of eight and thirty, half of whom were members of "conservative" communities—those that traditionally teach that women must be subordinate to men—and half of whom were members of "egalitarian" communities, where it is taught that the genders can hold all of the same roles in the church, family, and society. Interestingly, the greatest discrepancy the researchers found was not among the children, but among the women over the age of twenty. Women from both the conservative and the egalitarian communities described feeling more comfortable with themselves and gaining a sense of voice at this age. However, the difference lies in how they felt about that. Women from the egalitarian communities viewed it as a strength and a sign of maturity. The women from conservative communities, on the other hand, saw it as a personal weakness, a sign that they were too selfish or aggressive, which led them to "struggle to be more passive."[1]

The researchers write:

One 25-year-old woman, J., expresses the more comfortable she is in a relationship, the easier it is for her to express herself and to disagree with the other person. She views this as bad because a mature Christian should not disagree or be angry: "It's wrong, it's a sin. It's very much a sin to be angry no matter, I mean no matter what the result or why or whatever."[2]

A report in the Vatican newspaper based on a study of the confessions heard by a ninety-five-year-old Jesuit scholar, which was backed up by the Pope's personal theologian, found that the number one sin confessed by women is pride.[3] Yet I don't think this means women are more prideful than men. Rather, I think women are more likely to notice their pride and categorize it as sinful because it contradicts the gender expectations they've been raised with in secular and religious society.

> As opposed to a bat mitzvah or a quinceañera, evangelicals ought to have a funeral at the beginning of girls' adolescence. When you're a girl you're allowed to be who you are. But as you get older, you have to put that person to death. Because after puberty, you're dirty. So now you have to be what's expected of you. You always have to fit some kind of role or be whatever a woman is supposed to be instead of actually who you are. (Jo)

Sometimes just growing up—becoming confident, becoming self-sufficient, forming one's own opinions—can feel like a sin to a complementarian woman. But, what if it's just the opposite?

In her groundbreaking essay "The Human Situation: A Feminine View," Valerie Saiving Goldstein argues that the Christian focus on the sinfulness of pride is rooted in the faith's historic masculine leadership. She says pride may well be a sin for many men who hold power in our patriarchal society, making men's choice to check their pride in service of others very virtuous indeed. Yet women, not being in this position of power, are more likely to think too little of themselves than too much, suffering from an "underdevelopment or negation of the self"[4]—something Blue Jones saw in me from a mile away. And so, perhaps, for such women, pride is not a sin, but a *virtue*.

When I arrived back at Sarah Lawrence College as a sophomore—my friends having moved on to junior year—the plate of glass I felt between myself and my classmates, once cloudy, was now clear. Things I had gawked at like an obnoxious tourist when I first started there, I now watched with detached curiosity: the way people casually and comfortably touched one another; the unabashed strength I saw in so many of the women's strides. But clear or not, the plate of glass was still there, standing between me and the world I now lived in but didn't know how to enter.

I would stay up all night in the painting studio, emerging at four AM smelling of oil paint the way most college kids smell of alcohol. I'd sneak into abandoned buildings with my guitar and write songs alone. I'd create performance pieces with my friends so wild and dark I wondered if this stuff had been in me all along. And I'd spend whole afternoons just marveling over how little about life I really knew—which is perhaps the most rebellious thing one raised to believe she and her friends alone knew the truth can do. But once my pen was capped, my guitar encased, the studio door locked tightly behind me, I went right back to being the girl I'd been raised to be.

Blue Jones was deeply annoyed by my inability to recognize, let alone dig through, all the good-girl tendencies in me that were so utterly obvious to her. She wanted me to pull forth the most raw, real version of myself from the very depths of me. And I wanted to learn a few new chords.

Blue and I spent our semester together haggling over just what our independent study was about. I thought it was about writing music and lyrics. Blue had something else in mind. Sure, I wrote a few songs while working with her, but that wasn't the real work. And every time Blue had to explain that to me . . . again, I watched her become less and less certain about having taken me on as a student.

For Blue, art was ongoing. It was as much about the way the artist projected her voice when she yelled at her neighbor to turn down his music, or grumbled into her coffee in the morning, as it was about what she did onstage. Real art couldn't stop and start any more than life could. So either I was that little girl apologizing on Blue's answering machine, or I was the artist who knew how to sing from a place so low it made her gut shake.

I could be either.

But I couldn't be both.

Before I met Blue, I had no idea how much the gender expectations I'd grown up with controlled my thoughts, feelings, and choices—even down to the sound of my own voice. I had dropped from the evangelical hand that once held me, but the heartstrings that connected me to it were still there. Like a marionette, I still danced under the church's direction. And when Blue picked at the strings, the discordant sounds they made drowned out every other song I had in me.

After playing for Blue, I would often take my acoustic guitar off my lap and set it against her office wall, waiting for her response.

"Did you like it?" I would finally fill the silence.

"It was fine," she might answer shortly.

But eventually she would tell me what was wrong with it.

One response in particular has stuck with me.

"It was all about your daddy," Blue extrapolated. "I felt like it was supposed to be a woman-power song. But then, you actually used the word *daddy* in it."

I shook my head. She didn't understand. Perhaps I should play it again.

"And in your last woman-power song," she went on, "God played the same role as the daddy character does in this one. Why do you need some daddy figure to give you permission to be a powerful woman?" Her question hung in the air.

Verse

He was seventeen and my daddy laughed, he said,
"He'll be twenty-four 'fore he keeps up with you
You know you're a handful, pretty girl.
'Cause you've got a head and you've got a heart and

Most guys don't know where to start with a girl who knows
Where she's going."

Chorus
I said, "Daddy will I ever meet someone
To take me where I've got to go?"
He said, "Pretty girl,
Don't you worry your pretty little head
You don't need someone to take you where
You're gonna go.

"You're going somewhere like it or not.
You're going somewhere
'Cause what it takes my girl, well you've got, you've got
What it takes my girl you've got."

Verse
Seventeen left before my twenty-one, he said
"Listen girl, I just can't hold on.
You know you're a handful pretty girl.
And with another it may be easier
To get through the wear and tear
Of living this life than it is with you."

(Repeat CHORUS)

Bridge
My daddy don't lie to me.
I know that he's the only man who can handle
My most anything.
Yeah, Daddy don't lie to me.

If he tells me I don't need him
Then I don't.
'Cause he tells me, "girl you're all right
On your own."

Verse
Another one's knocking at my door.
"Listen boy, you don't want anymore.
They say I'm a handful, pretty boy.
So listen up and listen good.
My daddy told me everything he should
And lately I've learned I'm okay alone."

(Repeat chorus)

I walked out of Blue's office in a rage. Writing these "woman-power" songs, as she called them, was big for me. I wasn't asking for permission from some daddy figure the way she said I was. I was claiming my *own* power!

"Sometimes people just have empowering conversations with their dads," I railed to anyone who would listen over the course of the next week. "I can't help it if that's what happened!"

And then, it hit me.

That *isn't* what happened.

My dad never actually said what I had given him credit for saying in that song. Not in so many words anyway. It was within character for him—my dad is conservative in many ways, but he is a big supporter of women's leadership. Still, we never actually had the conversation the song described.

What *actually* happened is that I went out on a date with a guy from my church when I was almost fully healed from my last surgery. He called me the next morning and asked me out again. I told him that I'd love to go out again, but that next time we should just go as friends as I didn't feel that romantic spark. Then I heard a loud sigh of relief from the other end of the phone.

"That's probably for the best," he heaved. "You're kind of a handful."

Writing that song was my way of telling myself, *So you're a handful. So what?*

But, if the conversation was actually one I had with myself, I suddenly wondered, *why* did *I attribute it to my daddy?*

Crap.

I never told Blue of course. I couldn't give her the satisfaction. But I did begin to observe myself more closely—how I spoke, when, why. And for the first time, Blue and I got on the same page. When I began to speak in that high-pitched voice, Blue stopped me.

"Pay attention to what you are doing now," she would say. "Your voice just went up again. You hear that? The squeaky girl is back. Why? What are you thinking? What are we doing that brought you back there?"

"I don't know," I might say. "I guess I wanted to know what you think of the song I just played."

Blue would laugh. "You want me to approve of you? Then stop asking me to. How does your throat feel?"

"Tight."

"Tight. Right. So relax it."

I closed my eyes, dropped my tongue to create space at the back of my throat, took a deep breath, and rolled my head around on my neck.

"Okay, now finish what you were saying," Blue would prod.

When I did, it came out straight, without apology, without permission, without question, and with a mounting annoyance at the professor who it would've killed to give a girl a break, let alone a friggin' pat on the head every once in a while.

"Good," Blue said. "Now—sing."

The Virgin

"Jesus has never been more real, present, and personal," Katie told me, her hand wrapped around a watered-down White Russian at a local dive bar in our hometown. Her voice was steady and sure. She leaned over the small table and added in a near whisper, "I've never had a lover so good."

I cocked my head. I was pretty sure that Katie, who I had known since youth group, had never had a lover of any kind—good or not. But tonight, Katie looked and sounded sexier than I had ever seen her. We'd been friends a long time and I rarely saw Katie in anything but a boxy blue postal service uniform or baggy jeans and an oversized T-shirt. Now her voluptuous body was barely hidden behind a lacy black camisole and tight black jeans. She had curled her long dark hair into ringlets and done her makeup immaculately, tracing her eyes with black liner. It was like seeing Olivia Newton-John in the last scene of *Grease*, the one where she leaves her poodle skirt at home, walks into the carnival in black spandex and grinds her cigarette out with the toe of her shoe, making John Travolta drop to his knees and sing.

"Why are you smiling like that?" she asked.

"I don't know, Katie," I said. "You're on *fire* tonight."

It was the mid-2000s. An era when some single Christian women, having been too long told their life purpose could only be fulfilled in partnership with a man, took to saying: *I've got a man, thank you. His name is Jesus.* These women may have been virginal in the material world, but their dates with Jesus could be hot-hot-hot, and they could be hot too so long as he was around.

Despite the fact that Jesus was himself a thirty-something-year-old single man, prolonged singleness is frowned upon in evangelical purity culture. Author Joshua Harris sums up the attitude in his book *Sex Is Not the Problem (Lust Is)*, writing:

> Here's my advice: Get married. Unless God has removed your desire for sex and has given you a clear vision to serve Him as a single person, then assume that you're supposed to get married and either make yourself ready or begin pursuing it. . . . We're not just called to guard the marriage bed; I think more Christian singles should be running toward it![1]

When single evangelicals were asked by Claire Evans at London School of Theology,* "Do you think Christians view singleness as being equal or inferior to marriage?" 75 percent of the men said Christians view singleness as inferior. That seems like a big number! Until you hear that *98 percent* of the women feel this way.[2] Even within this pro-marriage context, men can get away with being single well into their adulthood (some even jokingly calling themselves "Bachelors to the Rapture") in a way that women rarely feel is permitted for them.

When researcher Dr. Kristin Aune asked, "What are the main issues facing single Christian women today?" the most common answer single evangelical women in the United Kingdom gave was "the church's attitude towards single women."[3] The second most common answer was

---

* Formerly known as London Bible College.

"men, sex, and dating." Many women supplemented their answers by saying they felt that the church pressured them to get married. Several said they felt that they were viewed as a threat to married people in the subculture. One even said it was difficult to know how to "function" in the subculture "without the leadership and 'covering' of a husband."[4]

Generally speaking, married people between the ages of twenty-one and twenty-five are more likely to attend church than those who are not married,* and the gap between the two populations is widening with time. Though the same percentage of married people who were attending church between 1972 and 1976 were also attending church between 1998 and 2002, the number of single people dropped significantly.[6] There are surely multiple reasons for this, but I don't think it is a leap to assume the church's negative attitude toward single people is one of them.

Meanwhile, purity culture does not permit women to solve their singleness by taking matters into their own hands and going out and getting a man (and certainly not going out and getting any other kind of romantic partner). A "pure" woman must wait patiently for God to bring the right man to *her*. All she can do is prepare herself. Say, work through any sin that might be preventing God from bringing the gift of a relationship to her.

Many purity advocates teach that women aren't very sexual, and so don't need a way to vent their repressed sexual energy in their single years. But that's not what I usually hear. Dating Jesus was just one of many work-arounds I heard about from women who wanted to remain pure but couldn't deaden their sexual, romantic, and relational impulses.

---

* Right now, around 80 percent of Americans between the ages of eighteen and twenty-nine are single, and nearly half of adults under the age of thirty-four have never married.[5] Between people getting married later in life, and the increasing rate of divorce, the connection between marriage and church attendance (and singleness and not attending church) provides an important insight into the rising number of people who consider themselves religiously unaffiliated.

One woman went on a yearlong "fast" during which she starved herself of romantic and sexual thoughts the way one might starve oneself of food during a traditional fast. Every date was turned down; every desire was shut down; and every insecure "Does this guy like me?" was caught, stopped, and replaced with prayer, meditation, and reading the Bible.

Another woman made celibacy sexy. Every time she wanted to have sex, she went out salsa dancing instead. She came home feeling sweaty, alive, uninhibited, and unafraid of her sexuality in a way that made her feel closer to herself, to the world around her, and to God.

The same year I spoke with Katie about her experience with dating Jesus, Agnieszka Tennant, columnist and former associate editor and editor at large for *Christianity Today*, wrote about this particular workaround:

In a popular book, I learn of women who set up date nights with Jesus. Christie enjoys her Friday nights by going to Barnes & Noble "to drink coffee with the Lord and to read whatever book from the Christian living section he guides me to" or by cooking a wonderful meal and setting the table for two, then "talking to God as if he is actually sitting there at my table with me, because I know that he is." . . .

My friend's mother took part in a "tea with the Lord," during which she and the other women wore their wedding gowns—those, at least, who managed to squeeze into them—and fancied themselves as brides of Christ. An influential Kansas City church teaches thousands of people the so-called Bridal Paradigm, which encourages a quasi-romantic relationship with Christ. And who among us hasn't detected an eerie resemblance between a contemporary Christian song and a pop diva's breathy rendition of a sensual love ballad? . . .

I don't question the devotion of anyone who says she loves Christ intensely, whatever language she uses to express it. But I have little patience for taking biblical metaphors too far and giving one's relationship with God an air of irreverent chumminess. Somehow, the scenario in which "his princess" shaves her legs for a date with Jesus seems to leave little room for fear of God.*[7]

The first time I read Tennant's article, I laughed with recognition at her reference to the sappy romanticism of modern Christian music, and *uh huh'ed* her dismissal of dating Jesus. But the more I listened to Katie and others talk, the less I laughed. Because I began to notice—when my friends were dating Jesus, they were awesome: strong, confident, and doing right by themselves in ways that I'd never seen them do before.

I looked across the table at Katie and smiled.

"I've never seen you this confident," I told her.

"Well, the guys I dated before make God look good," Katie answered, her winking face lit up by the multicolored lights hanging above us in the bar. "Anyway, for me sex is all in my mind. I'm a twenty-six-year-old virgin. I had my first boyfriend, Joe, a few months ago, and he was my first kiss.

"But God is giving me my dreams gift-wrapped with a chocolate on top. Jesus is saying: 'By the way, I love you. Put on your dress because I'm taking you out and the limo will pick you up at seven. And the flowers are for you. And I put $50 on your dresser. Hugs and kisses.' I feel like a honeymooning bride oozing love for God. You know how when you love someone, you want everyone to meet him? That's how I feel."

"What are the dreams he's giving you gift-wrapped with a chocolate on top?" I asked, reading her words back to her.

"Science!" Katie exclaimed as though I should have known. "I first started thinking about myself as dating Jesus right after my breakup with Joe. A guy sitting next to me at a coffee shop was filling out applications

---

* When giving me permission to cite this article in late 2017, the author asked that I inform my readers that she has not been a Christian for a decade.

for college and it made me think about applying to colleges and trying to get scholarships myself. I thought, 'I'm talented; I'm creative. Why am I working some dead-end job?' I wasn't calling out to God. But I just felt like God was there. Now I'm going to be a science major. I was scared out of my mind to do it, but I feel like everything is making sense."

"So," I began, trying to connect everything Katie just said, "your relationship with Jesus gave you the strength to change your life."

"Right," Katie answered definitively.

I cocked my head. "He doesn't sound like a bad boyfriend, actually."

In some ways, the modern-day evangelical trend of dating Jesus can be compared to the historic Catholic trend in which women joined convents to avoid gender expectations. Dating Jesus allowed Katie to take control of her professional life within a context that insisted that, after serving God, her top priority ought to be getting married. Another woman told me she often thought back longingly to the year in which she dated Jesus, though she now had a great earthly partner. She told me she was closer to God while dating Jesus than in any other period of her life but that she was also more *independent*. While dating Jesus, the women I spoke with asked themselves what the ideal boyfriend (which Jesus would obviously be) would want for them. And they answered that the ideal boyfriend would want them to *thrive*. So they gave themselves permission to pursue science, $50 to take themselves out for the evening, and whatever else they needed.

Though the dating Jesus trend has waned in popularity, the idea of taking one's frustrated sexual, romantic, and relational energy and turning it into something more useful—like the pursuit of spiritual endeavors—remains popular. I have personally taken plenty of conscious dating breaks during which my life looked a lot like these women's: I journaled; I prayed; I meditated; I went on spiritual retreats with God; and I held my sexuality close. I would be the first to say that celibacy served me well in these seasons, and that I came away better emotionally and spiritually as a result of it. But as time passes and one season turns into two, then three, then four, and perhaps a lifetime, its sweetness can begin to sour.

By the age of twenty-eight, I wanted to be a woman, and experience that side of life. I was feeling left behind. I wanted a house and a family and I wanted a man. But the longer I stayed out of it, the harder it got for me to even imagine entering in. I was almost on *Dr. Phil* because of that. I answered some question on Oprah.com. I said, "I'm twenty-eight and I haven't been able to kiss anyone yet. This is not normal. I'm so afraid." *Dr. Phil's* people called and said, "It's fascinating that you're straight and twenty-eight and haven't been able to have any affection." They said, "Can you send us your picture?" I sent them a picture and they were like, "You're not an ogre?!"

Then when I was about twenty-nine, I just went ahead and did it. Kissed the man I was dating. We later broke up, but I'm glad I kissed him. I *am*. Otherwise I'd have been too scared when my husband came along. *[What did you feel after that first kiss?]* I felt relief. That I could do it. That I was normal. (Jo)

Ten years after Katie told me about dating Jesus at the bar that night, she was still single. I sat down with a just-as-attractive, but much more casually dressed Katie at her kitchen table to talk about it. Now a science researcher, I asked Katie if she remembered telling me about dating Jesus and the role it played in her choice to pursue science in her midtwenties. She said she didn't. She remembered dating Jesus at other points in her life, but not this one. By then, Katie had tried so many different ways to make her singleness bearable that the experience wasn't even worth remembering.

The buzzer rang on the oven and Katie stood up.

"Should we check it and see if it's ready to eat?" she asked as she opened the oven door and pulled out a chicken dish heaped with seasoned cheese and cream of mushroom soup.

"Ready!" she announced to me as she surveyed the dish. "Ready Freddy!"

As we ate, she told me that she had approached several different religious leaders over the years about how to balance her desire to be a good Christian woman with her need for sexual expression.

"They didn't seem to understand what I was going through or how to help me, and there weren't books about that," she said. "There were books about how to dress modestly or, I don't know, books on 'okay, once you are getting married, here's what sex is and how to enjoy it with your husband.' But I was like, 'Just give me the man. I *know* how to enjoy it,' " she laughed.

In fact, enjoying it was Katie's biggest problem.

No matter how hard she tried, Katie couldn't stop her sexual feelings, her sexual thoughts, and, most upsetting of all, her sexual expression through masturbation. She set her fork down and looked at me seriously. "I began to feel like, 'This is probably something terrible in me and I'm just—'" She struggled for words. " 'I must be the only terrible, black-hearted, black-minded person. I must be weird; I'm a freak of nature; I must be a man.'" Katie was tripping over the purity culture stumbling block that tells girls *they* are to blame for their inability to meet a set of nearly unattainable standards, *not* the standards themselves. Katie even questioned whether she had been sexually abused or inappropriately exposed to sexual content as a child and had repressed the memory, as she couldn't think of any other reason why her sexual feelings wouldn't go away, as the purity movement demanded they must.

"I couldn't understand why I, as a girl, would desire sex so much when, supposedly, girls don't struggle with that. *You* know," Katie gestured to me, "in the evangelical world, sex is the deepest, darkest sin for a woman. There's an expectation that sex—or, anything to do with sex, so masturbation included—is only to be enjoyed within the context of marriage.

"But like eating or breathing or needing sleep, masturbation feels more like a need than a want," Katie said, forgetting her chicken. "There is no sexual outlet for me so I obsess over it. What is my outlet? What is a 'pure' outlet? I constantly talk to God about it: 'God, you made my body this way. What's up?'

"There are times after I masturbate when I'm like, 'Oh well. It's just part of life and it's that time again and whatever,'" Katie continued. "Then other times I feel bad and I beat myself up. I think, 'I should be able to choose, but it just feels like I can't. It must be a slavery to sin that I'm just not holy enough to overcome. It must be a lack of faith in me that I can't overcome this.' Guilt is a familiar friend to me. I beat myself up about everything, so that's just standard. I feel more comfortable with guilt than with pleasure or happiness. It seems like a natural state of being to me."

"When are you more likely to feel one way or the other?" I asked.

"Well, it can go to a lustful place, or it can kind of be somewhat clinical. Depending on how I approach it, I think I can feel more or less shameful."

"What's the difference between clinical and lustful masturbation?" I asked.

"Well, I've noticed as I get older how attached it is to certain times of the month, to hormones—"

I made a *really?* face.

"Oh my gosh yes!" Katie insisted. "It's just—it just *is*. I just don't need it most of the time. Then right before my period or right around ovulation, those are the times when it's almost like a physical need. My body's like, 'Go make peace.' And I say, 'Okay, it is now this time of the month. It's time to masturbate in the shower, where it's clean and I will not think about any particular man. This is just all physical touching and whatever.' Trying to keep it separate from that enjoyment you get when you are with somebody and the excitement of being with somebody." I nodded, remembering interviewees who told me about thinking about their laundry or trying to go into a Zen place of nothingness while masturbating so they wouldn't feel as much shame about it afterward.

"It's like, 'this is a procedure,' " Katie continued. " 'This is a procedure, and we are going to try to separate it from anything dark and horrible.' "

"What do you mean by dark and horrible?" I asked her.

"Fantasizing about somebody that I find attractive or somebody that I've been in intimate situations with before, and just recalling those feelings of being with them. Or imagining somebody touching me or saying things to me that I want to hear that make me excited. It's complicated," Katie summed it up. "I think masturbation is a comfort thing. The pleasure, the happy endorphins. It's a way for me—if I'm feeling super tired or super insecure—you get the good feelings and you feel better or relaxed, or whatever."

"It's a form of self-care," I suggested.

"But then there's the loathing that comes afterward. The fantasy helps you to get excited, and that gives you that physical reaction of happy endorphins, but then comes the self-loathing."

"When you describe the clinical masturbation, it almost sounds like you are trying to avoid shame by stripping sexuality of pleasure."

"Yes. Totally, yes," she agreed. "I think that it's hard to separate what may truly be . . ." Katie trailed off. "I *do* believe in sin," she began again. "And I do believe in a sin nature. But to what extent is true joy and pleasure robbed of me because I'm calling it sin when maybe . . . it's not?" She shrugged, picked her fork back up, and took a bite out of her now cold chicken.

I've spoken with a lot of women about masturbation. In fact, it is one of the most common topics to arise in my interviews. One of my most memorable conversations about it was with a childhood friend named Alma.

"I had an incredibly sexually active imagination," Alma admitted from an armchair in the corner of her living room, her legs tucked up under an afghan.

"Masturbation is what got me through so many years of chastity," she continued. "But I didn't use porn or things like that. I didn't even see my first porn magazine until I was twenty-six. I had to find ways to do it without totally breaking the rules so I didn't hate myself for it. I would fantasize that I was with my future husband and we were on our honeymoon. Or I would think about that verse that they always referred to in order to say, 'don't masturbate': 'If you sin with your right hand, cut it off.' I figured, 'Well, I won't use my hand then.'"

Alma raised her voice and mimed a scene: "'Oh, I have this marker that just happens to be here, or this pencil or whatever. Oops! I don't know how that got there!'" she laughed. "And I also used to arrange these little pointy tissues in my panties so that they would rub against me while I walked."

We both fell into laughter and Alma's husband, who had been doing the dishes in the adjacent room, came in to see what was going on.

"Now that I think about it though," Alma added thoughtfully, "I was scared. For a while, I thought I had used all my orgasms up. And that I had damaged my baby-making things and wouldn't be able to reproduce. I remember now, I was afraid I was doing it in my sleep. I was afraid that I would be caught by my Christian college roommate doing it in my sleep." She shook her head. "I was surprised that not everybody struggled with it. Either that or they were very good actors. I felt like I was a little bit of a freak. Really what it all equals is enormous psychological damage. It's amazing that this one subject can bring up so much pain in me . . . even now."

Alma's husband walked over and sat on the arm of her chair, putting his hand on her shoulder.

"Senior year of Bible college I decided to go to this woman who was a counselor," Alma said. "Everybody loved her, but I should've known not to go to her, of course. She was the same woman who said in class, 'If your husband beats you, you should thank Jesus for the opportunity to show your husband Christ's love by staying with him.'

"I was angry about that, but I had no place to put that anger. The glimmer of fury was put out by it having no other fire on campus. But I went to talk to this woman who taught this class. I threw up my arms and said, 'I need your help.' She told me to come in but she left the door of the administrative office wide open, so all the secretaries could hear.

"I said, 'I'm out of control sexually.'

"The woman said, 'What do you mean? Making out with your boyfriend? Masturbating? Having lesbian thoughts?' I said, 'Yes.' "

"You and Zach were making out?" I asked Alma with surprise. Zach was Alma's college boyfriend.

"Well, we were holding each other really tightly and that brought up sexual feelings in me, so . . . in that way . . . yes."

"That just sounds like hugging," I said.

"Whatever you want to call it, I'm sure the woman would have considered it making out. She said, 'How serious is this? Is there wetness down there?' And I said, 'Yes.' 'Okay,' she said, 'Let me go and get a chart.' The door was still open. I had no idea who was listening and was absolutely terrified about that. It seems strange now that it never occurred to me that I could just stand up and close the door. But I was in a place where I had no rights."

"She asked you whether you were wet?" I interjected.

"Uh huh," Alma answered, raising her eyebrows and tipping her head to the side.

Again, the greatest threat seemed to be pleasure.

"So then she came in with a book about how to fight sexual desires by denying yourself sugar, training yourself to go without a delight that is bad for you. The book implied that you could tell how sexually deviant someone was based on how much sugar they ate, because you could see their restraint or lack thereof.

"She showed me this chart, and proceeded to link all of my sexual misdemeanors to a poor relationship with my father. She said to me, 'If you confess to your father, your sexual sin will go away.' So a few weeks later, I told my father, 'I'm messed up with boys because you didn't care when I tried to commit suicide in high school.'"

I looked up from my notes.

"He cried," Alma said softly. "I regret saying that to him so much."

Then, "If we could just have the 'Masturbation Revolution' we could all get over it," she announced. "Our leaders probably could never get over the fact that *they* masturbate. That's why they're all making a big deal about it."

Her husband and I laughed.

"You know, I still masturbate," she said. "Less now that I'm married," she smiled at her husband. He smiled back, lifting an invisible glass and miming a toast.

"I still have lesbian thoughts. And today, I have to at least give lesbianism a passing glance. I mean, who knows? Maybe I'm gay. Maybe I'm a scientist. How would I know anything? I've spent my whole life pretending I am who they want me to be. My husband comes home from work and says, 'What did you do today, honey?' And I say, 'Oh nothing, just searched the web for hardcore lesbian porn. By the way, we've got these pop-up ads now that I can't seem to get rid of.'"

Alma laughed. I looked over at her husband and he nodded.

"I still have sugar," she continued. "There's still lots of wetness down there. And I think that woman was full of shit."

In the mid-2000s, when I was in graduate school studying American evangelical gender and sexuality messaging for girls, I decided to go to the Christian bookstore and find out what girls were actually being taught about masturbation.

"I work with a group of girls," I approached the clerk, "and lately I've been getting a lot of questions about . . . masturbation." It wasn't exactly a lie. But it wasn't the truth either. For some reason, I felt like I had to perform the part of an evangelical small group leader in that moment, as though I would get kicked out of the store if I told anyone why I was *really* there. The clerk laughed uncomfortably and took a small step away from me. "Do you have any books that address that issue?" I pressed. Now she laughed even louder. Too loud. Uncomfortably loud.

"I don't know!" she almost yelled. "Maybe Youth Ministry," and pointed to the Youth Ministry section. "Or Counseling," now pointing to the Counseling section. "Or Dating and Relationships!"

I went home from the Christian bookstore that day with five books—two addressed masturbation for men, two addressed masturbation for women, and one addressed it without being gender specific. Here's a snapshot of what I found: Masturbation is a gray area. The gender-neutral book and those written for males basically said that masturbation was bad, but not *that* bad, and obsessive shame over masturbating could be just as harmful to individuals and to their relationships with God as masturbation itself. For instance, the authors of *Every Young Man's Battle: Strategies for Victory in the Real World of Sexual Temptation* wrote: "If you're living with a deep sense of shame over masturbation, you need to stop masturbating, but you also need to stop the shame."[8] These books talked a lot about the individual's health and the health of the individual's relationship with God.

The books written for females were different. Masturbation was more strictly forbidden, and an emphasized reason given for why girls and women shouldn't masturbate that I didn't see much about in the books targeted at boys and men was protecting their future marriage, in part by protecting their future husband's feelings. For example, one book warned that if a girl masturbated, she might rob her future husband of the pleasure of giving her an orgasm without her stepping in and telling him what she likes (which she would have learned from masturbation). This logic is reminiscent of the logic of the princess story we discussed in chapter two, in which the princess lost her prince by telling him how to successfully kill the dragon. Basically it comes down to the hackneyed old story that men and boys don't like it when you know more than they do, so, just *don't*.

The gendered differences in the messaging I found in books on masturbation parallel the gendered differences in the messaging I am told many Christian couples receive when they go to their pastors or other religious leaders with sexual problems. If the wife admits to any premarital sexual expression, including masturbation, in a counseling session, she risks being told that their problems are rooted in her sin.

I think one of the reasons that masturbation is seen as so much worse when women do it, is that it is a subversion of purity culture's gender expectations around sexual and other forms of passivity.* As Jessica Valenti puts it in *The Purity Myth*:

> Staying "pure" and "innocent" is touted as the greatest thing we can do. However, equating this inaction with morality is not only problematic because it continues to tie women's ethics to our bodies, but also is downright insulting because it suggests that women can't be moral actors. Instead, we're defined by what we don't do—our ethics are the ethics of passivity.[10]

---

* As an illustration, the authors of *Every Young Woman's Battle: Guarding Your Mind, Heart, and Body in a Sex-Saturated World*, the counterpart to the evangelical book I previously quoted in regard to male masturbation, advises women tempted to masturbate to: "Place your sexual desires back into God's hands rather than taking matters into your own."[9]

This is something Katie understands well.

"I assumed—of course!—that God was going to bring the man that was meant for me," she told me, leaving our plates in the sink and walking back over to the table. "That it wasn't supposed to be me going out looking for somebody or making it happen. I definitely got the sense that if you were somehow spiritual enough, God would lead you through every choice, or presumed choice—because you don't really have a choice. And if you are faithful and trusting enough to listen and follow him, to obey his leading, then you won't have as many troubles in life. I thought, 'Surely I will find a wonderful man and we will make a happy family.'

"Then one day I said, 'Well God, where is he?' This was all I wanted my whole life, and it wasn't happening. I was just like, '*What* is going on? I'm young. I'm kind of cute, I could be cute to some people. I'm kind of nice. I'm very understanding. I'm not *outrageously* funny—like, people don't want me at their parties because I'm the funniest person alive—but I can be funny.'"

"For sure," I responded.

"So what is *wrong*? Am I just not a good listener? I must be sinful and not listening to God's guidance. Or am I just rebellious and he is telling me what to do and I'm just saying, 'No.' Or option three: he doesn't care.

"I just felt no guidance from God, and I started taking it personally after a while. I didn't feel like God kept his end of the bargain in terms of leading me and guiding me. I always thought that he had a plan and purpose for us and I was like, why wouldn't he tell me what that was, or at least let me *feel* what that was, or somehow shut the doors in some way so I have to go this other direction. I felt abandoned. I tried talking to him. Why wouldn't he talk to me? I just felt silence from Heaven.

"That was the first time I started walking away from God a little bit in my heart. I was kind of like, 'Up yours, God. You can't get me a man? I'm going to get my own.'

"I felt super secure with Raj right away. I just trusted him and I knew that he respected me as a person," Katie said of her only long-term boyfriend, who she started dating in her late twenties. Raj was a Catholic and neither Katie, nor her evangelical friends, considered him a "real" Christian so dating him was a serious insurrection. Still, she liked him. And she had been waiting a really long time to like someone.

"Even though I was in rebellion mode, I was a believer," Katie said. "I knew that if I ever came to a sexual line where I felt uncomfortable, Raj would stop. I knew that he would; I felt very confident about that. Still, most of my Christian friends were very like, 'I don't think that dating Raj is best for you because he isn't a born-again Christian. It doesn't feel true to who you are'—their just knowing how important my faith was to me. 'But if this is what you want, I will support you.'

"I think that in some ways, it hurt my friends when I threw my whole self into dating Raj. It was painful for them to see me choosing something that they thought would bring me pain someday. I definitely started disconnecting from my Christian friends at that time, and some of it was just feeling guilty about dating Raj when he wasn't a Christian, and not wanting to be reminded of that.

"I was almost at the point where I was like, 'I really like this guy. And maybe I could just even marry him the way that he is.' I was just so mad at God. I was really upset and disappointed. I wasn't finding a Christian man or a meaningful career—all the things that I wanted. So I was feeling frustrated. And after graduating from school, I had four or five avenues that I thought about as a vocation for myself, but I was just really looking for guidance from God: 'Where would *you* want me to be, God?'"

"What if God was asking you the same question?" I asked. "What if he was waiting for you to tell him what *you* wanted?"

Katie laughed under her breath. "It's funny because it really never occurred to me that maybe he was letting me choose. It never even occurred to me that he would be saying, 'And here's your life; do what you want.'"

In the end, though, Katie did choose. She and Raj had started to talk about marriage, but she still felt uncomfortable about marrying somebody who didn't share her faith. "What I finally came to was that I did still believe in the Bible and the God of the Bible, and I want somebody in my life who wants God in *their* life," she said. "So I broke up with Raj, which was a choice to put God first again. I hadn't done that in a really long time. And I think just the act of finally choosing brought me closer to God.

"Having gone to the dark side and back with God and with the Bible and the church, I think that I have a fuller appreciation for it now than I used to. Because I mean, there's a lot of crap in there. And a lot of really dark, scary, unanswered things. I went through a period of blame with the church, just as I went through a period of blame with my parents. Then I got to a place where I thought, 'I'm an adult now. I have to, at some point, stop blaming them for my problems and take ownership. I have to decide: Am I going to move on from the church and be with this man? Or not.'"

Katie has since resigned herself to the possibility that she will never get married. And that if she does, it probably won't be to the kind of man she has been holding out for—a born-again virgin like her. After all, what man would have waited all these years to have sex the way she had? It makes her sad. She'd be the first to admit it. But in the end, it is a trade she is willing to make for her faith.

7

The Tigress

When I pulled into the driveway of Muriel's small midwestern house, the midday sun was already hidden behind darkening clouds, warning of worse weather to come. Inside, Muriel's living room curtains were tightly drawn and the lights low. As we greeted one another, the words she had written to me over email when we were introduced by a mutual friend a few months ago came back to me: "I don't live the wide, vibrant life I expected. My life is quiet, my sphere small. I'm a poet, but the living itself is calm. Smallish. The result of an immune disorder that's slowly eaten away at my life so that I'm housebound, in a wheelchair when I go out, and occasionally bed-bound for weeks or months at a time."

I settled into Muriel's oversized La-Z-Boy, and she across from me on the couch. She had met me at the door, able to walk that far, but otherwise stayed on the couch for the remainder of our interview as it didn't take much to overexert herself. For almost an hour, we talked about her childhood in the evangelical church—years before her disease surfaced in her early twenties. Finally, the now-thirty-something-year-old broke into her first big smile.

It was her first day of Bible college, Muriel's eyes brightened as she remembered, and she met a guy. "Super handsome, but *so* nerdy," she laughed. "He had glasses that were huge and just sat on his face. And he would wear this Michael W. Smith—you know Michael W. Smith, the Christian singer, right? It was this white T-shirt with Michael W. Smith's super faded-out face on it with the '80s hair. It had torn and he had sewn it up with black thread. And then he would tuck it into black denim jeans that were tapered. That was Dmitri!" her smile widened. "By the end of the first week of college, I knew, he was the man God had for me to marry.

"That whole semester, we would just walk and talk—look at architecture, go to the lake, explore. We were just kids falling in love. We would hold hands, but that was all, obviously. We were on a Bible college campus where you couldn't do anything more than hold hands anyway, and I was terrified of getting anywhere near that slippery slope of sexual temptation.

"Growing up, there was a teenage girl who got pregnant and she and the guy both had to go up in front of the congregation and apologize tearfully and confess their sins," Muriel told me. "I remember thinking, 'Of course. Just another one. It's a slippery slope. It just keeps happening. It's just everywhere.' Sex just seemed inevitable if you even inched toward it. So I said to Dmitri, 'How about we don't even kiss until we're married? That's what I want.' And hubby-to-be, who'd never had a girlfriend before, said 'yes.'"

Like *stumbling block* the term *slippery slope* is used in reference to any number of things that might draw one away from God, but in the evangelical church it is so commonly used in reference to sexual sin that it's practically become shorthand for it. Many feel that engaging in even a "hint" of sexual immorality—such as kissing or hugging if done in a sexual way—is a slippery slope. And in the words of one interviewee, the sexual "slippery slope leads straight to Hell. It leads to flames and desecration."

I remember thinking about this message when reading evangelical Christian Dr. James Dobson's book *Life on the Edge: The Next Generation's Guide to a Meaningful Future* as a teenager. Dobson cites zoologist Dr. Desmond Morris's twelve stages of intimacy as described in his book *Inti-*

mate Behaviour. The first stage of intimacy, Dobson summarizes Morris's findings, is eye to body. The couple sees one another from afar. The second stage is eye to eye. Then voice to voice, hand to hand, hand to shoulder, hand to waist, face to face, hand to head, hand to body. However, the tenth stage suddenly becomes decidedly more intense, at least to the ear of a teenager like me: *Mouth to breast.* Now there are just two stages left: touching below the waist and sexual intercourse.[1] So you see? Although those first stages all seem to be safe, when a couple indulges in them, they find themselves just three stages away from having sex, and as it is often said among purity movement authors, speakers, youth pastors, and small group leaders, those last three stages *fly* by: Eye to eye, hand to waist, and the next thing you know, boy howdy, you're in bed.

By the middle of her first year of Bible college, Muriel and Dmitri were engaged. "I got a book, *The Joy of* . . . whatever . . . by Tim LaHaye and his wife, about sex," she told me.

"Okay, that's *The Act of Marriage*," I answered, referring to the Christian sex manual that came out in the mid-1970s.

"*The Act of Marriage*, yes," Muriel nodded. "And Dmitri explained sex to me some and I was like, 'You mean you have to move back and forth?' I didn't realize there was a friction aspect, I thought you just . . . stuck it in."

"Dmitri had some sexual experience?" I asked.

"No. He bought pornos to learn."

Desperate to have sex, Muriel and Dmitri's engagement was short.

"We got married at 9:30 in the morning so that we could have sex early. No lie, that's why we got married early! I was *excited* about sex! I thought, 'I don't want to wait all day,' because sex was this huge thing! It was what everybody talked about, in the negative. But then supposedly once it was in marriage it was supposed to be this amazing celebration. This was the flip side, right? Supposedly. But during our ceremony up there, the pastor says 'you may kiss the bride,' and we kiss. Our teeth

135

clanked. I was like, 'What is going on?' We, like, sort of used tongue. It was the weirdest thing in the world.

"There had been this whole promise: If you wait, then this kiss will be magical and divine. But oh my gosh, total opposite. I whispered in Dmitri's ear, 'Let's not do that again until we're alone.'

"There was a small reception and by noon we're in a hotel room. So we start stripping off. I see a naked man for the first time. I hadn't even seen naked pictures. I'd never seen any pornography or anything. So, naked man. And then I got to strip off. And now we're naked and this is weird and we start kissing or whatever and then I just bust up crying because this has all been way too much and I hadn't slept much the night before.

"So I take a nap. We take a nap. Then we wake up and we start trying it again. And I have no idea what hole or where anything is. We try that and Dmitri tries touching and he doesn't know. At this point I've read about the clitoris in *The Act of Marriage*. I know it exists, but I have no idea where it is, neither does Dmitri, and so he's, 'Does this feel good?' I have no idea. I've never let anything down there try to feel good before. So he keeps trying and I'm like, 'Is that an orgasm? I don't know.' So then he starts trying to stick it in. Again, I have no idea where. He's trying to direct. We don't get it in and then he's like, 'Well I'm kind of moved all the way here. Can you help me out?' So I start to do that, and then I'm just, like, left there. Not having done 'the sex.'

"We don't figure out sex for four months. We don't actually get it in. We keep trying. I mean, we're discouraged, but he does keep trying. Sometimes it hurts. We didn't get the idea about wetness or lubrication or any of that. I eventually figured out I had to stretch out beforehand, manually. I figured out where the hole was and I would stretch it out manually and then he would go in. It never felt sexy. Sex was never sexy. I never got off while he was in there, and even on his end, it was more like, if we did it, good, that's something we're supposed to do. But it was never 'this is so sexy, I want you.' It was just a check mark for us. I'm not sure when he gave up on trying as often."

"Did you ever talk about what you were experiencing with anybody?"

"No! Because it's embarrassing! I mean, that's just something you just *don't* talk about. We're married now. It's supposed to be a slippery, slippery, easy-to-fall-off-of slope. 'Where's the easiness? How's anybody accidentally having sex? How are teenagers accidentally getting pregnant? I don't know. How are they even getting it *in*?!'"

The purity movement teaches us that a "pure" woman comes to her husband an untouched virgin who has hardly (if ever) thought about sex before. And then, naturally and beautifully, the woman's new husband introduces his wife to sexuality for the first time and years of pent-up sexual energy which she was not even aware of come pouring out of her, allowing her to meet her new husband's every sexual want, which is also her every want, and together they live happily ever after. Both the repressed sexuality of the virgin and the fully surrendered sexuality of the wife are requirements in purity culture—one being fabled to lead to the other.

The Act of Marriage: A Christian Guide to Sexual Love,* the book that Muriel was given in preparation for her wedding night, insists that God wants everyone to experience sexual pleasure within the marriage bed. This was a breakthrough concept when the book entered Christian bookstores in 1976! Even today, this concept is controversial in some evangelical circles. Though most have embraced it, some still insist female sexual pleasure, in particular, is simply beside the point.

Attempting to ease the Christian couple's transition into sex, *The Act of Marriage* includes diagrams of male and female sexual organs, advice on how to bring a woman to orgasm, and what I consider to

---

* In a later edition, the subtitle for this book was changed to: *The Beauty of Sexual Love.*

PURE

be some really healthy relational perspectives around mutual care and mutual pleasure. But as bold as it is in shamelessly talking about sex in the (heterosexual) marriage bed, the book is still based in purity culture and thus follows a very gendered pattern—too often excusing men for sexual misbehavior and blaming women for sexual displeasure. For example, at one point the following story is related:

> A young mother of three came in to ask me to recommend a psychiatrist. When I inquired why she needed one, she hesitatingly explained that her husband felt she must be harboring some deep-rooted psychological problem about sex. She had never experienced an orgasm, could not relax during lovemaking, and felt guilty about it all. When asked when she first felt these guilt feelings, she admitted to heavy petting before marriage that violated her Christian principles and the warnings of her parents. She finally conceded, "Our whole four-year courtship seemed to be a continuous scene of Tom trying to seduce me and my fighting him off. I made too many compromises and am honestly amazed that we didn't go the whole route before our wedding. After we were married, it just seemed to be more of the same. Why did God include this sex business in marriage anyway?"
> That young woman did not require a battery of psychological tests and years of counseling therapy. She simply needed to confess her premarital sins and then learn what the Bible teaches about marital love.[2]

There is no mention of the possibility that the woman may not enjoy sex with her husband because he had not respected her sexual boundaries before marriage, forcing her to fight him off (in her words) for years. And no mention that perhaps the woman might have felt guilty about having sex because the church had embedded the notion that sex was shameful so deeply into her brain that she couldn't shake it now that she was married and it was suddenly supposed to be okay. No. It was

138

the woman's premarital sexual activity (not even the *couple's* premarital sexual activity, though the activity took place between the two of them) that was blamed for the couple's sexual problems. LaHaye's happy conclusion to this story is as follows: After the woman confessed her sin, "she became a new wife," and her husband's "spiritual growth since then has been exciting to watch—all because a wife caught the big picture that God planned lovemaking to be mutually enjoyable."[3] This illustration is picture-perfect purity culture. In short, *women's* sexuality must be just right, so that *men* can spiritually thrive.

I was about fifteen years old when I first heard a pastor say from the pulpit: "Every man wants a woman who is a lamb in the day, and a tiger at night." The congregation laughed. A few people clapped. My face turned red. I hadn't even had my first kiss, and already I felt myself on a tightrope strung between two opposing sexual expectations. I have heard the tiger/lamb language many times since. Interviewees share about it being said from pulpits, in Bible studies, and in Christian counseling sessions. Somehow, purity culture has turned a pornographic fantasy about a virgin turned vamp into "morality," so that now both a woman's nonsexuality before marriage and her hypersexuality *after* marriage are required for her to be considered good.

There are two messages happening. Somehow you have to be a lamb—chaste and pure as the driven snow until you are married. And then you have to be a tigress in bed. The vows make that instant transformation somehow. Then, if you don't satisfy him, he will have an affair, or he has a right to chastise you for not being amazing in bed or whatever, because you are responsible for his sexual satisfaction and whether his eyes wander. I remember Johnnie and I experienced some problems after we were married. I read the book, *Every Woman's Marriage*, which basically implies that if you are not satisfying your husband sexually, you are responsible for his having an affair and watching porn. I shudder looking back at it now, but at the time I really was being sincere in trying to be a good wife. (Jo)

Muriel had mastered being a lamb.

Growing up, she explained, "I was just absolute, one hundred percent nothing. Nothing, nothing, nothing. I would watch a movie that might make something tingle and I would just slap"—she pointed at her lap—"down there. Until I could feel nothing."

"Literally slap yourself?"

"Literally slap myself. Until I numbed it. That would make the feelings stop."

It was the tigress part Muriel had trouble with.

"There was just this anxiety and a general feeling of disappointment," she said sadly. " 'We're doing this wrong and why can't we do it right? There's something wrong with me obviously. I'm not working down there.' Or maybe there was something wrong with Dmitri. I wasn't desirable enough or he wasn't big enough or we're paying for his having masturbated before we got married. There were all of these messages about, 'If you wait, it will be perfect; it will be like a magical unicorn.' But it wasn't. Going straight from holding hands to having sex, I hadn't been able to develop sexual desire toward him in the normal way. Because I'd never let myself feel, I had no idea how to develop sexual attraction."

"You'd been slapping it down your entire life," I suggested.

"Yes. I'd been slapping it down my entire life."

Dr. Marlene Winell, a human development specialist and author of *Leaving the Fold: A Guide for Former Fundamentalists and Others Leaving Their Religion*, regularly counsels couples whose sexual difficulties are rooted in Christian purity culture.

"I've heard about numerous tragic wedding nights that often don't get any better," she told me in an interview. "Inability to be sexual is a big problem for both men and women coming out of the church. They've practiced turning themselves off so much that when they have a sexual occasion, they can't turn themselves back on again. Human beings don't have a switch."[4]*

For some, the issue extends beyond emotional blocks to physical ones. Some females experience what is called vaginismus—an involuntary physical tightening of the vagina that makes sex painful and sometimes even impossible. According to a sex therapist and an obstetrician/gynecologist interviewed by *The Sydney Morning Herald*, vaginismus is "more common among women who are saving themselves for marriage" and "women, who due to religious or cultural reasons, have developed an overriding fear of penetrative sex," though it is also experienced by sexual abuse survivors and those with a fear of childbirth.[5] Vaginismus can last days, or decades.

The first time I ever had penetrative sex with a man, I actually thought that there was something . . . that I had an excessively small vagina. I went to the doctor about it, and she was like, "I don't think so." It feels related to all the things that I was taught and not taught growing up. It's just like, you guard that shit with your life because it's everything. It's just a muscle thing. (Biz)

I heard rain begin to trickle on the windows behind Muriel's drawn curtains. The room had gotten darker, which meant the sky was growing darker too, and the storm was beginning.

"Go on," I urged Muriel.

---

*This book is not about men, but it bears mentioning here that within a society that equates masculinity with sexual expression, if not aggression, men who find that they do not have as high of a sexual drive as they are expected to—some perhaps due to the fact that they repressed their sexuality before marriage in order to be "pure"—face their own difficult challenges.

"The first year as newlyweds was just hard," she sighed. "All the stuff that was supposed to be fun and great, it was just so hard and miserable. Three years after we got married, I wanted to have a baby. But having a baby required sex, which we weren't that great at. But we tried the sex again."

"How many times had you had sex at this point?"

"A handful of times. I don't know. Five? So then there was 'the week of sex.' We tried to have sex every day while I was ovulating and it was so awkward but we got it done. We managed it four or five times, which put our total average up to almost ten. But it was enough to eke out a kid. Then we had barely any sex for ten years.

"At one point in the middle of those years, I laid down for a three-hour nap. I thought I had the flu and then I just kept sleeping. I went to doctors; they didn't see anything wrong and I felt complete condescension from certain doctors. And the church wasn't helping either. The church that was supposed to support and listen. I was so confused that it wasn't doing what it was supposed to be doing. I was this sane, rational person saying that something was wrong with me, but nobody—not the doctors, not the church—would believe me. The only person who believed me was Dmitri. He was the only one who I felt really understood. He was always, 'This is happening to *us*. It's happening to *us*. You're mine. So if this happens to you, it happens to me.'

"Dmitri and I would leave church crying some weeks because the sermon would be about church community and family and fellowship and stuff and I realized nobody is actually doing this; none of this is actually real. I was so sick. I was getting angry at everything in life, at God. I was in a wheelchair now, and I didn't mind when I accidentally ran into people's ankles. My son was small but I couldn't take care of him, because I didn't have the energy, so my mom was doing most of his caretaking. And Dmitri and I were thinking that we may not believe in God anymore. I repeatedly tried to go to the church elders. I was like,

'I'm having such difficulty with this, please help,' you know, 'help us with knowing how to deal with these issues of faith and illness.' They tried, but they didn't help. I even had some people tell me that they prayed I would get *worse*."

I looked at Muriel in shock.

"Oh yes. Because obviously getting this sick didn't do it, didn't make me a good Christian. They prayed that I would get worse and hit rock bottom because maybe that would bring me back to Christ. They told me that to my face. Just like my mom has told me she's prayed for my brother to lose his job. They pray for bad things to happen to people, so they might see their need for God. That will only happen if they hit rock bottom. If they are broken."

"It reminds me of what you and I talked about on the phone," I said. "How we both prayed for God to break us when we were young. How we asked to suffer."

"We were so dumb," Muriel answered. "Suffering is a bitch."

Muriel had calculated all of her life decisions around the equation that if she was pure, God would bless her. She would be gifted with a loving, romantic, sexual marriage. She would be kept safe in a strong, supportive, always-there-for-her religious community. "I was not one of those 99 percent faith, a little bit of question, people," she insisted. "I was 100 percent: I will be pure; I will believe; I won't crack." But when the purity and community equations proved to be bad math, everything "just crumbled." How could she believe anything evangelicalism taught her if the one thing they said was most important—remain pure before marriage and you will have a blissful sexual life after marriage and be supported by the larger community—wasn't true?

"To me, it meant there was no God," Muriel said, before going on to explain that, as an absolutist, she felt that if *anything* the church taught wasn't true, then *nothing* the church taught was true. I see this logic among many of my interviewees when they first begin to question the church's teachings. They hold on to the good/bad binary they were taught growing up; they just swap everything around on it. In their new reverse binary, evangelicalism goes from good to bad; the secular world goes from bad to good; sex outside of marriage goes from bad to good; abstinence goes from good to bad. But, most of my interviewees eventually have come to the conclusion that the binary itself is the problem. From here, they become uniquely sensitized to fundamentalism in all forms, distrusting any community that claims they have all the answers, that assumes they are all right and that those they oppose are all wrong, be that community conservative or progressive, religious or secular.

"I just didn't trust any kind of formal framework, because frameworks were problematic," Muriel said of her own journey away from the binary. "For forever it was Christians versus non-Christians, people who had the spirit of Christ in their hearts and the people who didn't. And thinking that, it made Christians seem completely different from non-Christians. But lives are just lives. I had to stop and see that dichotomy didn't exist. You know, no absolutist thing is going to work. So what were you left with? I didn't know. I really didn't know.

"I was the kind of girl who would walk around with my hand a little bit open when I felt lonely because I was imagining Jesus holding my hand, you know? And when I had insomnia, I would talk to God all night. To lose those things, it just felt devastating. It was like grieving a death. I felt completely lost, destroyed, confused. What do you do when there's no more absolutes? What do you fill that up with? How can you know anything? I'm left with this world and I don't know *anything*.

"My secret fear was, 'Well, maybe there *is* a God and I'm just not one of the chosen ones to be in a relationship with him. I don't see evidence of the Spirit in my life; therefore, maybe the Spirit is not in me.

Fair being fair, maybe I'm just not chosen.' I would go back and forward occasionally, breaking down and praying, 'Oh God, if I'm just not one of the chosen, please, please let me back in.' I would wake up with nightmares, terrified. I'd be about to die and in my last minutes I would quickly recant and accept Jesus into my heart. Right before I died I'd say, 'I'm sorry, I'm sorry, I do believe.' And God would always take me back.

"But then, I started to masturbate.

"The thing that you can*not* do if you're a Christian.

"The first time I masturbated it was like, 'It's really true. I really *don't* believe in God.' It was the last door shutting. Me saying, 'I actually don't believe.'

"I was terrified while I was doing it, and afterward I felt like crying. It was a weird shame/freedom thing. Both of those. I was freaking out. I thought, 'Because I'm masturbating I can't go back to God now. I can't ever be forgiven.'"

"How did Dmitri react to your loss of faith?"

"He was just like, 'You don't want to go to church anymore? Awesome.'"

"Was he being sarcastic?" I asked.

"No. He just said, 'Okay.' I was going through all of this angst and he was just 'okay.' Punk," she rolled her eyes.

After leaving the church, Muriel came out as a feminist. "I realized I had fought tooth and nail against feminism all these years because, secretly, I *was* a feminist," she exclaimed. "*I* was the person who'd started a Bible study in high school and college; *I* was the one leading these things. Dmitri and I would try to have these two-people Bible studies, where he was supposed to be the male and lead and teach and I was supposed to be submissive. So then he would try to do that but then he would wrongly, in my opinion, interpret the verse. I would be like, 'But no, if you look at it this way and this and this and this,' and then we would both just kind of sit there and stare at each other or get into a little argument and then be uncomfortable because I wasn't supposed to teach him."

But when Muriel finally gave herself permission to step out of the submissive position, it allowed her to do something "that had always felt ridiculous. I started writing poetry," the author of several poetry collections recalled.

In the years that followed, Muriel launched a new life. She went back to school for a graduate degree in poetry. She made several new friends. She was social for the first time in years. And accordingly, her health improved. But she was haunted by the feeling that the one thing other than her son that she carried with her into her new life—her marriage to Dmitri—was based on a lie.

"I started to question the marriage," she admitted. "What did we really get married for? The whole reason we got married when I was nineteen was so we could have sex, right? So we would not fall down the slippery slope and fornicate and do the sin. Which has worked out really great," Muriel huffed. "We'd never really been sexually compatible; we were more best friends than lovers." And so, after twelve years together, Muriel told Dmitri she wanted a divorce.

"He was brokenhearted. He wept and I felt horrible. I said, 'We're just best friends; we barely talk anymore; we have nothing in common.' Our lives had been separate. I said, 'We'll get separate apartments but in the same building so we can raise our son together.'

"We almost got divorced," she told me.

But when Muriel watched Dmitri lug her boxes and furniture to the apartment next door for her, Muriel still too weak to move them herself, she saw her husband with new eyes. They may have gotten married quickly because of the sexual purity rules, but somewhere in there, she realized, they really had fallen in love. Dmitri was a good man. He was carrying her boxes, for God's sake, *after* she left him! And he had stood by her when no one else had. She asked him to stop moving the boxes for a moment and to come sit next to her. He did and then, she asked if the two of them could start over. Letting everything go—her beliefs about herself and the world, her relationship with God, even her marriage—allowed Muriel to look at it all for the first time, and to choose which things she wanted to let go of, and which she wanted to hold on to.

"For the first time, I got to choose Dmitri for *me*," she said. "That night, I slept in his bed and we had sex. It was the first time it felt natural. It was just because we wanted to, because we needed that connection with each other. Then we kept doing it. It was like, 'Oh my gosh. *This* is how people have sex!' So we finally figured out how to do it."

"That's beautiful," I said.

"I think it's totally beautiful!" she exclaimed. "Our love story is gorgeous and I love him so *fucking* much. Like, he's the best thing. I feel like we will be one of those couples that lives together until a really old age and then dies together because we just literally don't function without the other."

Today, Muriel and Dmitri are still learning about their own and one another's bodies and finding creative new ways to connect. When Dmitri is masturbating, for example, Muriel snuggles up next to him and joins in. And when Muriel is masturbating, Dmitri does the same. "Getting used to doing that with somebody, the sin, the 'bad' thing, together," she said, "it brings us closer. I had no idea that my starting to masturbate would end up helping my marriage! We almost lost each other. We pushed it to the limit, but ultimately we decided we loved one another and could do our changing side-by-side. My husband and I are still together after fourteen years."

A month after the day Muriel asked Dmitri if the two of them could start over, her health failed again.

"I went from feeling the best I'd ever felt to feeling the absolute worst. I couldn't get out of bed for months. But instead of feeling horrible and angry and furious at the world, I felt totally at peace and joyful. I was like, 'This is not the way you're supposed to feel. This is not historically the way that I've felt when this has happened in the past.' And I realized, 'This is grace. This is an unasked-for gift from God. This *is* God.' "

"It made you believe again?"

"Not in a personal Jesus, or even a personal entity, but more . . . I'm open to God existing today. And I like to pray, so I do pray, but I have no idea if he's out there."

"So, suffering really did bring you closer to God."

"Not in that naïve way I expected. But eventually I have come to experience grace through it. In the church, suffering was a fanatic place. We wanted it so we could get past it: 'Break me so that you can remake me.' But now I can be silent and find joy in that silence, which is really helpful when you can't get out of bed or do anything, like I can't some days. It's very powerful. I feel God in the space of emptiness. I feel him when I am at my rock bottom, when I am in sickness, like those people wanted me to be," she laughed under her breath. "But it is through just sitting with it, being with it, learning to accept it." In these moments, Muriel says, she feels peace. Euphoria even. In her greatest moments of suffering, Muriel feels God—and he or she feels nothing like Muriel thought God would.

8

Family Values

"I'm so careful not to sound negative about the church," the mother of a childhood girlfriend insisted as she poured me a glass of Chardonnay. "I don't want to be that person who's tearing it down. There are so many good people there, who do good things, who have wonderful hearts. So . . ." She paused to look me in the eye before filling her own glass. "This is just within a framework of raising our girls there. And the impact the church had on our family. Within that context."

I nodded.

"Good," she said. She filled her glass halfway, thought about it for a moment, poured a little more, and then set the bottle of Chardonnay down and crossed her legs neatly at the edge of her couch. Then she gestured for me to begin.

"Right," I said. "The last time we spoke on the record was almost ten years ago. So one thing I want to do is read you everything you said then and see if you still agree with it all now and would be comfortable with my using it in the book."

"If Solange is comfortable," the mother smiled. She drew the name out in a long drawl—*Solaaaaange*. Moments ago, she had theatrically announced that this must be her pseudonym in the book.

"*Oui, Solange,*" I laughed.*

Solange is the only mother I interviewed for this book other than my own. Years before we drank Chardonnay, she had reached out to me, having heard I wanted to interview her daughters. She told me she was beginning to notice the effects of the church's sex and gender messages on her daughters' lives and wanted to be interviewed as well. I agreed.

"I chose our church specifically for their youth group," Solange had explained the first time we met for an interview. "I wanted it to supplement our work as parents, counteracting the negative impact of a secular high school and its peer pressure. I think that we viewed youth group as ancillary help to get them through those crappy, hard, teenage years. We wanted it to help us protect our little girls. I didn't realize until later that they needed me to protect them *from* youth group."

I looked up at Solange expectantly after reading aloud her own quote from nearly a decade ago.

Solange lifted her glass, took a sip, and set it back onto the table. The soft music that she had turned on in the background filled the silence.

"I was being polite," she observed quietly.

The first time I interviewed Solange, she was still part of the evangelical church. But over the past ten years, she had shared many a bottle of Chardonnay with her daughters as well, and listened to them tell her about their religious shame, fear, and anxiety. So when Solange's daughters left the evangelical church in their early adulthood, she understood why, and soon afterward, she and her husband left too.

"At that point I was still working it out," Solange said, reflecting on the quote from her younger self. "Talking with you that day was my first opportunity to put it into words, to search to articulate, to *tell* somebody. Because there was nobody to tell. My girlfriends, my peers, they were all

---

* Though these days many people think of Solange Knowles, Beyoncé's sister, when they hear the name, perhaps it's worth noting that I've read that *Solange* is the French form of a Latin name deriving from the word for *religious*.

in the same church. They were raising their kids there. I just felt lost and didn't know where to go. So I was being polite. But there's nothing in that I would change. Not a word. I totally support everything I said if not even more strongly. You can bold it, italicize it, and then underline it."

Several studies have found that, generally speaking, parents play a very small role in their children's sexuality education.[1] Parents who go to church regularly are even less likely to talk to their kids about sex than their peers (especially if they're white), and the conversations they do have tend to focus on their desire for their kids to make "moral" sexual choices, especially if they are talking to girls with whom they are more likely to emphasize the virtues of virginity than they are with boys.[2] The truth is, a lot of parents just don't know what to say. Many never received a proper sexuality education themselves, so they bring their kids to church hoping the institution will help them.

"I had hoped that the church would more than partner, that it would take the *lead*, especially about sex," Solange confessed. "I talked to my girls about it: 'This is A, B, and C; A goes into B.' I was very clinical and very specific about how you get pregnant. But I didn't know how to say the *romantic* part of it, the intensity of the feelings, and how things can carry you away when you're fifteen years old. I met my husband at seventeen; I was engaged at seventeen; I was married at eighteen. While it worked out for me, it's not what I wanted for my daughters. I thought youth group would be an extension of my teachings," she said. "But it wasn't."

"What did you hope the church was teaching them, and what do you think that your daughters were actually learning?"

"What I had hoped they were teaching was that you should want the best for yourself, sexually. And God wants only the best for you. I think abstinence protects women. Not that sex is bad, not that it's shameful, no. But it protects your body from diseases, from babies, et cetera. I thought youth group reflected those values. But I don't really know what my daughters were taught. I can't tell you. Because that wasn't shared with me. I asked the youth pastor if I could sit in on youth group because I wanted to know what was going on, and I was told 'no.'"*

"We actually talked about that ten years ago," I said to Solange. "You said then: 'It was all kept behind a shroud of secrecy. They said they wouldn't open up the space to us because if it was open to parents, then kids wouldn't want to come.'"

"Bingo. Absolutely true. Then you-know-who became the youth pastor," Solange said, referring to the youth pastor who was later convicted of child enticement with the intent to have sexual contact with the twelve-year-old girl from my youth group. "He did let me go, but it did not go well. Did *not* go well. I remember the night I visited youth group it was game night. They took a baby's potty chair and they filled it with Mountain Dew to represent urine, and a Baby Ruth bar to represent feces. They were making kids eat it and drink it as some kind of game. There was a girl gagging. In what universe is this acceptable behavior? I went to the head pastor and told him. I didn't go in there screaming and yelling, shaking my fist at him, but he dismissed me so fast it was so embarrassing. What I remember is being embarrassed. Because the times that I did speak with 'the men of the church,'" she said making air quotes, "I was so dismissed."

"Do you remember what about his response felt dismissive?"

"The nonverbals. You know nonverbally when someone's dismissing you. You've been dismissed by men. You've been dismissed *plenty*

---

* Many sexuality educators agree it is best practice not to have parents sit in on sessions about sensitive topics, such as sexuality. However, they also agree it is best practice for educators to openly share with parents what is taught in these sessions. For example, educators trained in the Our Whole Lives (OWL) program are encouraged to offer opportunities for parents to watch the videos their children will later watch and read the curricula their children will be engaging with in advance.

of times, Linda. It's in the lack of eye contact; it's in the tone of voice; it's in the words they choose and the utter lack of concern. The *utter* lack of concern.

"He said, 'Take it to the youth pastor.' So I took it to him. He was mad. I kept my composure. I didn't get angry back at him, but I was really upset. He didn't listen; he didn't care; he was defensive and angry. And had my husband been there by my side, I know I would've been treated differently. But I really felt as an adult, as a mother, as a parent, I should be able to talk to these people *myself*. The youth pastor said, 'Take it back to the head pastor.' After that, I was never allowed to go to youth group again.

"How do you fix things when you can't even find a voice to discuss them?" she said, looking away from me. "When you're not even comfortable talking about these things yourself? I would be very embarrassed and ashamed to talk about sexual relationships. That's not something I can do. But it's a conversation that needs to be had.

"I had always thought that if something was going on with my daughters, the youth pastor would talk to me. But after I went to youth group that time, I realized he wouldn't. The relationship was between the youth leaders and the children. It was almost like a secret relationship, a private, secret relationship, and you realize, now, that's how you control people. With really young ones, with teenagers—oh my God they're so vulnerable." Solange and I sat in silence for a moment, the thought of the twelve-year-old girl unspoken between us.

"I can't tell you what my daughters were taught in youth group," Solange continued, picking her glass back up off the table. "But I *can* tell you some of the results I saw: I saw them embarrassed about their feminine selves; I saw them more self-conscious about how they dressed and how they looked. They were just—I don't know. There was an underpinning of shame. When I read the Bible I see God's powerful love for women. I do not see in the Bible God treating women as second-class citizens, as little girls who aren't quite grown-up and will never be. But when you see your kids struggling at school and church, what do you do? Pull them out of school? I didn't realize homeschooling was an option. Change churches? The girls didn't want to leave their friends. How could I differentiate between what was normal growing-up stuff and what was abnormal? What was teenage angst and what was true anxiety?"

"Did you see other parents struggling this way?"

"No. I really didn't," Solange said. "The people I remember, they were all in. And in the beginning, I was too. I couldn't see it back then. I just could not see it."

"Did you ever try to talk to anyone about it?"

"I do remember trying to talk to some people who I felt had an education and an awareness. I did not try to talk to any pastor or associate pastor because the messages were so ingrained in them. I just wasn't going to bother with that. But some other parents, and some of the women who were actually working in ministry. And I either was not properly articulating my concerns or there was just this wall I was coming up against. It was like, 'If you don't agree 100 percent, it's hit the highway. There are other churches. Either be a part of this and get on board, or leave.'"

Over the course of my research, I have been surprised by how many of the conservative Christians closest to adolescents—parents, youth pastors, and other youth group leaders in particular—have told me they are concerned about the damage they see purity culture doing to adolescents' lives. Many silence their concerns, however, knowing they are not welcome within the community, and those who do voice them are often given the same message Solange was: The religious purity movement isn't going *anywhere*, so you can either get behind it, or you can go.

*   *   *

Around the same time I talked with Solange the first time, I met up with a former evangelical youth pastor from the area at a local coffee shop. "It was so important that everyone was in lockstep," Pastor Bob, who spent twenty-five years in youth ministry, told me through his long, bushy beard. "They would talk about it in pastoral meetings: 'We all have to be on message, on the same page.'"

Bob went on to describe a series of extremely troubling things he knew to be happening to some of the kids under his care. "It was somehow seen as, 'Oh great, those kids are here for this sexuality class,'" he continued. "But I thought, 'No! They shouldn't be in this class! We're just a church! We're not equipped to handle this!' I was disgusted, because the church put itself in a position of authority when it came to sexuality, and we had no business doing that. That's why I didn't want to teach the purity message anymore. I made up all these excuses not to do it, but I got hounded to. Finally I admitted, 'I just don't believe in it: the material, the delivery, everything about it.'

"My old head pastor, he is passionate, and one day he threw his arms out wide and he said 'Bob, you are waaaaay out here.'" Bob splayed his arms as an illustration. "'And we want you to be—'" he brought his hands together. "'We want you to be *here*,'" Bob made a physical box with his hands. "And it dawned on me. 'Of course! That's it!' I was starting to be more open. I was thinking 'maybe this narrow rail of evangelicalism is not the only answer; maybe there are more answers.' That was the soul of my decision to leave the church."

"Which is when you started The Bar Church?" I asked, referring to the experimental church Bob started and led in local bars for five years before leaving the ministry altogether.

"Yes," he said. "The Bar Church was for people moving away from shame in every way. At one point, we had every old evangelical pastor and youth pastor from the area there. The nicest way to put it is that a lot of them had had the crap beat out of them in their churches. Here. I want to show you something." Bob pulled a laptop out of his backpack. He searched for an episode of the series *One Punk Under God* about Jay Bakker, the more progressive preacher son of famed televangelists, Jim and Tammy Faye Bakker. Bob scrolled quickly through the episode searching for a particular scene.

"Here!" he said, moving the curser back a bit. I scooted closer to him to see the screen better. "*Here.*"

"Oh wow!" I exclaimed.

The cameraperson pulled away from Jay Bakker's sermon to pan the audience, and there, on the screen, was Bob. It turns out that the show visited The Bar Church at one point. Bob pointed at the screen and named various audience members. I saw more than one of my evangelical friends' youth pastors; I even saw the youth pastor that my teenage boyfriend, Dean, had confided in when I broke up with him for God.*

"These guys," Bob said, "a lot of them are just *out* now. They are the walking wounded. But some people felt, 'I need to go back to the mother ship.' If they wanted to be in ministry, they felt they had no other choice. I'm not in the church anymore, but I'm still connected by friendship enough to know that when it comes to sexuality, shame is still the thread that runs through it. Every time I hear another story about it, I think, 'The beat goes on.'"

Who knows how many of our youth pastors were like Bob and our mothers like Solange. How many of those who worked with evangelical young people day after day *saw* what was happening to us—the fear, the anxiety, the shame—but felt as powerless as we did to do anything about it. How many were told to get with the program or go. And simply made their choice. As we all did.

---

* Dean said the youth pastor had advised him to suggest incorporating more prayer and Bible reading into our relationship as a way to get me back. It was good advice. But my anxiety was far too great for such reasonable fixes.

*   *   *

The truth is, Solange's concerns weren't just dismissed by church leaders; for a long time, they were dismissed by her daughters as well. Until
they became adults, Solange's daughters didn't want to hear her counter the teachings of the evangelical church. They had been taught that
anyone who disagreed with its tenets was simply not a good Christian
and so shouldn't be trusted when it came to those things. (Even if that
person *was* your mom.)

"The church talked a good talk of 'we're going to support the family; this is all about the family.' You heard 'the family, the family, the
family.' You kept hearing that," Solange said, topping our glasses off.
"But the reality is they taught kids not to trust their parents. They told
the kids, 'Your parents didn't go to Bible college. They don't know what
they're talking about. *We* do. We've studied the Word of God in Latin
and Greek.'"

She's right. As adolescents, we were taught that, if ever they came
into conflict, the perspectives of the church—which we were taught was
God's representative—should be trusted over the perspectives of our
parents.

Youth group leaders were more trusted than parents. I longed for
the perfect Christian home. I criticized my family for not being as
spiritually minded as I needed, and neglected to nurture family relationships. I looked down on my parents for years. I had a superiority
complex because I was more spiritual than they were. I was a "real"
Christian; they weren't. I went to church every Sunday; they didn't. I
went to seminary, youth group, whatever; they didn't. (Jo)

My mom was supposedly a Christian, supposedly a born-again
Christian, but I definitely thought that I was a better Christian. I was

157

in touch with Christ and she was not at all because she was kind of horrible. (Muriel)

Meanwhile, parents were similarly taught to prioritize the perspectives of the church over those of their children. I have seen tremendous devastation result from this thinking. As an example, when one young woman moved in with her girlfriend, her parents announced they were disowning her. "They said they were selling all my stuff and they had taken down all my pictures because I had turned my back on Christ, and the Bible says that if someone's living a life of sin, that you're supposed to kick them out of the church so that they feel the pain of what they're doing, and then they'll come back," she explained. It took this woman years to create a new—and still deeply damaged—relationship with her parents. Many children are never so lucky.

It seems to me that the family the purity movement seeks to protect is *conceptual*, not actual. So-called family values are about preserving the idea of what a family *should* look like, not preserving actual familial relationships. In fact, I have seen family adherence to purity culture's black-and-white family values disintegrate families again and again.

Feeling powerless to change her daughters' trajectories as their relationship with the church advanced, Solange watched as her "brainiac, brilliant" daughters gave up childhood dreams and ignored big opportunities they no longer felt were appropriate for their religious identity. "We knew our girls would be told, 'You have so many gifts but you don't have enough testosterone so you'll never have it all,' " she lamented. "I knew they'd be taught that. But I didn't know how to fight it except to tell them that they could do whatever they wanted to when they were at home. They could follow their dreams. What would have been the course of their lives?" her eyes began to glisten. "What college would they have gone to, and how would they be expressing their passions and their true callings now if they had not gone to youth group?

"They were going to go to four-year colleges. That was my dream for them. That was my big dream. I'm getting emotional. We are third-generation Americans. I said, 'We are going to do it right. My girls are going to go to college and find their dreams and passions and live them.' Then you find something that's supposed to help them because the world is a scary world. You think the church is going to come along and be your friend and your helper, and it turns out to be just the opposite. I have them on this path and here comes youth group, and it totally changes the trajectory of what I was trying to do for them.

"Would I send them to youth group again? Never. I think the church hurt more than they helped. Do I want a do-over? I do. I want a do-over. Being my age—sixty-one!—my husband and I, we want do-overs all the time. We always want do-overs."

Solange wiped upward at the edges of her eyes with her pinky fingers. "You are going to make me cry, Linda," she said. "Those are my *kids*. And you have hopes and dreams for their lives. It changed the trajectory of their *lives*. I get very upset about that, because I feel very protective of my girls. I always felt very protective of my girls even when they were little. And they are still dealing with the ramifications, the effects of going to youth group today. They still live that *today*. You get it. Don't you? You get what I'm talking about? You know what I'm talking about? I think you do. Nobody else knows what I'm talking about."

9

The Stained-Glass Ceiling

Half of the women Jo went to Bible college with were there to earn their MRS, the thirty-one-year-old told me as she dug her spade around a weed growing in the flowerbed alongside her house. In other words, "they weren't there to get a degree; they were there to meet a man"— and become his *Mrs.*—"so they could get married and be in the ministry together." She yanked hard at the weed and it came up with a jerk.

"You mean the way some girls used to say their career goal was to become a pastor's wife," I suggested, sitting cross-legged beside Jo in the grass with a notebook in my lap.

Jo turned around. "Marrying youth pastors," she smiled at me with recognition. "That was a big deal."

Jo had no interest in getting her so-called MRS in college. She wanted to have her *own* ministry.

But, you know, Jo was a woman.

"I've felt from the age of . . . always . . . that if you were a woman in the church you weren't respected. I saw that the church intrinsically believed women were not as important to God as men. It was in how we were treated. Were we girls taught that God had amazing plans for us—married or not, with kids or not, that we had our own purpose? No. We were taught to support somebody else's purpose, and given biblical reflections on 'partner and submit.' Were we girls taught to be warriors?

To gird ourselves and be as prepared for life as possible? No. We were trained to be supportive, nice, and caring to a warrior man.

"I felt tricked. Like, 'Oh. I'm supposed to give my entire life to this God, and go into the ministry, which is supposed to lead to meaning, purpose, and fulfillment. But wait . . . I can't do it? Because I'm a woman?' For me, who gave up my whole life for Christianity, that was unacceptable," Jo said digging forcefully. "I wanted to give Christianity my all, and *be* my all. I felt like I had a lot to offer, but I was stuck. I became sexist in my own way. I thought being a woman was a handicap that I had to overcome, that to be feminine was to be weak and unthinking. I was ashamed of being a woman and wanted no part of that.

"I accepted my shamefulness as a woman as a starting point, even as I dared them to call me out on it. 'Yes it's shameful that I'm a woman, but I'm going to be brave enough to talk to you anyway. I'm going to rise above my shameful womanhood and I'm going to talk to you as an equal.' I thought, 'I am so strong a person that I'm going to embrace my *humanity*, not my womanhood.'"

For decades, what are often called "women's issues" have been one of the most divisive issues in the church. Two sides have formed: complementarianism (which you'll recall from chapter two teaches that men and women can only *complement* one another when men stick to leadership and women to following, especially in the church and the home) and egalitarianism (which I mentioned previously, teaches that the roles we play should never be determined by gender).

Scholars of feminist theology, womanist and African American theology, mujerista and feminista theology, Asian and Asian American women's theology, and other theologies have been working at the intersection of religion and women's rights since before I was born. Among these thought leaders are some who call themselves "evangelical feminists," "biblical feminists," or "egalitarians."

Egalitarian women began organizing in the 1970s. In the eighties and nineties, complementarians fought back. Hard. Christian colleges that had embraced egalitarian thinking in the previous decades, for example, now fought to prove their commitment to complementarianism as demonstrated by their hiring practices, course offerings, and assignments. One of my interviewees even recalls having to write a college paper titled "Why Feminism Is Wrong."

Tensions were particularly strong at Southern Seminary, the Southern Baptist Convention's flagship seminary. In the early to mid-1990s, the school made so-called women's issues a litmus test for whether or not a faculty member was conservative enough to teach there, its president calling them "clear dividers in our time."[1] As Dr. Julie Ingersoll writes in *Evangelical Christian Women: War Stories in the Gender Battles*: "Southern Seminary . . . moved from considering a candidate's views on the issue of women's ordination as only an indication of that candidate's views on inerrancy [that is, the belief that the Bible is without error, a standard litmus test for conservative Christians] to making hiring decisions solely on the basis of a candidate's views on that issue."[2] Faculty hired before the new litmus test was put into place were now required to articulate a complementarian perspective if they wanted to keep their jobs. Among many Southern Seminary faculty members, there was anger, crying, even vomiting.[3] The seminary lost about a third of its faculty and half of its student body to the subsequent firings.*[4] Many also left the Southern Baptist Convention.† But Southern Seminary had certainly proved its allegiance to complementarian thought.

---

* Specific reports vary.

† Jimmy Carter also famously left the Convention because of their views on women a few years later.

*   *   *

Jo took her orange Crocs off and threw them on the grass behind her. She wore an oversized men's button-up, a pair of jean shorts, and thick gardening gloves. Her short dark hair was tied back from her face with a bandana and she wore dark red lipstick, in rockabilly style.

"I remember Anne Graham Lotz came and spoke at my Bible college," she continued her story as she dug in the flowerbeds. "A group of men walked out because her tone was too authoritarian."

"Really?" I asked Jo. "They walked out on Billy Graham's daughter?" Jo nodded.

Though some evangelical college students are staunchly egalitarian—as demonstrated by the number of students who left Southern Seminary—some are just as staunchly complementarian—as demonstrated by the walkouts Jo told me were common when the school brought women whom students perceived to be preaching. And yet, women speakers still come to conservative Christian college chapels and stand on those stages, and professors still propose classes with content they know at least a few students will declare heretical, because they know that somewhere out there in that chapel and in those classes, there are students like Jo.

"As much as my college is this scary place in my brain, it was also a very safe, controlled place to become myself," Jo explained. "Because an underground of renegade people and professors were drawn to me, or I gravitated toward them." Among them, Jo began to believe that maybe things were changing in the church, and that when she graduated she could help move the needle even further, establishing the validity of women's religious leadership once and for all.

After college, Jo started working at a nondenominational evangelical church. By thirty-one, she had worked her way up the ladder and was just one step away from being director of children's ministries, the highest-ranking position available to women at the church. But her position always felt a bit tenuous. There was something about the daunt-less way she talked, the cocksure way she walked, the brashness, the grit about her that bothered people. Having purposefully tempered her femininity and embraced her gender-neutral "humanity" to get into religious leadership, she now found herself being told she wasn't femi-nine enough to lead.

"I was told that I speak too masculinely," Jo rolled her eyes.

"But your vocal register is actually pretty high," I countered.

"Apparently, it's the *way* I speak that's the problem," she explained. "Too straightforward, too direct. I've been told on several occasions it intimidates people." Jo scooted over again and began weeding a new section of the garden. I followed behind her. "About a year ago, I was co-leading a Bible study and a young man in the group said, 'I'd like to be a leader too,'" she continued. "I said, 'There are no open spaces for new leaders right now.' He called the next day and left a message on my voice mail saying that my tone and mode of communication was masculine and for the sake of the Bible study, the men in the study, and my marriage, I should read John Piper's book *What's the Difference?: Manhood and Womanhood Defined According to the Bible.* I skimmed through sections of the book and threw up."

"Literally?"

"Not literally. No. But have you read it?"

I shook my head.

"It is *so* offensive," Jo said, wiping her forehead with the back of her arm. "This guy blamed my 'masculinity' for why there weren't more men in the Bible study, though half of the leaders and half of the partici-pants were men."

I was pretty sure I'd heard this story from her before. "And he con-tacted the head pastor about it, right?" I said.

"Different guy," Jo laughed. "That was a different instance." She dropped a fistful of weeds into the grocery bag beside her. "That was somebody I had dated. He had confided in me that he didn't even know if he was a Christian anymore. Then after we broke up, he said he wanted to lead a small group in the singles' ministry that I ran. I said, 'If you're doubting your faith, then now's probably not a good time for you to be a small-group leader.' I said, 'Why lead a small group when you're not even sure you believe what you're saying? Let's take this time . . .' whatever. He freaked out. He wrote a letter to the pastor. He even had his *parents* write a letter to the pastor. He accused me of being an emotional woman and an example of why women should not be in leadership. He tried to get me fired! But our head pastor was like, 'This is stupid.'

"Privately, the head pastor actually tells me that he agrees with me about women's rights," Jo then said, turning and facing me. "We have little chats about it all the time. But he is only willing to go so far. He says, 'I agree with you, Jo, but this is not my battle to fight. I'm not going to back you up here.' He could create a lot of change, do a lot of good if he would. Actually, both he and my boss—a real steal magnolia type of lady—secretly agree with me on women's rights, but they refuse to take it up.

"So the guy *didn't* get me fired, but he *did* ruin my reputation," Jo turned back to the flowerbed. "He tried to get all the men in the group on his side and they had meetings about how horrible and power-hungry I was. Then the men tried to organize a meeting where they were going to confront me on my poor leadership skills, mostly because I was a girl, by putting me in a boat alone with them in the middle of a lake. True story."

"Did you go?" I asked.

"No," she guffawed. "I'm not stupid. I've watched a lot of *Law & Order*."

I laughed. "You know not to get in a boat with a bunch of men—"

"Who are mad at you. Yes. Yes I just know that. I've watched *Double*

Jeopardy. It's a bad idea. But what the church forgets," she said, standing up with the grocery bag in her hand, "and I'll preach it from the pulpit, because there are some who will let me—is that God is above gender. He sometimes expresses himself as a mother in the Bible. And so we are the image of God most fully when we are together as one. Equal."

It's important to note that Jo never attempted to break or change any of her church's rules. She wasn't advocating for women to be ordained, or publicly arguing that the genders should have equal authority. She didn't write op-eds. She didn't blog. She didn't post egalitarian content on social media. All Jo did was take the leadership roles that were offered to her, roles that had been approved by the church's male decision-makers for both her gender and for her specifically, and then, just be herself. And that was all it took to make people try and get her fired.

Some may see the existence of women leaders, like Jo, as a sign that complementarianism is on its way out in the church. Though I'd really like to believe that's true, it's important to look at the experience of women leaders themselves before we jump to this conclusion. In fact, many evangelical women leaders I've spoken with appear even more bound by complementarian gender expectations and other purity culture stumbling blocks than their peers. As a face of the church, they are expected to model the perfect woman—supportive of their husbands' leadership and of the leadership of men in general, gentle in spirit, and of course, undeniably feminine and pure. I've heard stories of everything from a pastor's wife whose congregants insisted she needed a more modest style, inspiring some of them to go out and *buy* her new clothes, to a female pastor whose congregants regularly approached her at the end of a sermon not to say how moved they were by her words but how they felt about her hair that day. In the words of Reverend Layton E. Williams, female pastors' "voices are critiqued for pitch and vocal fry" and our "hairstyle is regulated more ardently than our theology. . . .

We're faulted for clothing, make-up, identities, and even body shapes that reveal our existence as sexual beings."[5]

The aforementioned Dr. Julie Ingersoll documents devastating stories among women who are leading or in some other way challenging the gender-based status quo in evangelical churches and other institutions. She writes:

> They do talk about "war stories," they feel embattled, and they carry with them scars that include experiences of broken families, derailed careers, and, sometimes, abandoned spiritual lives. They suffer from fatigue, despair, cynicism, and emotional distress that often reach the level of clinical depression. They sometimes even long for death.[6]

Among the quotes Ingersoll features in her book is one from an evangelical faculty member whose struggle brought her to the brink of suicide:

> But as I started thinking through all this . . . I got seriously suicidal on several occasions. This spring, I just thought about taking huge doses of antidepressants. There were several times I had just made up my mind that this was "it." . . . Although God created me a woman and, one must assume, gave me those teaching and preaching gifts, He also made it impossible for me to please Him. . . . I can't please Him in the institution that represents Him. So the only way, ultimately, that I could please God would be to kill myself. Because nothing I could ever do as a living human being, because of being a woman, could ever please God.[7]

To be sure, egalitarianism is making inroads in the evangelical church thanks to the hard work of many dauntless individuals, but we still have a long way to go.

*   *   *

Ten years after we gardened together (or she gardened and I watched), I went back to Jo's midwestern house. We strolled into her backyard to sit at her mosaicked table where we talked for hours, her kids occasionally running out and yanking at Jo's shirt for her to *look-look-look-look-look*.

"I was offered the children's ministries director role when my boss retired," the now forty-one-year-old, who had been associate director at the time of our last interview, told me as we pulled our chairs out.

"That's awesome!" I said.

"But around the same time, an associate pastor position became available at the church," Jo continued. "And it struck me: 'I would be so good at *that*. *That's* the job I should be doing, not this children's position.' But I would have been laughed at if I had even applied for the associate pastor position. My only choice as a woman was to work with children, even though I knew by then I didn't want to.

"And then one day, Johnnie and I were holding our newborn baby girl in our arms. We looked at one another and we said, 'We have to make a choice. Are we willing to have our daughter taught the things that we were taught? This precious bundle who will inevitably come into the world and make mistakes—are we willing for her to be told that she is evil, a worm?' And I was like, 'Over my dead body will she ever be told that.'

"Then I thought, 'If I can't accept that for *her* . . . why do I accept it for *me*?' I realized, 'I'm beating my head against a brick wall trying to change the church and they don't want to be changed! I don't have to be in a system that is fighting with people all the time. I don't have to reform or revolutionize that system in some way for women's equality or whatever it might be.' Know what I mean? People are going to do what they want to do, and you don't have to judge them for that. Just accept them where they're at. But that doesn't mean you have to stay."

Today, Jo attends an evangelical Lutheran church. By some people's standards, this makes her still an evangelical, but the mainline/evangelical merger she aligns with now is less centrally located in the evangelical subculture than the nondenominational one within which she spent most of her life, so Jo herself would never say she was evangelical today. And neither would her old friends.

"I have friends who are sort of friends of mine in secret, because they can't be seen with me," Jo disclosed. "I'm the naughty person to get together with. They say talking with me is such a relief for them, and they will go on and on about how crazy their lives are at their churches, but they won't leave. They'll be like, '*This* is crazy, and *this* is crazy, and *this* is crazy.' But they still show up on Sunday with smiles on their faces because it's their whole world. And it's their kids' world. To leave would be to give everything up. When I left, this huge boulder came off my shoulders."

"What did it feel like?"

"Well," Jo paused for a moment, looking away, "terrifying. I mean, relieving, relaxing, awesome, amazing, but also, I would cry a lot. Because the boulder was holding me in place; it was anchoring me in one place. So it made me feel safe, in some way, even though it was terrible pressure. Without it, it was hard to know how to interact. I only knew how to speak Christianese. I only knew how to approach people who came from the same viewpoint as me. I was taught that anyone who didn't was unsafe. So my anxiety was high. But, I've always been anxious. I have a panic disorder. That's what my therapist told me anyway.

"It started when I was in Bible college. That's where I can pinpoint it. I would have very anxious racing thoughts and a racing heart, so I would shut the door and stay in bed all day. But the actual panic attacks— where I can't breathe, where I think maybe I'm dying—didn't begin until I started working at my old church. I loved my job, yet there was a part of myself that had to be left behind when I went through those doors. I had a talk I had to talk, a walk I had to walk. There was a role I had to play, and I had to play it very well in order to be trusted, to keep my respect, to keep my *job*. I had to play the part of the perfect evangelical girl effortlessly, perfectly, flawlessly. And that takes a toll on you as a person. Because you *can't* be perfect.

"I think the panic attacks in general just came from living in a world system that wasn't working. I was a mess. But I told myself, 'I'm a woman who has the right to vote; I have a healthy body; I have all my limbs; I'm not in a war-torn country; I have not been through the Holocaust.' I was using every other person's trauma to tell myself I had no business feeling anything."

"What kinds of things caused the panic attacks?"

"I've never been able to get a grip on that. It's like something subconsciously builds up, then suddenly, I can't cope anymore. I've been on Zoloft for six years now, and still, I experience almost blushing shame regularly. Just talking to the pastor of my church usually costs me nights of sleep."

"What do you mean?"

"I just have a physical reaction to talking to a pastor," Jo waved her hand, as though dismissing her feeling as ridiculous. "He's a perfectly nice man. He's never done anything to me, but it's like I've got post-traumatic pastor disorder. I'm so afraid of being diminished, talked down to, dismissed, patronized. Or of being looked up and down. I'm afraid that he's going to fail me in some—not in some minor way, not a slip-up—but in a fundamental way that is harmful. I just get really sick to my stomach. I feel so much shame. And I've always felt that. Talking to men who are pastors in the past too, or any kind of church leader. It's like I'm expecting to get slapped or something.

"Counselors say to me, 'It sounds like you have PTSD but I can't find the trigger; I can't find the trauma.' And I'm like, '*I* can! It's twenty years long!' They don't get it. This is a whole new field!"

"Actually, it might really be," I replied. "Some people are trying to get what they are calling Religious Trauma Syndrome recognized."

"That would be amazing and accurate," Jo asserted. "Put it in the DSM-5. Get it in there. Because it's real, and all of us who experienced it need therapists. So get it in there; make it a thing; and then get people trained on it."

Religious Trauma Syndrome (RTS), defined as "the condition experienced by people who are struggling with leaving an authoritarian, dogmatic religion and coping with the damage of indoctrination,"[8] was coined by Dr. Marlene Winell, the human development specialist whose work I mentioned previously. She suggests that RTS mimics other disorders, such as post-traumatic stress disorder (PTSD), anxiety disorders, obsessive compulsive disorders, borderline personality disorders, and so on, and describes symptoms ranging from depression to sexual difficulty to negative beliefs about the self.

"When you told your counselor you knew the trigger, how did she react?"

"She was a he, and he was useless. You know, some doctors, some psychologists are so locked into what they learn in school that they never move on or make their thoughts bigger or incorporate other things into them. I never went to him again. I found a different counselor who said she couldn't officially diagnose me with it, but said I had OCD tendencies around religion. So I went around accepting that for a while but then I was like, 'I don't know.'"

"Did she take into account external influences?" I asked. That diagnosis makes it sound like, 'There's something in you that is wrong, it's making you react to your religious community this way. But your religious community itself, and all of the traumatizing, impossible-to-meet expectations it's putting on you, we have nothing to say about *that*.'"

"I never thought of it that way before," Jo cocked her head. "I just thought the diagnosis didn't encompass the whole thing. But hey, you're right."

"I mean, I'm not a therapist," I said quickly. "But it seems to me that it would be different to say, 'Let's look at this highly authoritarian, shaming system you are a part of as well as some other more personal things, like your coping mechanisms, your genetics, your family history—'"

"Yes," Jo interrupted me. "I think my family of origin has a lot to do with my issues." Jo had previously told me that anxiety and mental illness runs in her family.

"That's important," I said. "But it doesn't mean that external influences don't *also* play a role."

"Good point," Jo reflected. "I'll take that one to bed with me tonight and think on it."

"What were you experiencing that made your counselor say that it looked like you had PTSD?"

"For some reason in my early thirties, I began to really enjoy alcohol and prescription narcotics," Jo admitted. "I described OxyContin as a down comforter for my soul and I was scheming about how I could lie to my doctor to get a prescription. So I started exploring why I wanted to numb myself. I was never a narcotics addict; I'm not an alcoholic; but I wanted to deal with this quickly so it wouldn't become a problem. I went to a therapist because I would have rather cut off my hand than go to my church and tell them I was struggling with it. I would have been taken off of every ministry that I was on; I would've been shamed; I might have experienced church discipline. Church is supposed to be where you feel safe and come for prayer, but no, you don't *do* that there. At church you show your shiny self that Jesus redeemed. You're together.

"Oh! That's something my counselor told me too! She said that I was a—there's a fancy word for it—that I had Dissociative Personality Disorder. It's the idea that you have two selves; you're not integrated; you're split in two. There's your shiny self that Jesus redeemed—that person goes to church and works with the kids—but the person you are when drinking yourself into a stupor while watching *24*, that self is not in church."

"Hmm," I grumbled.

"What?"

"Again, that label seems to ignore context," I said. "Hiding parts of yourself from a community that punishes people for showing those parts seems completely rational to me."

Jo paused and thought for a moment. "I've never thought about the difference between thinking that the problem is something that's innate in me versus a response to something outside of me. Even now, up until right *now*, I have been under the assumption that this is something that's in me, that I have done to myself, not something that was done *to* me. That's sort of mind-blowing. I really have to process that. That might change some things for me."

Since 1992, marriage and family therapist, certified sex therapist, and professor Dr. Tina Schermer Sellers has been requiring her graduate students at the Christian institution Seattle Pacific University to write a sexual autobiography. The intention is to help her students, who are studying to become therapists, come "to terms with their own sexual story so as not to inadvertently bring the implications of their sexual pain into the therapeutic clinical setting."[9]

In the early 2000s, the professor saw a shift among her students' autobiographies: a sudden rise in religious sexual and gender-based shame.

"The symptoms I'm seeing are exactly the same symptoms I might see in someone who was sexually abused," she told me in an interview.[10] Having grown up in a very sex-positive environment herself, she couldn't understand why so many students whose sexual autobiographies did not include sexual abuse would be experiencing symptoms traditionally associated with this form of trauma. What's more, she didn't understand why she saw the rise in shame when she did—in the early 2000s. (I have since learned that most of her students are in their early twenties—making her class in the early 2000s full of young people who, like me, would have been among the first to come of age under the influence of the purity industry.)

The shame spike she saw in the early 2000s became a plateau. Year after year, the stories of sexual shame came pouring in. The professor began to research religious sexual shame, and eventually authored a book for helping professionals (like therapists!) to address people's religious sexual shame. The title of the book is *Sex, God, and the Conservative Church: Erasing Shame from Sexual Intimacy.**

The lack of therapeutic understanding around the damage that growing up in the purity movement can do comes up often in my interviews. Christian therapists are often too deeply embedded in their religious worldview to guide us, and secular therapists, who are generally tragically under-trained in both religion and sexuality, aren't always much help either.

My counselor, she's wonderful, but she doesn't have any tools to help me. Both she and I have said that. I love her. She's amazing. She's been enormously positive and helpful. But she's not equipped to help me. I'm not blaming her. She just isn't. My whole background, being raised in the evangelical world, she will listen completely, and I can tell she's intently trying to understand. She just has absolutely no ex-

---

* Dr. Tina Schermer Sellers and several of her former students also launched an online platform to disseminate and address stories of sexual shame called Thank God for Sex (thankgodforsex.org). There you can see, among other things, videos of real people sharing real stories—a big leap within a space known for secrecy and anonymity. "The big thing we hear over and over is thank you," one of the volunteers who runs Thank God for Sex told me. "'Thank you, thank you, thank you. This is so needed. I didn't know anyone was talking about this. *Thank you.*'"

perience at all with anything I'm saying. She'll go into my romantic relationships; she'll go into my relationship with my parents; she'll go into everything except the spiritual part of it. And when I bring it up, I will talk about it in depth and she has absolutely nothing critical to open up in that vein, and that's really hard. (Scarlet)

Some therapists have told me they believe the lack of training they receive on religion is due to a long-standing divide between religion and psychology. This divide results in some therapists being so dismissive of religion that they won't even touch it. Others, meanwhile, are so afraid of being seen as *anti*religious, recognizing that religion and spirituality can also be healing tools for people, that they refuse to consider that religion can be anything other than good for a person. This is puzzling to me. It is well documented that religious communities function as extended families, and we all know every extended family looks different—from one another, and from one moment to the next. Sometimes our families affect us positively, sometimes negatively, and most often, both at the same time. Therapists don't shy away from exploring these complex and often contradictory familial dynamics. So why shy away from exploring complex and contradictory religious dynamics? What makes us think that religious networks, unlike every other network in our lives—our families, our work communities, our friend groups—can only be either "all good" or "all bad"?

Lacking support elsewhere, those coming out of the purity movement turn to one another. Often, its informal—two friends talking, a small group of people meeting for an intimate dinner—but sometimes, these informal conversations grow. Two friends decide to launch a Purity Culture Rehab Project, blogging about experiences like losing their "kissginity";[11] a group of college women host a Shed the Shame event on their evangelical campus, encouraging students to talk more openly about shame; and several hundred evangelicals and former evangelicals gather every day in online communities, at least one of which is a women-only group centered around the topic of shame.

> I get 5–10 pings from the online group a day and am getting more and more sucked in. We are going to therapists and the therapists don't know what we're talking about because spiritual abuse is the form of abuse that we are trying to come out of. But we go to this group and they totally get it. I wore a dress the other day and it showed a crack of cleavage. My husband's friend was over, and I could feel my cheeks flame the whole time, like, "Oh my gosh, I'm so immodest. What if he's looking at me and having sexual thoughts?" That's something that I can go to the group with, and they're like, "I totally get you." But if I try to explain that to somebody else, they're like, "What?!" (Muriel)

Were you to look for these groups, you may not find them. Most are closed and require you to have a trusted personal connection already in the group to be accepted in. What's more, online group participants often use pseudonyms, sometimes even creating fake social media accounts and email addresses so they can feel safe conversing about taboo topics. In fact, pseudonyms are common throughout purity culture recovery, even among content creators. People run online platforms, host blogs, host podcasts, and even write books under fake names in order to keep the vitriol they receive for speaking out away from their professional and personal lives. But as the number of people willing to talk about religious sexual and gender-based shame grows, the desire for anonymity that has driven so many of these crucial conversations underground is beginning to dissipate.

Jo is part of two of these private online groups. "You can just go online and say something like, 'Does anyone else have shame about having private thoughts because you were always accountable to somebody in the church?'" she told me across her backyard table. "I shared that recently and people were like, 'Yeah.' They got it. PTSD symptoms, disassociation symptoms—these are constant conversations there. Some people just claim that they have it: 'I have PTSD; I'm having triggers everywhere today.' They just claim it! The need for better diagnostic labels is talked about a lot too, and counselors needing to pay more attention to the religious context we're coming from."

But therapy, medication, and DIY support groups aren't all Jo has tried to cure her anxiety. "I've tried diet changes. I've tried natural stuff like 5-HTP and lemon balm and Holy Basil with varying degrees of dosages. I've tried yoga. I've tried meditation. I've tried just about everything to control whatever creates these panic attacks," she told me. "I had a whole life; I had a church; I had a support system; I had friends; I had a job in the embodiment of evangelical America. I had a *whole life*. And I gave it up. *Everything*. I gave it all up at the same time for the same reasons," she explained.

"It's been excruciatingly lonely, because where do you go with that pain? It's been so tempting to go backward sometimes. Just to give up and go back and just say, 'Fine, you win. Will you just love us? Can we just be part of your community again? Just whatever, you win.' It's too hard. It's too exhausting to reframe your entire worldview and to heal through all the things and to get through every obstacle. It's painful. It's scary sometimes. Fear is everywhere. Like that scene in *Jurassic Park*. That part in *Jurassic Park* where—you've seen it right?"

"Mm-hmm."

"The part where the kids are in the car and then they hear the stomp. And then the water in the jar jiggles a little bit, and you know something just awful is coming. And you're like, 'Get out of the car now!' The first time that I saw that movie I thought, 'When I'm not on medication, this is how I live *all* the time. I've never told this to anybody, by the way. So now I'm telling it to somebody who's writing a book."

"In *Jurassic Park* the thumping was the dinosaur," I said. "What's the thumping for you? What are you afraid of?"

"I don't know," Jo looked up, squinting into the sun. "Condemnation, shame, Hell, death, eternity, responsibility, commitment, being responsible for something I can't handle, that I'm not ready for, not being able to receive what God's will is, making mistakes, disappointing people, making the wrong choices, ruining my children, not being lovable, getting older, I can go on for days. The fear is palpable. Like that T. rex is just the world."

At the beginning, often all that those of us who let go of a shaming worldview know is that we are tired. Tired of hiding ourselves, tired of hating ourselves. We yearn to be who we are, to live honestly and authentically. So we start to run. Toward what? We don't know. And then one day—like Wile E. Coyote spinning his legs at top speed—we realize that we have run off the edge of a cliff. We had been sure there was solid ground beneath us just a moment ago. But suddenly we look down and there's nothing. No old worldview. No new worldview. Just . . . space. But unlike Wile E. Coyote, we do not fall. We float. Because we didn't just lose our grounding; we lost our gravity—our entire way of being, of understanding ourselves and the world around us. We have no compass, no sense of direction. We don't know what's up, what's down, what's forward, or what's back. We are confused and, all too often, we are alone. We float above an abyss and, as the Bible tells us it was before the world was created, darkness is over the surface of the deep.

This is what I call "the gap"—the expanse of space between the way in which we used to look at ourselves and the world, and the way in which we will come to see ourselves and the world once we've found our footing on the other side of the ravine.

I don't know what the other side is yet, but you know it's kind of—It's like in *Indiana Jones and the Last Crusade*. He throws the pebbles down the chasm, and you see them hit something, that there is an invisible bridge. And then he can find his way across the rest of the thing. That's where I'm at. I'm just kind of throwing the pebbles out to see the next step I can take. Then as I get more confident and realize that the world isn't going to explode, I can visualize the other side. (Val)

On one side of the gap lies our indoctrinated brains; on the other side lies our searching spirits. And the rest of us is somewhere in the middle—sometimes stretched, other times bouncing from one gravitational pull to the other and back again, getting close to living in a way that aligns with our spirits only to have our bodies jerk us back or punish us in ways that make us feel we haven't gotten very far after all.

"But I'm not hiding my face from any of it anymore," Jo said, turning back to me. "Okay," she smiled. "So I don't know who I am or where I'm going or what my identity is. So I might regret my entire life's choices up until this period." She laughed under her breath, and shrugged lightly. "It is what it is."

Stumbling Out of Church

10

Trapped

"Before we do the X-ray, is there any chance you might be pregnant?" the nurse asked as she entered the examination room.

I looked up from where I had been squatting in the corner of the room, caught in the act—burying my panties between my T-shirt and my jeans so the medical staff wouldn't know the color or quality of my undergarments. I straightened abruptly, flattening the front of my paper dress with my hand.

"Uh," I hesitated.

The college nurse lowered her chin, a look of concern coming upon her face. We sat in silence for a moment. Then she tilted her head and raised her brows as though to say, *Well?*

"What would happen if I were?" I asked.

"Your child could have severe birth defects," she answered matter-of-factly.

When I didn't respond, she added more gently: "A pregnancy test only costs five dollars."

Just talking about the possibility of pregnancy was enough to make my eczema flare. I crossed my arms over my chest and rubbed hard at my itching biceps before forcing my hands to meet one another in front of my body so I wouldn't keep scratching at the rising red skin.

"Maybe you should do the test," I gave in, wrapping my hands even more tightly together. "Just to be safe."

I decided I would not mention to the nurse that I already gave myself pregnancy tests regularly. That I was on birth control. That my boyfriend and I often used condoms, even when we were just fooling around. Oh and, right, that I was technically still a virgin.

By now, I was a junior at Sarah Lawrence College, where there were so many love-your-body naked parades that it felt as though there was sperm floating in the air just waiting to impregnate my innocent egg at a moment's notice. I'd show up to dances feeling risqué for showing cleavage and notice two people wearing nothing but body paint before even getting in the door. I'd sit outside the school's sadomasochism-themed dance with my mouth gaping open, watching my classmates stand in line to be whipped by fellow classmates wearing shiny black leather bodysuits. And I'd listen, wide-eyed, as my roommate regaled my friends and me about the campus workshop she'd attended where students were instructed on how to find a woman's G-spot on themselves and others, after which the facilitator invited those who were interested to put on a plastic glove, insert a finger into *her* vagina and locate her G-spot as an illustration. One thing was clear: I may not be an evangelical anymore, but I was still a *serious* square here at one of the most experimental colleges in the nation.

One day, a classmate who, for a short period of time, asked people to please refer to him as The Empress from now on, lounged on my dorm room bed flipping through an old copy of *Martha Stewart Living*.

"You have got to be the only one on campus with a monthly subscription to this magazine," The Empress said, looking up me.

"Well that's crazy," I answered, flopping down next to him. "Because it's amazing. Did you see my Ode to Fall?" I gestured to the bowl full of cinnamon sticks, leaves, and apples artfully displayed on my dresser. "Very Martha," I informed him.

"Linda," The Empress laughed. "Seriously. How in the *hell* did you end up at this school?" Then he sat up straight. "So!" he announced excitedly. "I wrote a role for you."

"Really?"

"You said you used to do improv comedy, right?"

"For a while after high school."

"Perfect. I want you to play Martha Stewart."

"You don't want me to audition or anything?"

"Honey, you don't need to. No offense, but you already *are* Martha. You kind of even dress like her."

"Hold on—" I protested.

"Not every day," he assured me.

"I do *not* dress like Martha Stewart."

The Empress held the magazine up. Martha was on the cover wearing a taupe button-down collared shirt and a pair of white jeans.

"Really?" he said, directing his eyes to my own outfit.

"Shut up," I said, throwing a blanket over myself. "Anyway," I poked my head out from under the blanket, "my shirt is blue."*

Soon afterward, I found myself onstage in front of half the school performing a very dirty version of Martha Stewart, in which Martha taught her TV viewers how to use household items for sexual purposes. For instance, Saran wrap as a dental dam. It was a decade before Ana Gasteyer essentially did the same thing on *Saturday Night Live*. Performing my most salacious role before hundreds of my classmates, I remember staring out at them as they almost fell out of their chairs with bawdy laughter and asking myself, *Can they tell I had*

---

* I ran into The Empress a few years ago in a Manhattan Home Depot. We were both in our midthirties by then. He startled me by coming up behind me and saying, "Of course I find you in the Martha Stewart paint section . . ."

to ask my roommate what a dental dam was the first time I read the script?

In many ways, I was still *playing* sex. The scripts had gotten more explicit, but my role—that of an actress—had remained the same.

Religion has a way of getting inside the most private parts of your life. Though I no longer attended an evangelical church, I still found myself analyzing my thoughts, obsessing over my mistakes, and seeking out even the tiniest sins in hopes that confessing them could free me from the feeling of impurity that was always there. When your inner life looks like that, sometimes the safest place to do something "bad" is in public.

Standing onstage playing Martha Stewart, I must have appeared to those who didn't know me like a completely normal twenty-two-year-old healthily exploring her sexuality through comedy. But inside, I was a wreck.

The first time my now-boyfriend Sebastian and I tried to have sex, things did not go well. My head said it was fine for me to have sex with the long-term boyfriend I loved. Yet every aspect of the actual attempt triggered a physical reaction: the removal of each individual item of clothing made me tremble, the introduction of the condom made my head flame, the condom coming out of the packaging made my eczema flare, and the kissing that I knew was meant to lead somewhere this time, not just be what it was, sent a shudder through me that screamed: *You. Are. Bad.*

I fought it back.

This is just like when I realized that I speak in a higher register than is natural for me, I told myself. *Your body is just stuck in an old way of being. You don't have to let it control you. You can control it. Just close your eyes, Linda. Reset your equilibrium. And go on.*

I pushed forward. I tried to force my body to behave. But this wasn't like the other times that I had resisted the gender and sexuality messaging with which I had been raised. Sex was just different for me.

Before I had decided that I was open to the possibility of having sex before marriage, sexual exploration didn't terrify me in the same way that it started to once the loss of that all-important "virgin" label was a legitimate possibility. But since I told Sebastian I thought I was ready to have sex, everything about our intimate lives changed.

Sebastian called them my freak-outs. In the midst of them, names that I would never use for anyone else—*slut, whore, harlot* (a term that isn't used in secular culture much but that I certainly heard growing up a lot)—ran through my head as though on ticker tape. My eyes would get watery. Sebastian would ask me if I wanted to stop. "No, no," I would say. "Let's just do this. I have to be able to do this." But then the tears began to roll down my cheeks, I was scratching at the raised red skin from my flaring eczema and, before I knew it, I was huddled in a corner of his bed crying and scratching myself until I bled.

"I remember we would just be talking," Sebastian told me recently when I asked him what he remembered of the years—literally, *years*— that we endured these freak-outs together. "Then something sexual would come up," he continued, "even just talking about another couple having sex, and suddenly you would be curled up in the fetal position. During your freak-outs, it was like you weren't really present. Your emotions took over and you spoke and acted from that place. You were always looking to pick a fight with yourself. It was like you had a chip on your shoulder for you. There was a lot of self-accusation: 'I'm terrible, I'm the worst.'"

Even after an attempt to have sex was over, the anxiety Sebastian saw stayed with me—along with new layers of self-hatred at having humiliated myself in front of him again. If I got close enough to having sex before the freak-out came, I couldn't help but anticipate the terrible consequences that I felt would undoubtedly follow. Surely, something horrible was about to happen to me. Some punishment was coming. Some terror was about to arise. After all, hadn't I been taught all my life that this was simply what happened to girls who did the kinds of things I just did?

Of all the ways I imagined the sky might fall, pregnancy seemed the most likely. My irrational fear could only be quelled with a store-bought test. I could breathe easy again when that beautiful minus sign proved to me that, for now, no one would find out what I'd—almost—done.

A common adage in neurobiology, Hebb's axiom, states: "neurons that fire together wire together." In other words, if two neural circuits—such as those for sexuality and shame—are fired simultaneously often enough, eventually firing the neural circuit for one will automatically activate the neural circuit for the other. Dr. Norman Doidge refers to this phenomenon in his book *The Brain That Changes Itself: Stories of Personal Triumph from the Frontiers of Brain Science*, at one point describing the work of Dr. Michael Merzenich.

Merzenich has described a number of "brain traps" that occur when two brain maps, meant to be separate, merge. As we have seen, he found that if a monkey's fingers were sewn together and so forced to move at the same time, the maps for them would fuse, because their neurons fired together and hence wired together. But he also discovered that maps fuse in everyday life. When a musician uses two fingers together frequently enough while playing an instrument, the maps for the two fingers sometimes fuse, and when the musician tries to move only one finger, the other moves too. The maps for the two different fingers are now "dedifferentiated." The more intensely the musician tries to produce a single movement, the more he will move both fingers, strengthening the merged map. The harder the person tries to get out of the brain trap, the deeper he gets into it, developing a condition called "focal dystonia." A similar brain trap occurs in Japanese people who, when speaking English, can't hear the difference between "r" and "l" because the two sounds are not differentiated in their brain maps. Each time they try to say the sounds properly, they say them incorrectly, reinforcing the problem.[1]

I believe that the merger of sex and shame that I experienced is just such a brain trap. Even if we eventually come to understand that our sexual nature is natural, normal, and healthy, we may find that our upbringing in purity culture, which has dedifferentiated shame and sex over years of messaging, observation, and experience, ensures that our brains fire those shame neurons when the subject of our sexuality arises, with or without our permission, trapping us in a shame spiral. The first time an adolescent girl feels shame about her sexual nature, it may just be because she knows she is "supposed" to feel this way. But if this same girl continues to feel shame when having sexual thoughts or feelings over years, repeatedly firing those neurons at the same time, sex and shame will eventually become very difficult to disconnect in her brain. Her neural pathways have been paved, physical and mental habits formed, metaphors for how sex will change her internalized, methods for fighting off sexual feelings made habitual, and on and on.

"It's negative," the nurse announced brightly.

"Great!" I replied from the edge of the examination table, hugging the paper dress around my waist.

"Let's get you a birth control prescription though, okay hon?" the nurse continued. "You really shouldn't be having sex without protection."

"Oh, I'm good," I responded. "I'm actually already on birth control."

"You're *on* birth control?" the nurse repeated me, her face contorting.

It was one of those moments in which you suddenly see yourself from the outside. When things that had seemed relatively reasonable to you mere minutes ago—like the fact that you felt it was necessary to take a pregnancy test before undergoing an X-ray despite the fact that you were on birth control (to say nothing of your virginity about which she didn't even *know*)—are suddenly exposed as not normal at all.

"If you're on birth control," the nurse said slowly, "then why did you think you might be pregnant?"

Because I'm crazy? I wanted to answer. *So okay, I grew up in a really conservative religious community and I've been a little messed up about sex ever since. It's complicated, but . . .*

"I missed my period," I sputtered out instead. "So. You know. Better safe than sorry, right?"

It wasn't exactly a lie. After all, taking birth control for my particularly painful periods over the past few years had completely messed up my cycle. Most months, I didn't get a period at all. The technicality of my truth felt very important to me at the time.

The nurse smiled, though the look of suspicion didn't leave her eyes. Still, she probably just thought I was having unprotected sex, I thought to myself. Which felt a lot less embarrassing to me at the moment than what was *really* going on.

So I just nodded and smiled back.

What is wrong with me? I prayed as I threw the paper dress into the trash bin after the X-ray was finally done. I put my clothes on as fast as I could, desperate to get to my dorm before the tears began to fall. *None of the other girls I go to school with are experiencing these things*, I told God as I ran across campus. *They aren't having nightmares in which people call them horrible names. They aren't having freak-outs every time they try to have sex. And they sure aren't making the school nurse give them pregnancy tests when they're virgins.*

I jammed my key into my dorm room door, burst inside, and shut the door tightly behind me. *So why am I, God?* I railed. *What is wrong with me?*

I thought I had been ready to leave my sexual shame behind. And yet, the very choices I was making in an attempt to circumvent that shame wound up triggering it! And it was a lot more difficult for me to deal with this than it had been to deal with the original shaming experiences that started everything. When other people shamed me, I could resist, differentiating myself and my values from the values of the purity movement messengers. But who could I push against now? Who could I fight? Whose values could I differentiate myself from? When the only person left was me.

For a long time, I thought I was irreparably damaged. That I'd never be able to have a healthy romantic relationship. Then, around my senior year of college, a childhood friend left her position as a faculty member at a conservative evangelical college. Talking with her over the phone, my friend confided in me that she had been overwhelmed by fear and anxiety for years. She was always walking on eggshells, afraid she would do something to upset the all-male administration. Only recently had she found the strength and the acceptable excuse—getting married—to put in her resignation and move several hours away from the school. Yet even since leaving, she was still haunted by recurrent nightmares of her school's deans raping her and found herself scared that they had found ways to watch her from afar.

The next time I went back to my hometown, I helped my friend riffle through her plants, Kleenex boxes, and picture frames to reassure her that the school's administration was not recording her in an attempt to find some information they could use to "pulpit shame" her, as she had seen happen to so many others. I watched the relief spread across my friend's face when no recording devices were found, and realized, that look on her face? It was the same one I was sure spread across mine every time I took a pregnancy test.

My friend and I had taken opposite paths after high school. Whereas I had left evangelicalism, reforming myself as a spiritual-but-not-religious person who was really trying hard to have sex with her boyfriend, my friend had attended a college even more conservative than our home church, pursued a career in Christian education, and remained sexually "pure" until marriage. And yet, here we both were—tormented by the same fear and anxiety.

One day, this friend told me a story about when she was a student at the college at which she later taught. The school had a strict policy, she told me: Women were not allowed to wear pants on campus or, in fact, anywhere other than their hometowns (presumably because they were in their fathers' jurisdictions then).

In the first few days of my friend's second semester of college, she was called into an administrator's office.

"One of your fellow students reported that she saw you wearing jeans at a mall over Christmas break," the administrator accused her.

"Yes," my friend said, her stomach turning over. "But the mall is in my hometown," which was several hours away from the school. "It's okay for me to wear jeans in my hometown, right?"

Once the administrator verified my friend's claim about her location at the time of the pants sighting, he let her go without punishment. But the message that someone was always watching stayed with her.

Within a context in which one is not safe to walk around her hometown mall hours away from her religious school without the fear that someone, somewhere, might be watching her, was my friend really paranoid for combing her home for recording devices? Or was it possible that the administrators actually *would* plant recording devices in her home to maintain their control over her after she left her post? She didn't know. Just like I didn't know if there was an actual risk of my getting pregnant if my boyfriend's genitals and mine were in the same general vicinity. I didn't *think* so, but . . . what if? That not knowing, the constant question of whether we were being crazy or we were just being smart was maddening.

Today, my friend isn't sure what to make of the paranoia she experienced after leaving the school at which she taught. She is the first to say that the college was more conservative than most Christian colleges and she struggles with the knowledge that some of her fellow female faculty members seem to have been unaffected by even the extreme doses of shame and control doled out at her school.

But for me, seeing somebody—particularly somebody who had followed all of the purity movement's rules—face challenges similar to my own at a time when nobody in my new secular world seemed to be was big, regardless of the details. It would be several more years before I would begin interviewing individuals raised in the evangelical church, but it was then that I first knew this was what I needed to do. Because if I was not the only one experiencing these things, then perhaps there was still hope for me after all. When I eventually began my twelve-year tour through the stories of evangelicals and former evangelicals like myself and my friend, interview after interview filled me with the same feelings I had with my friend that day—relief, anger, and the righteous knowledge I was anything but alone.

As I mentioned in the opening, evangelical young people are the most likely religious grouping to expect that having sex will upset their mother and cause their partner to lose respect for them. Evangelicals are also among the least likely to expect sex to be pleasurable, and among the most likely to anticipate having sex will make them feel guilty.[2] And yet evangelical young people are basically just as likely to have sex as their peers are.[3] In other words, most evangelical youth are a lot like I was in the years after I left the church—sexual, and ashamed of it.

Several of my interviewees, whether or not they were still in the church, attempted to sidestep their shame by telling themselves they were still technically virgins, despite what many would see as evidence to the contrary. They engaged in other forms of sex, but avoided penis-in-vagina sex. Or they had penis-in-vagina sex, but promised themselves they were going to marry their partners someday so they could at least say, "I've only slept with one person" or "my husband was my first," tricking the untrained ear. This logic led more than one of my interviewees to marry men they said they might not have otherwise.

The summer after my freshman year in college, my boyfriend and I, who I had sex with when I was fifteen, broke up. I quickly started to become afraid: "Wait, if I ever get into another relationship, I am going to have to tell them that I am not a virgin. And how am I going to do that?" That conversation seemed so insurmountable and humiliating for me. I couldn't even imagine it. I didn't want to have to say to someone, "I'm dirty and used and not pure. Will you accept me?" I thought, "I need to get back together with him because he is the one that I did this with and we need to be together, right?" And once the ball was rolling and all the stuff was happening—invitations were out and all the people from this church I had grown up in were going to be there—how could I leave? I thought, "There's nothing I can do about it. I can't change anything. I can't get out of this relationship. I just have to figure out how to make it work." (Andrea, recently divorced)

Others justify having had sex by calling it a crime of passion, which somehow feels less "bad" than having premeditated sex.

A Christian friend had been having sex for a few months and I bought her some condoms. She was so mad, because they never planned to have sex. It just "happened." Had they bought condoms, that would be planning to do it, planning to have sex. It's almost like getting drunk. You don't plan to get drunk, so you don't make a plan; you don't have a way to get home or whatever. But then you do, and you're stuck. (Rosemary)*

Yet the sex/shame brain trap is set and sprung all the same, ensnaring many of us raised in the purity movement in fear and anxiety.

Over the course of my interviews, I learned I wasn't the only one having freak-outs.

We're rolling around naked; he would be rubbing his penis on my vagina but not in it; I would have orgasms from it. But I still, in my brain, I could be like, "We're not having sex." I would still be a virgin. And you know what happened . . . an inch, quarter-inch, whatever, would start to go in and I would recoil and freak out. (Scarlet)

I wasn't the only one afraid of getting pregnant though I hadn't had penis-in-vagina sex either.

Surely you've heard of "the phantom baby"? How nobody has had sex but they all think they're pregnant? I've never met an evangelical woman who doesn't irrationally believe she's pregnant at some point.

---

* Studies have found that abstinence pledgers are less likely to use protection against sexually transmitted infections and pregnancy when having sex than their nonpledging peers. To be sure, the lack of accurate information young people receive in abstinence-only-until-marriage programs is likely at least partly to blame for this. After all, over 80 percent of the abstinence-only-until-marriage curricula reviewed by a 2004 House Committee on Government Reform minority staff report included "false, misleading, or distorted information about reproductive health."[4] But I believe there is something deeper going on as well. Prophylactics are demonized in religious purity culture. A condom, for example, isn't just a piece of rubber in a plastic sleeve; it is an instrument of sin, which can make shopping for protection feel like plotting your immorality. Some serious mental gymnastics have to be done just to get your credit card down on the counter, let alone get the prophylactic out of the packaging and into use. Somehow, it seems easier—and, some hope, less sinful—if sex is unplanned.

I dare you to find me one who's well adjusted enough that that hasn't happened to her. I don't think she's out there. Since I started dating after my divorce, I even feel it coming back. My period was three days late this month and I was like, "Well crap! I'm pregnant and I haven't even gotten any action yet! I haven't even kissed anyone!" But the thought that I must be pregnant is there. It's just there. It's like a goiter. It's just living with me. I don't know how long it will take to get rid of it. (Val)

And the friend who I helped search her home for recording devices wasn't the only person paranoid that people were watching her.

When Johnnie and I got engaged, everybody felt like they had a piece of our relationship, and he and I both experienced a sense of fear. We would go out on dates and I would be looking in my rearview mirror the whole time being like, "Is someone following us? Are people from the church watching me right now? If I buy this wine, am I going to be reported the next day? If they see my car at Johnnie's house too late, am I going to lose my job?" There is this idea that you're accountable to everybody for your sexual behavior, for your dating behavior, for everything, especially as a woman. If you were not telling something, it was because you had sin in your life. You don't own anything, even your thoughts, and it matters more how the culture and the community thinks about your thought than what the thought itself is. Their judgment determines everything. (Jo)

For me, the sex/shame brain trap was the most difficult to escape. But my interviews revealed that sex and shame weren't the only purity culture concepts around which people developed what appeared to be brain traps. For instance, one interviewee told me her body reacted in almost precisely the same way when she tried to have sex as when she preached a sermon, as she was breaking the purity movement's rules about what she was and was not allowed to do as a woman when doing both.

"Sex with my husband is terrifying," she admitted to me on a hacienda in the Southwest. "I think, 'It's going to start; I'm going to panic; and then I'm either going to be a disembodied person while it's happening, or I'm going to freak out.'"

"What do you mean by 'freak out'?" I asked her.

"Sometimes I end up watching us having sex from over here," she said, gesturing upward toward the bright sky. "And sometimes I'm just starting to enjoy myself, right? I'm just starting to feel good, and then it just hits. It's just a real visceral thing. Panic. A feeling of not being able to breathe. Like, 'I'm going to die.' And I end up in a ball and I'm crying and I don't know why. I used to have a panic attack 75 percent of the time my husband and I tried to have sex. Now it might be more like 50 percent or even a little bit lower, but that's just because we have sex so rarely. Neither of us wants to take the risk and start something sexual that might end up with me crying.

"I became a pastor because I needed to get control of this thing that was so hurtful to me. Especially the cruelty of it I experienced in the religion as a child. But when I was first in a full-time pastor position, in the outfit every Sunday, sometimes it was hard. I'd have these experiences of depersonalization exactly the same as I do with sex. Feelings of, 'I'm no longer the person who is here. I'm watching myself from afar.' It's like it's too dangerous to be fully present to it. I don't agree with that logic, but it's deep in my bones."

"You feel the same things you feel when trying to have sex, while you are in the pulpit?" I verified.

"Yes. Just standing."

"Why do you think it happens?"

"Because here's a thing I'm doing that I was taught from a very young age is wrong for me to do. I'm not supposed to be doing this, and I am."

"Just like sex," I said.

"I think at a very basic level, that's it," she nodded, her hair blowing in the wind. "So suddenly, I'm gone. I'm standing in the pulpit, but at the same time, I'm ten years old again. Back in that place."

Sebastian and I did eventually have sex, though it was, in his words, "a brief and bungling affair." Both virgins, neither of us wanted to call *this* our sexual debut. In time, Sebastian and I broke up. In the years that followed, he got a new girlfriend and says he was shocked by how easily sexual intimacy came with someone who wasn't religious. ("Thanks man," I rolled my eyes at him.)

It would be another three years before I would finally relinquish my virgin title, having claimed that the things I'd done before that day just "didn't count." I was twenty-six. In a quaint Japanese hotel room with a long-term boyfriend that I was certain I would marry, in the way in which we are absolutely certain of just about everything in our twenties. And the sex/shame brain trap just . . . broke. I prayed the whole while. Thanking God for the moment, the man, and most of all, that I might finally be free. And a holy presence filled the room. My boyfriend startled. "Is someone else in here?" he asked.

"Yes," I answered him.

11

Frozen

"So, the book is about sexual shaming—what it does to us, how we struggle through it, and ultimately how we might rethink our approach to sexuality. Any initial thoughts?"

It was a hot summer day in New York City and Eli had traveled a long way to get to my Manhattan apartment, plopping himself down by the air-conditioning unit immediately upon his arrival. "Initial thoughts?" he heaved, his short hair ruffled by the air-conditioning vent. "Oh God," he rolled his eyes. Then he pulled back to face me. "My initial thought was, 'I need more Pirate's Booty,'" he said gesturing toward the bowl of pirate-branded cheese puffs I had just put out on the table between us.

I laughed. "To talk about sexual shame you need—"

"*Lots* of salt," Eli finished my sentence, grabbing a handful of the snack. "And probably some gummy bears." Still laughing, I pushed the bowl of gummy bears toward him.

Nine years ago when we first met, the clean-cut, conservatively dressed thirty-year-old man who sat across the table from me was still going by his given name, Elizabeth. About two years later, he transitioned genders. But Eli's name, physical appearance, and voice weren't the only changes I noticed when he walked into my apartment all these years later. I remembered Elizabeth, who I first met online, as skittish, almost scared. Elizabeth had literally trembled through our first interview, but Eli—though unabashed regarding his discomfort talking about sexual shame—didn't shake at all.

Eli and I have discussed it and decided I should use female pronouns when referring to the period in which he presented himself as Elizabeth and male pronouns when referring to the period after his transition.* Though Eli is a man, I am including his story in this book because he was raised with the same girl-specific messages that the rest of my interviewees were. Whether or not he felt like a girl growing up, he was certainly *treated* like one. So Eli's story too sheds light on the impact of the purity movement's gender-specific messages for girls.

Elizabeth was raised in the South. She thought of herself as a good Christian girl who'd never break any of the church's rules. Then, in high school, she got her first crush. On another girl. "And I was like, 'This does not compute,'" Elizabeth told me the first time we met. When the feelings didn't go away, Elizabeth volunteered to join an ex-gay ministry. Some of these ministries focus on trying to get queer people not to think about or act on their sexual desires, whereas others go so far as to literally try and turn queer people straight. Elizabeth's was more in the former category. "There wasn't even a question about whether or not I would go to the ministry," Elizabeth continued. "I had been taught this was my problem, and this was what I had to do about it, because . . . *of course* I do. I didn't even think to question it."

Elizabeth participated in the programming from late high school to early college. "Part of me was totally not believing any of it and then, another part of my mind was just, 'What if they're right? I could go to

* Though this was Eli's wish, as they say, "you've met one trans person, you've met *one* trans person." In other words, every trans person is different and it's best to check in with someone about how they want to be referred to at various points in their lives.

Hell. Oh no! I should do the right thing, the biblical thing. I should try to get straightened out.' No pun intended," she smiled.

When Elizabeth began attending a state college in the South, she stopped going to church as often; she came out to her friends as a lesbian; she even got a long-distance girlfriend.* But she kept attending the ex-gay ministries, holding out hope that one day they would cure her of her attraction to women so she could go back to being a good Christian girl.

"I was just bouncing back and forth all over the place with no sense of groundedness at all. I loved growing up in the church. That's the thing. It hadn't been this horrible, traumatic experience for me. I hadn't gone to one of these mean, scary churches that was overtly angry or hostile. My church put on this face of, 'We love everybody and we're all about grace.' That was always the message. But when I started confessing to people in church, 'I'm dealing with this right now, it's really hard for me, I don't know what to do,' the only thing that they could seem to think about was how to convert me back to their way of thinking: 'Well, you're wrong, because we already know the answer.' Nobody was like, 'Okay, let's just talk through this. It's your life, and whatever you decide we'll still care about you.' The only thing they cared about in the conversation was giving me 'the answer' and making sure that they got me back on 'the right path.' Treating the whole thing like a debate instead of a conversation.

"I realized, 'This community's ideology is more important to them than anything else. It's more important than people. It's more important than keeping their relationships with each other intact. The ideology is the only thing that matters here.' I guess on some level I knew that they would respond that way. But there was a part of me that was like, 'But surely, I've grown up in this church. All these people care about me—

---

* Eli has asked me to share that although the person he was dating was living as female at the time, the individual has also transitioned since then.

surely they're not going to react that way to *me*.' When they did, I felt like, 'Other than being a person who comes to their church and believes all the right things, do I have any value to these people? And if I stop believing the right things, then do I lose all my value to them?'"

This inner turmoil took a toll on Elizabeth. Her depression became so severe that her therapist put her on an antidepressant that she now thinks made things even worse. Second semester of her first year of college, Elizabeth began cutting herself.

"I kind of zoned out. And when I snapped out of it and realized I was cutting on my arms, I freaked out. I was like, 'I can't believe I was doing that!'"

"Do you remember what you were thinking when you would cut yourself?" I asked.

"I remember *exactly* what I was thinking about. I was thinking about all my struggles with the whole sexuality thing. That's what was on my mind when I did it. It was sort of this self-punishing thing. I was thinking about all these things that I had been taught were bad and wrong—like having a crush on somebody. Some weird part of my mind thought, 'Well, if I punish myself, maybe it will go away. Or maybe I'll feel better. Or something.' Once I started doing it, it was hard to stop. I was just very depressed about the whole gay thing. And honestly . . . I still haven't completely stopped."

In her book *I Thought It Was Just Me (But It Isn't): Making the Journey from "What Will People Think" to "I Am Enough,"* Dr. Brené Brown writes about the way in which shame and subsequent isolation can drive an individual to desperate acts.

While dealing with shame and feelings of disconnection can be a normal part of developing and growing relationships, disconnection can become more serious when it turns into feelings of isolation . . . Jean Baker Miller and Irene Stiver, Relational-Cultural theorists from the Stone Center at Wellesley College, have beautifully captured the overwhelming nature of isolation. They write, "[. . .] In the extreme, psychological isolation can lead to a sense of hopelessness and desperation. People will do almost anything to escape this combination of condemned isolation and powerlessness."

The part about this definition that really strikes me as critical to understanding shame is the sentence "People will do almost anything to escape this combination of condemned isolation and powerlessness." Shame can make us feel desperate. Reactions to this desperate need to escape from isolation and fear can run the gamut from behavioral issues and acting out to depression, self-injury, eating disorders, addiction, violence, and suicide.[1]

"A week before Thanksgiving I checked myself into the hospital because I was starting to get really worried about what I might do," Elizabeth continued. "I'm not very good at asking for help, and it kind of felt like a way of asking for it. I was having thoughts of suicide. I was just cutting constantly. I wasn't getting any better, and I didn't know what else to do. I was afraid."

"Did your parents know you were in the hospital?"

"My roommate called my dad and let him know." Elizabeth's parents were divorced. "I was on my best behavior in the hospital and I convinced them to discharge me after four days because I was scheduled to see my dad for Thanksgiving. Over Thanksgiving, I was just sleeping and not talking to anyone. The day I was scheduled to go back, my dad brought me to the airport. I had all my suitcases and stuff. I had already told him that I wanted to leave school and my dad said, 'Well, go back and finish the semester. It's just a few more weeks.' But then I just freaked right in the middle of the airport. I broke down crying and I couldn't even walk up to the plane. I was like, 'I can't go back.' I couldn't even function at that point. I was doubting my ability to even just go to class and sit there for a few more weeks. So my dad said, 'That's fine; stay with me.' And he drove me back to his apartment."

It took Elizabeth a year and a half to recover to the point that she was able to begin school again. In that time, she got a job, changed antidepressants, quit attending the ex-gay ministries, and church as well. "I was like, 'Wow! There's this whole world of people who don't care if I'm gay, or if I'm bi, or if I'm whatever. They're just going to let me do my thing. And I'd rather be around people who aren't going to always be trying to influence me over to their way of thinking.' I took one little step away from the church, and then another little step, and then another little step . . . and then everything fell apart and I just never went back."

When Elizabeth did begin attending college again, it was as an out lesbian.

Eli scooted his chair away from the air-conditioning unit, having sufficiently cooled down.

"Deep down, did you always feel like you were a man?" I asked him.

He cocked his head. "Looking back, I had some thoughts of that nature as far back as my early teens," he responded. "But the idea that I might be trans seemed so 'out there' compared to the idea of being gay that I managed not to think about it for a long period of time. I knew I didn't want to be a guy's girlfriend. That just felt too weird. So I just said, 'I don't like guys.'"

"You were only aware of two options at that point: being a lesbian or being a straight woman," I offered.

"Yes. And the straight woman option was the *least*-preferred option. It was actually when I was in undergrad for the second time that I started thinking about transitioning more. By the time I started grad school, I had changed my name, but I was still trying to decide whether to take testosterone." This was when Eli first realized he wasn't only interested in women. He was attracted to individuals across the gender spectrum. In other words, it wasn't until Eli knew who *he* was that he could identify who he wanted to be *with*.

"I guess I was ready to come out with being bisexual around the same time I was coming out about being trans," he explained. "And I became very quickly a lot less prone to depression after I started taking testosterone. It was like I had gone on some kind of mood-lifting drug or something. Literally a few weeks after going on testosterone I felt like I'd been put on uppers. Suddenly I felt different. Just bang. Moods leveled out, more energy, depression gone, just immediately. Now I have the physical and emotional energy to deal with things that used to upset me or stress me out." Eli said he also became much more comfortable with himself—a fact which was obvious when he walked into my apartment.

"I've always had problems with the physical aspect of performing," Eli—who is a professional singer—illustrated. "I could stand there and sing, but when I had to get up and act, I used to freeze up. It's like I couldn't relax and loosen up and sort of get into it before. I would just kind of stand there, very stiff, because I was never comfortable in my own skin. But now that I've become a lot more okay with myself, I can actually perform instead of freezing onstage. I can actually do the whole theatrical thing that I was never comfortable with before."

But there is one area of his life around which Eli still isn't comfortable.

He grimaced at me across the table. "Since this is what this interview is about, I guess we should probably talk about the sexuality thing, right?"

"Yes," I smiled at him.

Eli sighed heavily, pulling the bowl of Pirate's Booty into his chest.

"Most of my friends are a lot more—certainly a lot more sexually active than I am and also just a lot more casual about sexuality," he began. "I look at them and I'm like, 'That would be nice to be that relaxed about this,' but I just can't seem to be. Honestly, I kind of just avoid the whole thing, which is not very helpful or constructive, but that's usually what I do."

"What whole thing?"

"Like if I'm attracted to someone, I don't do anything or say anything. I don't know, I don't really know what I'm afraid is going to happen exactly."

Eli went on to explain that his first relationship, the long-distance one he had in college, was his longest to date. They were together about a year, but only saw one another a handful of times. Since then, Eli has had one four-month relationship, and one brief sexual encounter with another trans man.

"And honestly, that's been it," he sighed out heavily, his shoulders falling as if relieved to have gotten the information out. "If I'm completely honest with myself, I'd like to be having more experiences like the last one I had, where it's just casual and fun," he continued. "But the only reason it happened that time was because the other guy initiated. If it had been left up to me, it never would have happened. Not because I wasn't interested. Just because I wouldn't have actually done anything. I just don't know how to get there. I have no idea whatsoever how to flirt with people.

"I had my thirtieth birthday last month and I had a bunch of people come to this karaoke—you know those karaoke doo-wop places? I invited a bunch of friends, and I was talking to my best friend beforehand. I said, 'There is this guy in this choir I'm in, and he's bi and I think he's really attractive and, you know, I would really like to go on a few dates with this guy and maybe just have some fun.' He'd RSVP'd 'yes' to the party and I didn't even know him that well.

"So I was saying to my best friend, 'He's coming to this party.' Because my friend is so good at this. We were roommates for about two years. The whole time that he and I were living together, he was usually dating two or three different people simultaneously. And sometimes I'd be like, 'That looks like fun. I wish I could do that.' And he would say, 'Well go do it then.' And I would just be like, 'But I *can't*.' And he'd be like, 'What are you talking about? That's ridiculous. Of course you can.' And I'd say, 'It's not that I'm incapable of doing it. But. I just . . . something in me is just like, "No, but you don't do *that*!"' Even if I consciously decide I'm going to, that it's totally fine, and if I get myself into a situation that might go in that direction, I just freeze. I said to him, 'I just want to follow you around and watch you flirt with people until I learn how to do this by osmosis.'

"So my friend was like, 'Well, you should hit on this guy over karaoke.'

"I said, 'But I don't know what I should say. I don't know what I should do.'

"And—he's so funny—he was like, 'Okay, here's what you do.' He gave me a list: 'First you do this, and then you say that, and then you do this, and then you do that.' It was really specific.

"And I was just like, 'Okay. You're hilarious. Sure. All right. I'm going to try this and see what happens.'

"And then . . . I just froze up."

"You couldn't remember what he told you to do?" I asked.

"Yes. I mean, what happens is I blank out. I can't think of anything to say, or I know what I want to say, but I just freeze. I just can't do it. The conscious thought that I'm having when I freeze up usually is, 'I'm going to look like an idiot.' But there's plenty of other areas in my life where I've gotten over my aversion to being embarrassed and looking stupid, and I'm like, 'Whatever, I'm going to go try this thing, and I'm probably going to look like an idiot, but that's fine.' But this, I can't get past.

"There was no reason for me not to do it. I had, like, six drinks. But I was sitting there at the party and the guy and I were chatting, and every time I thought, 'Okay, I'm going to do this,' I would just go blank. My mind would blank out. And I would just be like, 'I have no idea what to

say right now.' Absolutely none. I froze. And that was it. I've never figured out a way, when I have that brain freeze reaction, to psych myself
up to go for it anyway."

"It's interesting," I said. "Because researchers have found that shame
can actually create a kind of confusion in our brains similar to the freeze
that you're describing," I said.

Dr. Curt Thompson describes it in *The Soul of Shame*:

> When shame appears, especially in malignant forms, we are often
> driven to a felt sense of *stasis*. Our mind feels incapable of thinking.
> We may feel literally physically frozen in place when experiencing
> extreme humiliation, and if we are able to move, we feel like going
> somewhere we can hide and remain hidden without returning to en-
> gage others. We don't necessarily experience this with minor insults,
> but there is no question that our ability to move creatively in our
> mind is slowed.[2]

"So I wonder," I continued to Eli, "if you are freezing in these moments because you're approaching doing something that you've internalized so much shame around."

Eli nodded slowly. "Even now, I was just sitting here thinking about—
as a manifestation of everything we're talking about—how awkward it
feels for me to even be having this conversation," he admitted.

"It feels awkward?"

"Yes. But it's not because of anything that you said or did. It's just
because I don't know how to talk about sex or sexuality. It feels really
uncomfortable to even just say, on a recording, 'There's this guy I'm
really attracted to and I was conniving with my best friend to try to
figure out how to get him into bed.' That feels like such a weird thing to
say. It's really hard to just admit that's what was happening. Just to even
say that feels like I'm breaking some weird rule of, 'You're not supposed

to talk about these things. You're not supposed to want that. You're certainly not supposed to discuss it with people. What a shocking thing to do!' I tense up and get that feeling of, 'Uh-oh, I'm breaking a rule right now. And everybody else is going to see me breaking this rule. And they're going to judge me.'"

"But—help me understand this," I said. "Because you've already made all these public declarations about who you are and who you are attracted to that feel so big. You came out as lesbian, then came out as bi, you transitioned genders, and you are not secretive about any of that—"

Eli crinkled his nose and pursed his lips. "It is definitely possible to come out and say, 'I'm this and I'm that' while avoiding talking about sex. Especially now that everybody knows what these words mean. I'm like, 'I'm bi,' and they're like, 'Okay,' and then that's the end of the conversation. Like the Christian singer you were telling me about earlier—"

"The one who I was told had said it was easier for her to come out as a lesbian than it was to come out as someone who had sex outside of marriage," I said.

"Yes. I think that in the church, there's a lot of shame about having a sexuality at *all*. There was this sense that I was bad and I needed to punish myself for having sexual feelings, and also having *wrong* ones, because they were toward a woman. But also, if I'm attracted to anyone I should be falling in love with them and thinking romantic thoughts about marrying them or whatever, not thinking about having sex. Do you know what I mean? And *that* message is *everywhere*, not just in the church.

"In the gay community, there's an aversion to talking about sex in external messaging because the people shaping the messaging want to make it more palatable to people. They make it totally about falling in love and wanting to get married. And it's worked! That's the thing. I think that's the thing that makes more people accept it now. Like, 'Well,

I understand falling in love and wanting to get married. Falling in love and wanting to get married is good. So how can I judge someone because they just fell in love and wanted to get married with someone of their same gender?' But the sex part, they leave that off. Nobody wants to talk about *that* part.

"And I think that is a big thing that is driving me to continue to feel bad about myself. Because I've come to the realization that I'm not really interested in having a serious relationship right now, and I'm not interested in getting married possibly ever. That doesn't mean that I'm not still interested in having sex. But in my mind, if you don't want to get married, then the appropriate response is to not date anybody and be a hermit.

"I am just beginning to realize how much my upbringing has had and still has all these effects on my personality and my approach to life that I don't even notice a lot of the time. I still have this urge to be the kind of person that I think this community would have wanted me to be, even though I don't believe in the religion part anymore. Just trying to be this very respectable, appropriate, wholesome person who follows all the rules and does everything right. And the most respectable and acceptable alternative to serious monogamous relationships in the evangelical frame is to be totally single, and I don't know, get ten cats. No relationships. No sex. Either you get married or—" Eli searched for the right words.

"You get a lot of cats."

He laughed. "I have one cat. I'm working on it."

Eli isn't the only one I've spoken to whose sexual shame triggers are so sensitive that simply brushing the triggers with something as small as a thought can activate them. Whereas my own body didn't react until I began making bold sexual choices, some other people's bodies react long before such a choice is even on the table, preventing them from ever being in the position I found myself in in my early twenties.

Some of my interviewees have tried to get around this by turning their brains off using alcohol, drugs, overworking, and so on.

I'd been saving myself for marriage, but with this increasing ambivalence, which is entirely—well, I'm sure a huge part of what my drinking is about. I have several female friends who did this thing too, who sort of became drunks so that when we had sex for the first times we didn't have to choose it. You know. Because, to choose to have sex is almost impossible. The way that—for me—the way that my mind was set up, the way that the world was set up for me, I couldn't do it. I would either have to decide to do something, consciously and deliberately decide to do something that I was absolutely certain was completely wrong, which is a really hard thing to do. Or I would have to somehow change what I believed before doing the thing, which is also really hard. It's hard to change your beliefs in the abstract. You know. So. So I drank. And then I didn't have to decide. (Simone)

I had to stay busy all the time. If I stopped to think, I knew I would go back to the way I was raised, because I was taught so many ways of justifying believing the way I had and I hadn't yet developed enough of an argument away from it. I knew it didn't feel right anymore, but I didn't know why. So I didn't ever slow down. I would run myself to the point of exhaustion, which also helped with the nightmares. The nightmares were still there, but they started to go away just because I was so tired all the time. If I was exhausted when I fell asleep, I wouldn't dream, and then I also wouldn't have time to lay there and think either. So it was kind of this perfect solution in my mind to get away from thinking about any of it. I'd either be really busy or I would drink a lot, so I wouldn't think very much. (Holly)

But not everyone is able to find a way around their sexual shame triggers.

I am reminded of the story of a young woman named Jasmine, who is in her early twenties, about the age that Eli was when I met him as Elizabeth nine years ago. Jasmine was raised an evangelical Christian in the rural Mountain West. She studied abroad in Europe for a year in high school, where many of the religious ideas with which she was raised fell away. But not the shame.

"Even as a child and a teenager," she explained, "I wouldn't even be able to say that I liked someone to my closest friends. I couldn't even say it to my*self*." Jasmine went on to tell me a story about a crush she had while studying abroad at the age of sixteen.

"There was this other foreign exchange student who was Australian or something, and I think I liked him a little bit. Not a lot, but a little bit. Nothing ever happened, but my friends kind of knew. We were flirting, and—" She stopped talking suddenly. "Even now, I can barely talk about it, because I'm so repulsed by my own feelings."

"What does it feel like?" I asked her gently.

"I don't like to talk about him, or any of the guys or girls that I've even had anything with. Even those I've had *nothing* with. Just mentioning them, I cringe. I start fidgeting. I get really, really hot. I start laughing because it makes me nervous. I feel repulsed and I feel really nauseous."

"What are you repulsed by? By the fact that you liked this Australian guy?"

"Yes," Jasmine answered. "This is how I feel a lot. It's weird because on one hand I'm very liberal socially. I totally believe that people should be as sexual as they want. But at the same time, *I* can't be like that. It's like, physically my body won't allow it, and I've never been able to figure out how I can think one way and feel another way. I don't know how to start. I really want to be able to. But I always feel this disgust. I don't even know how to explain it except disgust. It's like, you see a plate of worms. I feel like I'm being forced to eat a plate of worms. I feel disgusted and disgusting. Disgusted at myself. This is even hard to talk about because I just feel gross. I feel bad. I feel ashamed. I feel really ashamed even having this conversation."

But Jasmine continued.

"Once people started saying, 'You like him, this Australian guy?' I just woke up and I was like, 'I *hate* him,' " she continued her story. "I started hating him. I just felt so much hatred toward him and hatred toward myself for ever putting myself in that position, and that's kind of how it always manifests. I think my body just doesn't allow me to do a lot of things. I identify as bisexual, but there is no reason for me to say that, because I am never in a relationship, so it doesn't come up.

"I feel like my body even controls the way I think. So not only would I not ask somebody out, but I wouldn't even allow myself to *think* about it. If I ever have a thought, 'I like that person,' immediately, my body will shut that down: 'Don't think about that. Don't even do that.' Whether that takes just not thinking for a while, or physically removing myself, or going over and talking to someone else about something else, I don't allow myself to think, so action cannot happen.

"For a long time, it's been easiest for me to use the 'I'm a strong independent woman and so I can't' excuse when I've really always known that that's not true," she continued. "I've always known that I wanted it. I wish I didn't, because then I wouldn't really have to deal with this. But I have a deep aching for a relationship. And at the same time, I can't touch it."

"I'm thirty and I'm just now reaching a point in my life where I'm realizing how negatively the church affected me," Eli told me near the end of our conversation. "For the longest time I was like, 'No, I'm fine.'

Because I didn't go to some big, scary, hellfire church where I was overtly traumatized and left. I'm not having panic attacks and nightmares about going to Hell and whatever. Because I didn't have those experiences, I thought 'I'm fine. My church was harmless. They were kind of homophobic, but whatever. Other than that, they were totally harmless.' I've looked back on this community with all this fondness. I would talk about my old church, about how great it was, not realizing that they had raised me with this message that made me feel I had failed to be what I was supposed to be. I had failed to be a good Christian and be part of this community. And that the reason that I had to leave was because of that failure. I hadn't been able to fit in. I hadn't been able to just do what I was supposed to and believe the right things and remain part of this community. I wasn't good enough. That's something that the church did to me. But for a long time I didn't think of it that way. I was just like, 'I'm fine. I'm not traumatized. I'm not scarred for life by this.'

"I look back and I think of the ex-gay thing as a really, really short period of my life. I'm like, 'That was this weird thing that happened, and now it's over.' But I look back at the religion in general as this huge, all-consuming part of my life. A lot of the other things about my religious upbringing and community seem to have had more of a continuing impact on me than that. I'm trying to figure out how to explain this." He paused and thought for a moment.

"Ex-gay ministries and things like that sound extreme," I suggested, "and like they would have a bigger effect on a person than everyday shaming messaging."

Eli nodded. "Those were the things that you would think would be the most traumatic things. That would continue to haunt me, or whatever. But a lot of the things that I feel still affect me go back way further, like things that I just grew up with and that were an ongoing part of my life. I'm kind of curious whether anyone else has said similar things."

"Well, I'm not always hearing about cataclysmic experiences in my interviews if that's what you mean."

"What? They don't have those experiences, or they just didn't have that big of an effect on them?"

"A lot of people don't have those experiences at all. Some do. But for the most part, I'm talking to people about these really small, intimate experiences that influence their lives more because of their frequency more than their size. I'm actually glad you brought this up because it's easy to scapegoat. To be like, 'Well, ex-gay camp, that's the only problem,' right? 'It's not the deep sexual shaming that is laced through almost everything.'"

Eli nodded. "It's not 'this specific thing that happened when I was nine is the problem.' It's not like that. It's just . . . I was for so many years in that environment that I feel like I was really strongly affected by it. Just, in general. I should stop being nostalgic and pining away for this community that probably wants nothing to do with me anymore anyway," Eli said.

Then he turned to the window and stopped talking.

12

The G(od) Spot

"Big emotional cannons started going off after I told you some of my story on the phone," Scarlet admitted. She sank down into the beloved orange couch that she had told me she'd carried with her from apartment to apartment over ten years. An abstract artist who referred to painting as her first language, Scarlet wore a pair of black leggings, black leg warmers, a black T-shirt, and long silver earrings. Her hair was tied up to one side with long tendrils hanging around her face, and her feet were bare.

"Flashes of fear, flashes of anxiety, of memory," she continued, leaning into my space opposite her on the couch. "But super-fast, like a billionth of a second—boom, boom, boom—I saw maybe twenty parts of my life or my history."

Doctors and nurses screaming . . . the certainty that she was about to die . . . waking up in the hospital bed . . . seeing the photojournalist . . . seeing her sexy red underwear discarded on a chair . . .

"Like a flip book," I suggest.

"Yes. Punctuated at the end. Like when you're in an airplane with turbulence and it drops really fast and your stomach drops. Kind of like that at the end. Jarring panic that was unfounded because what happened, it already happened!

I have synesthesia, which means I relate colors with experiences or feelings or concrete things like days or people—definitely people, months, years. And *The Incident with the Photojournalist*—that's what I call it—it's like an open circle. No top and no bottom. It's just, like, black. This black thing. Growing up was afternoon sunshine and hot pink and peaches sky. You are earth tones in sienna and umbers with a thread of creams, Linda. I'm reds, mostly darker wines changing into crimsons and scarlets. But *The Incident with the Photojournalist* is just black."

"I was a very late bloomer," Scarlet, who had been raised in the southern part of the Midwest, said when I asked her to go back to the beginning. "I was chubby. I was wearing my combat boots and writing poetry. I was in theater. Surprise!" She laughed. "And I've always been a very sexual person. As I got older, my baby fat rolled off and I got a do-over genetically. I have a really sexual, curvy body."

But having grown up in the evangelical church, Scarlet guarded that sexual, curvy body like "a little woodland creature. Like a bunny in my hands that I had to keep safe while walking on a delicate, little, tiny tightrope. Keeping it safe was supposed to be the most important thing, right? It's so easy to misstep; it's so easy to fall. And if you fall, the whole thing is going to explode into this big avalanche of fire and death and nightmares. Really! That's how it's really presented! At the time, it sort of made sense because it seemed like you had to protect it because it's so sacred. But in the meantime, my body was like," Scarlet threw her head back and growled from the pit of her stomach, shaking her head from side to side. Then she looked back at me and smiled: "It was ready to rock."

During her twenties, Scarlet attended art school, launched a career as a professional artist, and engaged in a series of intense, monogamous relationships with evangelical men: "Adam was bonfire crimson, oranges and black; Evan was an indigo blue changing into metallic blue-gray;

Ben was a midnight blue and flare of auburn." Though she didn't have penis-in-vagina sex with any of these men, she went what she referred to as "99.9 percent" of the way with them.

"I would cry because I was so lost. I loved being sexual and it felt so right but I knew, 'This is so bad. I'm going to have to suffer because this is what I've done.'" The feeling manifested physically for the first time when she was in college.

"One day I went to my anthropology class and I was feeling really weird. I started low-level shaking. I went back to my room and my heart just started beating so fast. I'd never felt anything like this. I couldn't stop it. The shaking took on a greater rising. Then I remember I tried to stand up and I fell on the ground. I thought I was having a heart attack. I really thought that I might be having a heart attack. I called one of my closest friends. He ran over to my apartment and took me to—I can't remember. But I ended up at the hospital. A doctor gave me Valium which made my body be like—" Scarlet made the sound of a robot shutting down, collapsing her body into a heap in her lap. "The doctor was a Greek woman who I really liked," Scarlet continued. "She asked, 'Can you tell me what you think brought this on?'

"I said, 'I think I'm not supposed to be with my boyfriend.' I recognized how embarrassing that was to say when I was in the hospital, but I really thought this is what brought it on.

"I hadn't told her anything about myself, but her second question to me was, 'Did you have sex with him for the first time? And do you feel ashamed and bad about that?'"

"I wonder what led her to see somebody having a panic attack and think—"

"I grew up in a very, very evangelical state," Scarlet interrupted me. "It is a hotbed of evangelicalism. Almost everybody there. There are almost no liberal Christian people, really, at all," Scarlet said, seemingly implying that she might not be the first person this doctor saw whose religious sexual shame manifested as a panic attack. "I was scared to even answer her," Scarlet continued. "I was like Bill Clinton: 'Have I had sexual relations? What is the definition of "relations"? Have I had "sex"? I've had *oral* sex.' I remember asking these questions of myself. Eighty-five percent of the rest of the university is having full-on sex and probably a portion of them are having orgies, and threesomes, and crazy stuff. And I'm literally going to the hospital because I've had oral sex with my boyfriend. For real!"

"So the doctor's question struck at some truth in you."

"Of course! But my answer to the doctor was still 'no.' Because I was holding desperately onto being a virgin at the time. The doctor said, 'I'm not going to tell your mom and dad; it's better if you tell me than if you don't; it's totally natural; you're nineteen years old.' She was very loving and sweet. I remember she made me feel very human, confident and strong, even when I felt completely messed up and crazy. She definitely didn't believe me about not having had sex, and she shouldn't have.

"The doctor was like, 'This was a classic anxiety attack.' She had been seeing my grandma and my parents and said, 'Anxiety attacks run in your family. You're probably going to have them for the rest of your life.' Anxiety disorders *do* run in my family," Scarlet informed me, "but definitely all my experiences in the evangelical church set all of those nodules on fire for me."

Finally, Scarlet met Chris: "moss green and dark river blues and earth tones."

Scarlet and Chris dated "an epic, a whole eon," she told me. Seven years. "He was the male version of me in terms of sexuality. Desperately, deeply wanting it, but Chris had a much scarier, cutthroat religious voice in his head. There's a whole different version of shame that goes on with guys too. Meanwhile, I kept growing closer and closer to being ready. Finally, a little over a year into Chris and my relationship, I was twenty-five and I just wanted to. I remember it was a very quiet night, very calm. I totally trusted him. I didn't feel any shame whatsoever after it. None. But he would do a pendulum—'I can't, we shouldn't be doing this'—that lasted our whole relationship, which was very hard for me. So after seven years, I ended it."

By the time Scarlet broke up with Chris, she no longer considered herself an evangelical, in large part because of the way in which the church separated the body from the mind and the spirit. "The sexual and the spiritual had always felt like one to me," she explained. "And in my twenties I came to a new spiritual identity, a new place in which I saw sexuality as embodied in the supernatural mystery."

Having come to see sexuality as an integral part of the spiritual experience, Scarlet was no longer willing to be part of a religion—or a relationship—that would restrict her spiritual life by restricting her sexual life. And so, she grieved the loss of her relationship. And then, six months later, she got online.

"My friend helped me create an OkCupid profile. I put it up and it was explosive. I had no idea. There was a whole world I didn't understand. The best way to describe it is I kind of felt like I was at a party when I was twenty-five, the age I was when I started dating Chris, and I'd fallen asleep in a room. And I woke up at the party seven years later and walked outside and nobody I knew was at the party anymore. It was a very strange sensation. People were writing me left and right. Really crazy, weird people. It was very daunting.

"And then this dude wrote me who was *hot*. Really, really hot. But also seemed really earthy. He was an artist. His work is absolutely gorgeous. He used to be a photojournalist covering international conflict and now he is a fine art photographer. He was one of the very few I actually wrote back. Deep autumn-day sky-blue and a rapid mosaic of grainy colors to jet black," she said.

Eventually, they scheduled a date. "I remember every tiny little thing about getting ready. I was excited. I was very, very attracted to him. I remember all of it. Then when I saw him, I was stunned. I was blown away. I learned later, you're never quite sure when you meet people online exactly what they're going to look like. He was *way* more attractive than the picture. I had to realign quickly."

Over dinner, the photojournalist, as she called him, told Scarlet stories about his life that made her fall for him even harder. When it was her turn to tell her story, she tentatively mentioned that she was raised an evangelical Christian. In reply, "he told me that he had people very close to him who were also raised in an evangelical home and church, and he was actually very defensive of their experience with other people." Sensitive to binary-based judgmentalism, as many of the former evangelicals I know are, his words sent a chill down Scarlet's spine. "He had no idea how big of a turn-on that was for me. And then he just kissed me out of the blue when I least expected it. Just started kissing me. Touch-wise, hunger-wise, we are made of the exact same things. No question. His past and my past, completely different. But how we were as sexual animals was identical."

Over the coming weeks, they texted, talked on the phone, had lunch, and when he had a crisis one day, it was her that he called for help. "A bond had begun to form," Scarlet summed things up. Then one day he asked her if she wanted to see his apartment. "I went over there and it was amazing," she gushed. "He'd created this beautiful environment. He had built all of these things. We went into his backyard and I remember looking at all of the millions of plants he had planted while his two cats were wandering around being lovely and affectionate. It's all slow motion to me in my memory. This whole time at his apartment, right before, I remember every tiny, little thing in slow motion.

"It was gray out, and spitting rain a little bit, but nothing bad. He looked out and stood on the porch. He didn't say a word, but his eyes were like, the only way I've ever described it to my best friend is they were like 'Wolf Sex Eyes.' They were! He just stood there, eyeing me in this primal way. I've never experienced anything like that.

I barely got back up to the step with him. It was absolutely crazy. Things on the table. It was really wild and awesome and I was so into it. It was like a movie, it really was. And I was completely loving it. It was that one time in my life I was like, 'Yes!' In that moment, I was like, 'This. Is. Me!'" she said, slapping her palms on her legs as she hit each word, as though grounding herself in the experience. "This is the part of who I've always been that I've wanted to sink my teeth into! I want to be doing this; I should be doing this; he wants to do this; and we *are* doing this.'

"That was the very first time I had ever experienced that wildfire with absolutely no regrets whatsoever in my body or his body. He had this really cool bedroom with this huge, fluffy, European bed thing. Of course, right? And I had on my hot red panties and maybe my bra was still on. And then a streak went through me, a millisecond in the middle of it where my old self was seeing what was about to happen, and I was like 'This is about to happen, I'm really about to—' It was like a lightning bolt striking through me. He only had boxers on at that point. Then they came off and the flash was gone and I was totally unaware of anything like that existing in the world.

"It was just incredible, and otherworldly in every way. It truly was real ecstasy, an out-of-body experience. Then I remember we laid in his bed and talked for a long time. Then there was a whole second round. The second time was even better than the first time! I was loving it. I was like, 'I'm probably going to be here all day!' That was maybe one of my very favorite times in my whole life. Ironically. Because then it was over, I was totally laying there, tingling kind of, again in this otherworldly place. I was happy. Not connected to the earth at all. Floating . . ."

And then the photojournalist got up to go to the bathroom. As he stood, Scarlet saw that he wasn't wearing a condom. "I knew that he had put on a condom the first time because I watched it, but when he stood up after the second time, it was like the bottom dropped out inside of me. I was so unbelievably turned on and then it was like the record scratching.

"I said, 'Wait, were you not wearing a condom?' And he was like, 'No.' I remember, in a weird way, he looked equally shocked that I was shocked. Even though, I now personally feel like his response was BS. He was like, 'I thought we were in this wild phase and we made this eye contact, and I thought that you knew that that's what I wanted to do and you wanted to do it too.' Saying we had this extensive conversation with our eyes that I was not aware of."

Suddenly, the panic set in. Diseases, pregnancy, all of the threats Scarlet had been warned would befall her if she had sex outside of marriage flooded her mind "like a cloud of locusts or something from the Bible, a black storm from Hell. I was desperately trying to look normal. I was trying to say in a totally natural way, 'Have you been tested?' I was too scared to ask him, 'Do you regularly have sex without condoms with people that you barely know?' I'd never thought of these secular things before. I was like, 'What am I doing? I don't even speak this language. I'm so ashamed. I'm so embarrassed.' I was trying to say to myself, 'Okay, okay, okay. This is the irrational side. You are on the irrational side, for sure. This is the far end of the irrational side. Reality is probably in between.' I was trying to ground myself, but my brain kept being like, 'You barely know this person! You don't even *know* him!'

"And then, I distinctly remember him saying, 'Wait, there is . . . What's on your back?' I reached around and it felt like an enormous mosquito bite the size of your palm. And then I looked and they were on my arms, like this—" She took half of the rind of a large orange that she and I had split earlier and placed it all over her body to demonstrate the size of the welts. "And I am watching them rise on my stomach, on my breasts, like a horror movie. And then my coughing—I was struggling to breathe, to catch air, and this was all escalating so quickly.

"He was like, 'Oh my God, what is happening? Go and get in the shower. Maybe you're allergic to my detergent or something. If you wash it off, maybe it will alleviate it or something.'

"I was like, 'Okay, okay.' And I ran completely naked through this guy's apartment to the shower, and that's the first time I looked down at my vagina and I was like—" Scarlet breathed in abruptly. "I gasped. I've never gasped before in my life. It was like—" She cupped her palms and held them, face up, side by side, the edges of her pinkies touching.

"That large? Are you kidding me? How is that possible?" I asked.

"Probably that's how it is when people give birth," she said. "Blown up. Open. The size of both of my palms open. I would say it's the scariest thing I've ever seen in my life. I had no idea what was happening to me. And my legs, my face, everything was bright red. It felt like I had absolutely no control over these horrific, nightmarish things that were happening to my body. That's when the ringing in my ears started. I couldn't hear anything. Just like after a concert, when you can't hear? Like that, exactly like that. I stumbled outside. The door was open. The photojournalist was standing there. I stumbled out and I said, 'I have to go to an emergency room.'

"He was like, 'Let me go and get you Benadryl. I think maybe if you drink some Benadryl, it will stop.' And I could hear his voice like a far-away, faint angel voice through the ringing.

"I was like, 'No, no. I can barely hear you. I have to—we have to go.'

"The next thing I distinctly remember is yelling. We just went right into the hospital. He was yelling, 'We need to get through! We need to get through!' There was no stopping in the waiting room or anything like that.

"Then I remember sitting in this weird bed-chair thing and there was a nurse doing all the things with my pupils, like shining light in my eyes. The nurse was talking. I was really trying to understand him but I remember, it was so hard to stay conscious. It was so hard to hear and process what he was saying, and not black out. I was trying with every grain of my being not to. I just kept saying, 'I feel so sick. I don't know what's wrong.'

"Later I remember the nurse asked the photojournalist what happened. He said, 'We had sex two times. Nothing happened while we were having sex. This happened ten or fifteen minutes after we had sex for the second time. I have no idea.' They asked him, 'Were you wearing a condom?' He said, 'First time I was, second time I wasn't.' The nurse wrote it all down. They came back and they shot me with something. Then, I blacked out. I couldn't do it anymore.

"I came to for a split second. The photojournalist was yelling and this nurse dude was yelling to other people. I don't remember what they were saying, but everybody was yelling. And I was out again.

"I know," Scarlet looked at my face, which must have registered shock, though I'd heard the shorter version of the story on the phone with her already. "It's surreal to talk about. I never talk about it. I'm actually shaking a little bit right now talking about it."

"Are you okay?" I asked.

"I'm fine," she said quickly. "I woke up on a table. They were pulling my clothes off and yelling numbers. I don't know. I guess blood pressure. Scary stuff that makes people yell." Then she stopped again. "I'm totally shaking, talking about this . . ."

"Do you want to squeeze my hand?" I asked, reaching out.

"I really will be fine. It's just so weird because I don't talk about it in this much detail, almost ever." But then she did take my hand, and she squeezed it hard. "Thank you," she said breathing out audibly.

"Somebody was holding my eyes open," Scarlet continued. "Saying, 'Okay what is your name? Can you say your name? Can you say your name?' And I couldn't say my name, which was also really weird because I could say it in my brain, but it wouldn't come out of my mouth. She was like, 'Do you know where you are?' And I nodded because I knew I was at the hospital. And she was, 'I don't want you to— Don't go away. I want you to stay. I want you to stay with me. I want you to stay with me, stay with me.' Over and over. Holding my eyes open. I don't think I've ever physically tried harder to do anything in my whole life than that moment and I couldn't, and I was out again."

Since this day, Scarlet has talked to countless doctors about what happened to her. None of them have been able to explain it. It looks as though she went into anaphylactic shock, they've said, but they don't know why.

"They asked me about allergies. I said, 'I'm allergic to cats, and he did have a cat. If I pet them and rub my eye after, my eye will get puffy and itchy, but it really didn't match the extremity of what happened obviously. And not all things cause anaphylactic shock. Latex condoms can cause anaphylactic shock, peanuts, sometimes shrimp, but not animals.

"At that time, the best guess was that I had some sudden allergy to the condom. That's the only one that really made sense. They asked me if I was allergic to condoms and I said, 'Not that I had ever known of.' I went through a million allergy tests. They tested me for everything in condoms and it came back completely clear. I have never been allergic to peanuts. I didn't eat peanuts that day. I have eaten peanuts a million times since and nothing. Nothing. They tested me so many times for a million bazillion things and the only things that came back were cats and a random dust bunny. Weird little side stuff that wouldn't cause anaphylactic shock. I don't think I'll ever know, because every doctor I've shown my case to looks at it and kind of—" Scarlet shrugged. "Not one person can make any sense of what happened. The most anyone can tell me is that I might have a very mild version of some kind of allergy— maybe to cat fur on his bed or some kind of lubricant on the condom. But I mean, these are really stretches. Some people I've told the story to have suspected the photojournalist tried to roofie me, and it went wrong. But I did not have any food or drink with him that day. All of it remains a perfect jet-black mystery. No answers."

"What do you think happened?" I asked Scarlet.

"I cannot with 100 percent certainty explain what happened on that day. Obviously, something medical happened. And in my mind, just as obviously, something spiritual happened. I had thoughts like, 'Maybe this is actually what happens when you tempt Satan. When you go that far and you feel like you know better than God knows.'

"Doctors don't understand it. They bring their colleagues in and they say, 'When did you feel the body change?' And I tell them the truth. I say, 'It was right after I realized he wasn't wearing a condom.' My gut tells me that if, when the photojournalist stood, I had seen his butt instead, and he had shuffled off to the bathroom and I never saw his penis and had not found out he hadn't worn a condom, none of this would have ever happened. I have no scientific proof for any of it. But I don't know what else to say. What if my head was turned, and he got up and he moved to another room? A tiny shift could have changed everything."

This is how Scarlet's story ends:

"I woke up in the hospital and there was nobody in the room except for the photojournalist. My robe was soaked; my body was soaked; the mattress was soaked; I couldn't talk; I didn't even know what had happened, but it was very calm. Everything was very, very quiet."

Then Scarlet saw her sexy red underwear discarded on the chair by her bed. And flashes of memory struck her in reverse chronological order—a more extreme version of what she had experienced after telling me her story on the phone. "Just little things. Again, part of my synesthesia is I remember details—a question the photojournalist asked me at dinner, something weird he did with his fork. Just this little, tiny"—she moved a pen sitting on her coffee table over a quarter of an inch, illustrating—"but really fast. Domino-fire fast. Then there were flashes of my relationship with Chris. Of all of my past romantic relationships. Then back to my parents, what I was taught and how lovingly they brought it to me. Then I was thirteen years old in my youth camp and this volcanic shame overcame me. I heard all the demonic things you hear growing up come from the bottom of the ocean of my mind. I was hearing, *This is what happens when you go against the will of God*.

"The photojournalist came over to me and he started talking to me. He was actually very sweet. He was rubbing my hand and saying things to me that I don't remember. But I just know that it was very warm and comforting. He told me it was nighttime. I believe it was around midnight. I think we'd gone there in the afternoon, probably like two, three, four, something like that. To this day, the time that passed doesn't seem possible to me, but I mean, it happened.

"I remember the staff came in and asked me 'Do you have family? I really think you should call them and they should know this happened.' But my family would have been horrified in so many ways. So they looked on their paperwork and said, 'The last time you were here your emergency contact was someone named Chris. Should we call him?' I said, 'No.' I thought of him being totally disgusted and sickened by what I had done. I didn't want to talk to anyone. My best friend was on her honeymoon so I couldn't call her. My other friends, I love them, but this was not—I'm not going to call them at 12:45 AM to please come over to the hospital and help me.

"The doctors wanted me to spend the night and I didn't want to be there. I was like, 'Please let me leave. I really don't want to be here. Please let me leave.' I begged and begged. Finally, the doctor was like, 'I will let you go against my better judgment. If anything happens, you need to come. If anyone finds out I let you leave, I could be in really big trouble.' It felt very, very serious.

"The photojournalist took me home. He walked me in and sat me in that chair," she said, pointing to the chair in the corner of her living room. "And then he suddenly became a different person. He was like, 'I have to leave. Like, I need to go. Look. Right now. I need to leave.' Something switched inside of him.

"And now, I was alone. It was the most alone and ashamed I had ever felt in my whole entire life. I just felt stripped of all my dignity and stripped of all my value. And I thought back to what the Greek doctor said after my first panic attack."

I nodded. I had been thinking about her too.

"Then I fell into a death sleep and woke up and was just a zombie wearing old clothes and sitting here on this orange couch," she said patting the couch. "Just staying in the same red underwear for days, though I could never wear them again afterward. There was heavy shame all over my body. Everything hurt. My vagina hurt. My full body hurt. I was an ocean of shame. Talking about it still drops my stomach out."

"Did you ever see the photojournalist again?"

"We had some texts back and forth. I hadn't heard from him so I was like, 'Look, I know you're totally freaked out, you have every reason to be freaked out, but you understand that I basically almost died and I'm having a complete crisis right now? And you were the only other person in the whole world that was there when this happened. Actually, you know more about what happened in the hospital than I do.' I became really upset and really angry and scared. I needed some kind of conversation to understand what just happened to me. And he would not engage with me at all, but I could see on OkCupid that he kept looking at my profile all the time.*

"Then three weeks later, he was like, 'Can we talk? I think we should talk,' and basically apologized for how he was acting. He said, 'I don't

---

* As of summer 2017, OkCupid no longer allows users to see who visited their profiles.

even have an operating system to process what went on and I'm so sorry. I handled it so badly. It was so scary because we were basically having a relationship at the very early stages and I didn't even know what to do.'

"I needed that. We'd lived through this very frightening thing together. Suddenly we were back on planet Earth and then things started between us again on the orange couch," she said. "I remember him carrying me, like a movie, back to the bedroom. I told him, 'I so want to, but I'm really scared that it's going to happen again,' and he was like, 'But I'm the person that was with you, so I know how—I'm here.' He was weirdly very comforting.' So we had sex again, a different kind of sex. My whole body was still numb. I was not there.

"After it was over we talked for a little while and I said, 'I think we should go to dinner next time. I think we need more just talking and being together.' And he was like, 'I do too.'

"He left.

"And we never talked again."

13

Dementor

Finding Harry Potter fan fiction changed everything for Rosemary.

"A big part of why I started reading all of that—fan fiction, hentai, because why go mainstream porn when you can go nerd porn?—was just because I wanted to know about sex," the twenty-five-year-old former evangelical homeschooled student explained from the other end of the tweed couch we shared. "Having learned about sex from fan fiction though, I genuinely couldn't imagine how you could have sex without magic," she laughed. "And I became very concerned I was addicted to porn. So I told my mom, and she sent me to an anti-gay counseling center for porn addiction. I was about sixteen. I had never kissed a boy. I hadn't even been on a date at this point. And my counselor, who was gay—or 'ex-gay'—had me reading books about people having promiscuous affairs that were ruining their marriages and things."

Rosemary slipped her Birkenstocks off and tucked her legs up under her long patchwork skirt, beginning to get comfortable in my friend's house. We had both taken long bus rides to get there that morning, as my friend's city was, conveniently, halfway between Rosemary's and my homes. "In a weird way though," Rosemary added thoughtfully, "I think being treated for a porn addiction made me feel important. At the time, I felt very small and ignored. I was depressed. And my brother—who is two and a half years younger than me—was acting out really aggressively. He threatened to kill me a lot. He was even hospitalized for a while. I never really took him seriously on the murdering thing, but I started locking my door all the time. My parents really hated that I did that. I think they thought I was hiding out in my room. Which, I was. But, I mean, what are you going to do?

"I brought up to my parents how unhappy I was several times, but they weren't really receptive to it. My brother was verbally sexually abusing me—asking me to have sex with him or describing sex to me. When I was maybe fifteen, I told my mom. She burst into tears and just didn't say anything to me for hours. When my dad came home, he said, 'Do we want to talk about this?' My parents made me confront my brother about it in front of them. I was like, 'Oh. Yes. Robert, stop propositioning me.' My brother was like, 'What does that mean?' And I was like, 'It means stop asking me to have sex with you.' And he was like, 'What are you talking about? What? That's so gross.'

"And then it was dropped.

"When I was seventeen, I mentioned it to my mom again. I remember intentionally making it nonthreatening: 'Hey, I know he's joking, but it's really irritating. Can you tell him not to say this?' And she was like, 'Yes, yes.' And then that wasn't a big deal either. I think that's the whole reason I told my mom that I had a porn addiction. I was going through all this stuff and I just really wanted attention."

Talking about her fear and discomfort around her brother didn't get Rosemary the attention she needed. But she knew she'd be seen if she confessed a sin. Rosemary's parents' reactions to the two varieties of sexual "issues" Rosemary brought to them—her reading Harry Potter fan fiction, which resulted in her being sent to ongoing therapy, and her brother's sexual propositions and threats, which resulted in brief conversations—reflect the purity movement's values and norms. Generally speaking, purity culture excuses male sexuality and amplifies female sexuality, and it shames consensual sexual activity and silences nonconsensual sexual activity.

Sexual violence perpetrated by those within the community in particular is strictly censored, as it challenges the pure/impure binary upon which the purity movement is based. The binary demands that predators are outsiders, though seven out of ten rapes are perpetrated by someone known to the victim (this is even more likely among juvenile victims, 93 percent of whom know the perpetrator) and 55 percent of sexual assaults take place at or near a victim's home.[1] One of the results of *othering* perpetrators is that victims can be psychologically unprepared to protect themselves when threats come from closer to home than they ever imagined they could.

"My parents wanted me to know how to defend myself against back-alley rapists," Rosemary said. "I even took a self-defense class. But none of that prepared me for someone I loved and trusted disrespecting me." She took a deep breath. "I was home for the summer after my first year of Bible college," Rosemary began. "The assault itself wasn't physically violent. I had never even heard of 'consent.' I didn't hear that term until I started studying feminism when I was twenty or twenty-one. My brother just came in, did his thing, and I was just like, 'What the fuck is going on?' No options even occurred to me."

"You froze," I suggested.

"Yes. I'm pretty much at peace with that now. I mean, my understanding is that's a very normal reaction. When you're scared, you're just trying to get through the situation and a lot of times, it's your body deciding what it will do, not your mind. I remember staring at a globe the whole time. I remember fluorescent lights. I also remember having my eyes closed. It's one of those sensory jumbles. I just wanted him to leave. It was just, 'If I compromise with him enough, he will leave; it will be like nothing happened.'"

A few weeks later, Rosemary told her parents. "My mom screamed like I have never heard her screaming. My dad was really angry. And then," Rosemary looked down, "I guess they talked to my brother." Rosemary's brother told his parents that Rosemary hadn't fought him off. "And my parents took that to mean it was kind of my fault," Rosemary said. "My dad said he didn't have a video camera in my room so he'd never know exactly what happened. I hated him for saying that, though he's since said he never said it. The church views men as animals with no agency. The whole 'as a girl it's your job to stop guys from doing stuff' line of thinking. So my parents treated my brother like he'd messed up but nothing more, and I felt really blamed. They acted like it was consensual, like it was sex. Sex is so penalized in evangelicalism, it's easier to chalk rape and abuse up to sex and be done with it. But I don't think what happened between me and my brother was sex at all. This was *abuse*."

Though purity culture messaging about girls and boys is very different, the gender-based messages are absorbed by all. For instance, boys hear girls being told that they must cover their bodies and avoid flirtation in order to protect themselves from boys' and men's uncontrollable sexual virility. *What does that say about men?* some of these boys may find themselves wondering. Or, more specifically, *What does that say about* me?

Several years ago, writer David Ellis Dickerson spoke about his experience as a young evangelical man on the radio program *This American Life*.[2] At one point, David called up his childhood friend, Derek, the son of a missionary, and they exchanged stories. "I, uh, developed a technique of seeing girls as just floating heads," Derek admitted to David. "You just learn you're just not—*not* going to look below the neck. . . . I was a cartoonist for my college newspaper, and I didn't actually know how to draw girls really. I mean you can see—you can see when I would draw a female figure, uh, top-to-bottom in a cartoon, there's an awkwardness to it, because I didn't actually know what they looked like," Derek laughed. "It's funny to look back and talk about them now, but it was all very dead serious back then."

David understood. He *did* notice women's bodies, and the shame was tantamount. He recalled, "On warm days I would walk across campus feeling like a monster, because I believed that noticing a girl's body was the spiritual equivalent of something like sexual assault." Every accidental glimpse of cleavage or a little extra leg was terrible. And at the same time, wonderful. Eventually, he found himself walking around campus, the library, the supermarket, perpetually "hoping to see another accidental glimpse of . . . something."

Finally, he admitted his secret to his pastor. His pastor advised him to go to Sex Addicts Anonymous. When David, a twenty-two-year-old virgin, told his story to the group of gathered sex addicts there was, as one might expect, "an awkward silence." A few days later, he went to a Christian counselor. The counselor advised him to go home and masturbate, to David's great shock. He bought a porn magazine, went home, masturbated, and, as he tells it, was immediately cured. "It felt like a miracle," he said. "It was so fast, so life-changing, that it was like converting all over again."

I don't believe that stories such as David's and his friend's are as uncommon as many might first assume. As my interviewee Jo said, "women are taught their bodies are evil; men are taught their minds are."

But when I listen to stories like Rosemary's or that of the Duggar family—whose reality show *19 Kids and Counting* regularly reiterated the family's commitment to ensuring their kids' "purity" only for it to come out that one of the sons was accused of sexually assaulting several girls, including some of his sisters—I cannot help but wonder if, while some men worry that they are monsters because of this gender-based messaging, others may feel their monstrous behavior is justified because of it.[3] When boys are repeatedly taught that they cannot control their sexual impulses and that it is a girl's responsibility to protect her own purity, how logical it must seem for perpetrators attempting to justify their actions to come to the conclusion that if a woman dresses or acts a certain way she is "asking for it," making rape at least partly (if not totally) her fault?*

At the insistence of the adult Rosemary first confided in, Rosemary's parents sent both her and her brother to therapy. But when Rosemary begged her parents not to leave her alone in the house with her brother anymore, she found "it was inconvenient for my parents to make sure they were in the house with me. Their attitude was just minimizing, like I should just get over it."

Again, it is important to note that Rosemary wasn't the only one receiving the message that she should just get over what happened to her in moments like these. Her brother received that message too—making it more likely for him to follow the very common pattern of abusing again. So Rosemary began house sitting for people around town, moving from couch to couch, anything to not be left alone with her brother. Between house-sitting jobs, she stayed with the adult in whom she first confided.

"I had to survive. I felt I was just going to die. Just drop dead. It just felt like things were going to be over. Or that they were. Like somebody had just dropped me in someone else's head with someone else's memories and I could play them all in my head but they didn't mean anything. It felt like I had just been beamed into my life. Sexual assault is so degrading. You treat a person like they're not a person. It

---

* To be sure, not all sexual violence is male-on-female, and that which is not is often even more silenced than that which is. Sexual violence against males is deeply stigmatized, and violence against gender nonconforming people, which is disturbingly common, is often entirely ignored.

was just hard to fight my way back to feeling like a person. And that was really what kind of started my break with evangelicalism. Because the church makes abuse easy. Elizabeth Smart, the kidnapping victim, talks about this," Rosemary said, referring to the child safety activist who was kidnapped at the age of fourteen. "She was raped by her captor repeatedly," Rosemary continued. "They found her alive, which is amazing because that doesn't always happen. But she talks about being raised in the Mormon church [where purity culture also thrives] and feeling like she was worthless because she was no longer a virgin after the rape."

In Smart's own words, spoken at a human trafficking and sexual violence conference at Johns Hopkins University:

I was raised in a very religious household, one that taught that sex was something special that only happened between a husband and a wife who loved each other. And that's what I'd been raised [with], that's what I'd always been determined to follow: that when I got married, then and only then would I engage in sex.

And so, [after] that first rape, I felt crushed. Who could want me now? I felt so dirty and so filthy. I understand so easily, all too well, why someone wouldn't run because of that alone. . . . Can you imagine turning around and going back into society where you're no longer of value? Where you're no longer as good as anybody else?[4]

Elizabeth Smart's sexuality "education" included an object lesson. She remembers learning that a virgin was an unchewed stick of gum and that a person who has sex is a chewed-up stick of gum. After being raped, Elizabeth said, "I thought, 'Oh my gosh, I'm that chewed up piece of gum. Nobody re-chews a piece of gum. You throw it away.' And that's how easy it is to feel like you no longer have worth, you no longer have value. Why would it even be worth screaming out? Why would it even make a difference if you are rescued? Your life still has no value."

"Did you experience that feeling of worthlessness that Elizabeth Smart talks about?" I asked Rosemary.

"Yes," Rosemary responded. "I remember, with shame and the whole purity culture thing, I just kept thinking, 'If someone I loved and knew that well could treat me like that . . . what if they're right about me?' I never considered pressing charges, ever. Supposedly it's one of the most underreported crimes, and I totally believe that. You just want to move on with your life. But the really awful part," she said shaking her head slowly, "is I would come back and stay at my parents' house when my brother was gone. But when he would come back, I had to leave again. It was like, 'Really? Your rapist kid, maybe he could get a hotel. Yes?'"

"Or *he* could couch surf," I insisted.

"Yes," Rosemary replied. "He had friends in the area. I'm sure he could have stayed with people. I slept on a futon in my bedroom when I was home, but I wasn't sleeping there while my brother was there. So, one time I'd taken the sheets off the futon, put them away, and put the futon back up into being a couch before leaving. My mom called me, and she was mad. She thought I'd hidden the sheets, and she wanted to make up the bed for my brother. I was like, 'He doesn't have to sleep in my bed. He raped me in my bed!' And she was just pissed at me about the sheets. 'For evil to succeed, all that is needed is for good men to do nothing,'" Rosemary continued. "That's Churchill or someone.* To side with the perpetrator we must do nothing, but to side with the victim, we're asked to stand with them, which is so much more emotionally taxing."

"So they chose him," I said sadly.

---

* The origin of this quote is a matter of dispute, but it is often attributed to Edmund Burke.

"Yes. They chose him. They chose his comfort over my security."

"You deserved better," I responded.

"Yes. I did," Rosemary replied. "A lot of people do." She reached across the table for the Tupperware container I had set there earlier. "Are you familiar with Harry Potter?" she asked me.

"I've read the first few books," I answered.

"Did you read the third book, with the dementors?"

"Yes. Or, I saw the movie."

"Okay. Remember how the dementors bring out horrible memories? And the way to deal with the aftermath of that is to eat chocolate?"

"Okay, yes, I totally remember," I said.

Rosemary picked up the Tupperware filled with fudge brownies and dropped it in her lap.

Listening to my interview with Rosemary again now, I am struck by how appropriate the metaphor she drew about the dementors really is. In the Harry Potter books, the dementors are like trauma-triggers. They "force their victims to relive the worst memories of their lives, and drown, powerless, in their own despair."[5]

For many of my interviewees, the church has become just such a dementor. The way in which it wrongfully classifies sexual violence, for example, can re-traumatize survivors, making the church—a place that many would hope to be a safe haven—a very dangerous place for survivors. Laura, whose story is shared in chapter four, illustrates:

I have this really weird reaction of crying every time I enter a church. Uncontrollably. Embarrassingly. It's just like everything boils out. I just feel it coming out and I can't stop it. I think part of it is I really wish someone could see my pain. I don't know if that's exactly why I'm crying when I'm there, but . . . I just feel . . . like . . . all the pain

I've ever felt, and I can't keep my face on anymore. The songs are all about God's love, redemption, different themes. But as someone who was raped, the church doesn't have any message for me. I used to think, "Maybe there'll be a message for me there someday," but I don't think it exists. (Laura)

Even those who have not personally experienced traumatic shaming can be affected by the church's purity teachings in this way. For instance, one former evangelical woman who told me she has a panic attack every time she enters a church has no explanation other than the fact that she saw her sister pushed into marrying a man she had slept with and who later abused her. When the woman's sister went to the church for help, she was advised not to report the abuse. Having watched the way that the purity message contributed to her sister marrying an abusive man, and later not leaving that man, is enough to now make the woman cry every time she enters a church.

But the church isn't always and certainly doesn't *have* to be a dementor. It *can* be a healer, as the continuation of Rosemary's story illustrates.

Near the end of her summer of couch surfing, Rosemary prepared for a trip to Europe, where she would spend her sophomore year of college. By the time she was packing her bags, she told me, she was so depressed that she was seriously planning her suicide. She would kill herself in a European library, she told herself. She had always loved books so much. But when Rosemary arrived overseas, things began to change.

"I think evangelicalism means something a little different where I was in Europe than it does here," she explained, her tone growing light again, as it had been at the beginning of our conversation. "Evangelicalism here is about purity culture: you don't have sex; you have to wear these clothes; you only listen to this music; you only watch these movies.

In the part of Europe I was in, they were more concerned about creating fellowship with each other and doing service. It was one of the few times that I was really in a 'Christian fellowship.' Not everything about it was perfect, but it was really honest. People didn't try to fake who they were. There was a lot of love. We cared about each other a lot. Some of us were European; most of us were Americans; and the fourteen of us on the program just got very close."

One day, Rosemary told me, she and her peers were given the assignment to share their testimonies, the stories of when they were first born again. The structure of a testimony story, which is often shared publicly, is strict: it begins with a review of the individual's former life of sin and/or suffering, during which people's most painful life experiences are often shared (for as the saying goes, "no test, no testimony"). Next there is the story of the moment in which the individual gave his or her life over to God. And finally, there is the blissful picture of the individual's new life as an evangelical Christian—which, though not without struggles, is so full of grace, love, and support that the storyteller can truly say some version of: "I once was lost, but now I'm found."

Becoming born again can literally be lifesaving for some people, and many people's testimonies are the most intimate, heartfelt stories they can tell about themselves. But other people's experiences simply don't adhere to the structure. And some of these people find they need to bend the truth a little—or a lot—to make their stories fit, which some have told me makes the testimony structure feel more like a marketing pitch for evangelicalism than anything else. As a result, testimonies have waned in popularity over the years, making people like Rosemary say: "I've never been a big fan of the testimony-sharing thing. I think they're kind of the worst.

"But then," she warmed, "I got into the classroom. And someone stood up and said a bunch of things that I had never heard someone say in a testimony story before, things that must have been horrible to share.

And I just felt like I could stand up and say exactly what was going on with me. And so, I did. I don't really know why. I think I just thought, 'It can't get any worse.' I was open to anything at that point. And I think everyone else went there with this kind of mind-set too, just embracing whatever came. And everyone in the room was amazing. One random guy even came up and told me that if I ever needed to talk, I could talk to his wife, which I always loved. Because of course I wouldn't want to talk to this random guy about how I'd been raped, but he was just trying to do something. He didn't know what to say, so he was like, 'Here. Have my wife.'"

We both laughed.

"And a bunch of other people said, 'We're really glad you're here.' And they didn't say anything else. I thought, 'Okay. They don't hate me because, I don't know, I was abused.' That just felt freeing. So the class was great."

The next day, Rosemary's class joined another class for a weekend retreat. There, she and her peers were asked to share their testimonies again, this time with the larger group. "I was like, 'I'm not going to share my testimony again. It's exhausting. I'm tired of crying,'" Rosemary said. "But I was sitting on this hill, and I just felt like it had been so freeing to tell my story. And I realized there was no reason not to tell any part of my story. I would tell people if I survived an earthquake, so why hide this? And I thought, 'All right. You know what? I'm going to. Why not?' So I did. This time with forty people instead of fourteen. And the room reacted really well again. And I think after that retreat thing, I just started feeling free. Really feeling like I didn't have a secret anymore. I think the more you tell your story, particularly within safe spaces, the freer you are. That's part of the reason I'm willing to tell you my whole story . . . within reason, I'm not going to give everybody all of my dirty laundry. But if there are things that you can't tell anyone, they have power over you.

"Then I got my testimony paper back," she frowned, though her eyes were still light. "And the teacher told me my testimony wasn't 'happy enough.'" Rosemary began to laugh. "That my testimony wasn't going to inspire people to want to be Christians. I was suicidal at that point, and miserable, but I laughed. Because it was just so ridiculous. And fortunately, everybody else was lovely, so it was not traumatizing to get that response, but it stands out. Let me tell you how 'happy' I was, laden with PTSD that had been totally not dealt with. I was like, 'I don't even know what I'm doing right now! I'm miserable. Fuck no, I'm not happy! I've just lost my family. I've been homeless for a summer.' But I was still there. And that alone was the accomplishment of my life. That summer, I felt dead. But in Europe I felt alive again. I was walking around and trying to figure out everything from scratch. And it was a good place to start doing that. It was a safe place. I was cared for there. But that's a snapshot of evangelicals, right?"

"It is," I said—both the students' warm embrace, which literally saved Rosemary's life, and the teacher's admonishment that her life didn't look like it was "supposed to" and that she had best go back and rewrite it. It is a tension I suspect most evangelicals and former evangelicals would identify with.

"When I came back to college after my time in Europe, I felt like I had to fake it in order to be accepted in the evangelical community again," Rosemary continued.

"Fake what?"

"In Europe we all wanted to know who each other were, but back at my evangelical college in the US, it didn't feel like that was an option. You're just supposed to be 'a happy Christian.'"

Rosemary gave her evangelical college another year, and then she dropped out.

"I felt like I was starting from a blank slate," she told me, "and it was terrifying. I believed in God, but I didn't know what that meant at that point. I started researching some other spiritualities, looking into Native American spirituality, Celtic, neo-pagan spiritualities. I'd always loved mythology growing up. Some of the time I was praying. Some of the time I was journaling. Sometimes I was reading. Sometimes I was just looking for space to just be. My brother had moved out and I moved back in with my parents while I was looking for another house. And then my brother—surprise!—came home for a month, and I ended up couch surfing again."

Rosemary still lives in the east coast community in which she grew up. She's maintained a relationship with her family, which sometimes forces her to see her brother, which she hates. But she does it, because he isn't her only sibling. Rosemary has another brother and sister—both much younger than she and her brother—over whom she is understandably very protective.

"I actually have a picture of them," she said to me. "Want to see them?"

"Yes," I smiled.

"Yeah," she said, holding up her phone. "That's my little brother and sister."

"Aww. Cuties!"

"They're great. I love them. Zach is a teenager now. He's super cool and will only talk when he gets excited, and my little sister is just adorable."

Rosemary held her phone in front of her for a moment longer and just looked at it.

"Today, I am a feminist," Rosemary told me near the end of our interview. "The first time I heard in feminist circles that 'an enthusiastic yes is standard consent,' it was freeing. With my brother, it was always, 'Oh, I could have done more. I could have screamed. I could have run upstairs where my mother was.' But it never even occurred to me to ask for help. Not even remotely.

"I have had to learn instinct, to learn how to stop distrusting myself. Now, it would be different. Now, I could walk out.

"A couple of years ago at a party, I got drunk. This guy came out and tried to have sex with me on my friend's porch, and I kicked him and chased him around the house yelling, 'No means no!'" She laughed. "Yeah. Drunken me is a badass. Surviving gives you a very unique set of skills. It costs a lot. But it also makes you powerful."

How We Get Over

14

Going Home

I was thirty years old when I called my parents and told them I was coming home again.

"Oh Linda!" my mom exclaimed.

"To write a book about sex and the church," I finished my sentence.

"What's that now?" Mom said.

It had been five years since I started doing interviews, and it would be another five before I would finish them, going back and re-interviewing many of the people I began this journey with. But if you had told me I was only at the midpoint then, I never would have believed you.

For the first time, my path appeared clear of purity culture's stumbling blocks. I was sure I was healed. And I was ready to help heal others. I quit my job in New York City, put my things into storage, and purchased a ticket to my hometown so I could write full-time from my parents' house, where I didn't have to pay rent. All I needed now, I thought, was the gumption to get up and go.

But all the while, my shame was still there. Waiting to rise into a new kind of stumbling block, one I wouldn't even recognize until I lost my balance. Until I tripped. Until I fell.

*   *   *

One of my first nights home, my mom and I sat together talking on the couch until late.

"So you're actually doing this," she began.

"I actually am," I replied.

Mom shook her head, pulling the afghan off of the back of the couch. She wrapped half of it around her shoulders.

"Why?" she asked, offering the other half to me.

"I just have to," I answered, taking the afghan from her.

"To what? Talk to these girls about . . . womanhood and . . . sexual things?" she said, still shaking her head. "Just be sure you don't wreck your salvation, Linda. Even if your intentions are good, if people misconstrue what you say and get bad feelings about God, that isn't good for you. For your salvation."

"Mom," I tried to explain, "God is why I'm doing this. I feel called to write this book."

"Did he *say* that to you? Did he actually *tell* you to do it?"

"Not in words."

"Then are you sure that it's God who's calling?" she pressed. "That it isn't someone else?"

I felt the blood rush to my face. "Are you talking about Satan?" I pulled away from her. "Are you saying that Satan is making me write this book?"

"No," she hesitated. "I'm just saying that . . . he *may* be."

"Mom," I groaned. "It's so not cool for you to say that I'm a tool of the Devil."

"Linda, Satan is the Prince of Lies," she said with fear in her eyes. "I don't want him using you. What if people turn away from God because of what you say the church did? Those people will go to Hell. Which is a lot worse than whatever is happening to you and your friends. So, it may seem like a good thing to bring this all up now but—don't you understand? I don't want you to get *hurt*."

Under the afghan, I could feel her shaking.

"Here," I said, handing my half to her.

"Just promise me you're praying, Linda," Mom pleaded as she wrapped the rest of the afghan around herself.

"Just because I don't go to church anymore doesn't mean I'm not praying," I answered.

"Well, *are* you?" she demanded.

"*Yes,*" I retorted.

"*All right,*" she wiped at the tears gathering in her eyes. "*Good!*" Then she sighed and said more softly, "Good Linda, good."

Conversations like this one were common in the five months I lived with my parents at the age of thirty. And they weren't all with my mom either. Several of the people I had interviewed five years earlier expressed concerns over having their stories told publicly when I said I wanted to write them down in a book. They worried their stories would lead people away from the church, costing them their salvation. They told me they didn't want me to make their God look like "a meanie," and that they struggled with whether or not they could trust me—as someone who had left the community—not to "twist" their stories.*

I never stopped knowing I had to tell this story. But the more my friends and family expressed their fears and concerns, the more self-conscious I became about *how* I told it. When I tried to write, my head was clouded by all the ways I might write it "wrong." Some days, I would sit frozen in front of my computer screen. Other days, the words poured out of me and my laptop was wet with tears. I was writing some of my most painful personal stories, and some of the most painful stories I had been told by others, but the hardest part, for me, wasn't how writing these stories made *me* feel. It was my fear around how reading them

---

* This book does not include any interviews with individuals who remained uncomfortable with their stories being told.

might make *others* feel. People like my parents, my youth pastor (the one who was there before and after the one who was convicted of child enticement), and the people from church who had supported me and my family when we needed them.

The church is like a bundle of sticks, I remember an evangelical leader once saying. *As long as we stand together, we are strong. But when someone leaves the bundle, they weaken themselves and weaken the rest of us too.* The stories I heard as an adolescent about women ideologically leaving the bundle by demanding equality or evangelical insiders challenging the church's positions on other issues came back to me along with the fear of being seen as such a damaging dissenter.

And there it was. The shame I was sure I was over.

One afternoon while my parents were out, I went into my childhood bedroom, now my father's office. The Bible verses that had papered the walls had been taken down, and the white, crib-like daybed replaced with a desk. Still, if I closed my eyes, it was easy to see the way it used to be. *The tall white dresser there by the big window*, I rearranged the room in my mind. *The short white one here. And the daybed, just there.*

I thought I was so grown-up, I realized as I opened my eyes again. But it was all right here where I left it—not in this room, not in this house, but in me.

Research shows that when we challenge old ideas about ourselves and the world and replace them with new ones, we can break down old neural connections through what's called synaptic pruning and strengthen new ones. And if we keep at it, eventually we can create a new way of looking at the world long enough to pave *new* neural pathways, to shape *new* memories, to internalize *new* stories—narrowing the gap between what were, in my and my interviewees' experience, the ideas our bodies long ago internalized and the freedom our spirits now called us toward. This is the miracle of brain plasticity. A miracle I had thought I'd already finished experiencing. I had learned how to listen to my inner voice, even when it contradicted the voices around me. I had won the freedom to reinterpret the religious texts of my childhood and to listen to the voice of God *I* heard. I had learned how to express the full range of my emotions, and how to speak freely about my thoughts, my feelings, and my beliefs. And I had liberated my intimate life from purity culture's control, making me believe I could have a healthy romantic relationship.

But under every layer of shame is another layer. And this latest layer—the shame I had around telling this story publicly—felt as hard as granite. Every day, I sat down with my computer, hoping the shame would splinter as I metaphorically rammed my body into it, but the shame wasn't breaking. I was.

My parents watched me closely as the months wore on. They both became increasingly determined to stop me from writing this book, each for their own reasons. And I fought them hard, pushing back in ways I didn't when I was a "good Christian teenager," which was unsettling for us all. Mom and I talked often about her fear that my exposing the damaging effects of the purity movement would be akin to my committing mass murder on an eternal scale as my words could turn people away from faith and secure their fate in Hell; her fear that God would hold me accountable for the blood on my hands and I would be sent to join them in Hell as a punishment; and even her fear that what I was doing was so taboo that I'd be utterly destroyed by the evangelical community for doing it, that even if this *was* God's will and I wound up in Heaven where I would be rewarded for having answered God's call, it would be only after years of experiencing Hell here on earth at the hands of the community whose harmfulness she begged me not to expose.

It had to stop. So I sent what I had of the book to agents, even though I knew it wasn't ready. More than one replied with the message that the book was too dark, too painful to read, one even saying that it "hurt to turn each page." They asked me to write with more levity or at least to offer readers breaks from the intensity. I laughed at the request. I had no levity in me, and I hadn't taken a break from the pain since I left New York City. I thought to myself, *Their comments may as well be about my life*. My *life* had become dark. My *life* had become painful. It hurt for me to turn the page of each day.

So I stopped.

I stopped writing.

I stopped interviewing.

I told God that it would be great if someone else could do this book.

I moved back to New York City, took my things out of storage, got a new job, and told myself it was over.

But the call remained.

A few years later, I was lying in the grass in Brooklyn's Prospect Park at dusk, talking to my mom over the telephone.

"When in your life have you felt most alive?" I asked my mom wistfully. "Like you were really living?"

"I've never thought about it," she answered me.

"Think about it now," I said playfully.

"I don't know, Linda," she protested.

"*Think* about it."

"I don't think about things like that. I don't ask myself questions like that one."

"Well, start now then."

She was silent. I waited. A breeze ran over me.

Finally, Mom sighed. "It's when I'm with God," she said.

"Really?" I asked. "Like, alone in your room?" I pictured her sitting on the floor by the window where she often goes to pray.

"No. When I'm with God."

"Right. But otherwise, you mean, alone?"

"Mm-hmm."

"Why do you think that is?"

"It's the only time that I can really be myself," she said quietly. "God is the only one who loves me unconditionally. And approves of me. Unconditionally. No matter what mistakes I make. So I can just . . . be myself."

"I understand," I answered her softly. It was what I had wanted from religion my entire life, perhaps what we had *all* wanted. But maybe we were looking in the wrong place. Looking for it from one another, when all the while only God could give it. We sat in silence together for a moment. Then, I heard myself ask her, "Mom?" My voice was high, the way it used to be when Blue told me I was acting like a child. "Do you still think God has his hand on me?"

It was something she used to tell me almost every day. *Don't you ever think that you aren't something, Linda*, she would say while rubbing my head at night when I was small. *Because you are. You are something special. Like Moses and the other saints. I knew when he protected you in my womb after my miscarriage. It was his way of saying he loved me. Because he was trusting me with something very special.* As I drifted to sleep, she once leaned over me and whispered into my ear, *I feel so privileged to be allowed to raise you, Linda.*

I waited.

She didn't answer.

"Like you used to say when I was a little girl?" I continued. "That I am special? That God has his hand on me?"

"God doesn't take his hand off you," Mom finally answered. "You will always be special, Linda. And he is still willing to guide you. I just don't know if you are following him anymore."

I lay in the grass for a long time after that, as night fell around me. I wondered why I had asked Mom that question. It was the question of a child, and I wasn't one. I didn't need my mom to tell me whether or not God had his or her hand on me. I felt God's presence every day. I asked, I realized, because I wanted *her* to believe it.

Evangelicalism has always been about Mom for me. When I was an adolescent, both my mom and my dad told me on separate occasions that their favorite part about me was my Christianity—my mom because she thought it was the most valuable, precious thing in the world and she loved that she and I shared it, and my dad because, after having lost his faith as an adolescent, he saw in me what he wished more than anything he could have for himself. I knew my dad would be disappointed when I left the faith, but that he would understand. But deep down, I think I feared leaving the faith might mean losing Mom.

When my mom continued to love me despite my having lost her favorite part about me, I counted myself lucky. Not every former evangelical gets this. And then, I had to go and push my luck. Talk to people about gender, about sex, and expose the harmfulness of some of the church's teachings. I worried that if Mom ever felt forced to choose between evangelicalism and me—as she might when the book comes out—she might not choose me.

And suddenly, lying in the dark grass, I realized, that's why I went home. Not, as I told people, because I had been working at a nonprofit and had no savings and so needed to go somewhere I could write without having to pay for food or housing (though that was true). Those were reasons; they just weren't *the* reason. After all, I had had other options: friends offered guestrooms in both Fort Worth, Texas, and Atlanta, Georgia; a several-month-long house-sitting opportunity for a five-story mansion surfaced in New York City, and the man I had been dating said he would pay for me to write full-time from India for a year, where he himself was moving.

But I turned them all down.

I wanted to go *home*.

To convince them, to convince her, that I was doing a good thing. Who am I kidding? To convince them that *I* was good.

I didn't receive the blessing I went home for.

But in time, I realized I could go on and tell my story without it.

And perhaps, that is what I really needed.

They say going home is the hardest part of any journey. It is there that we risk losing the gains we made elsewhere. There that we may ignore our hardest-won lessons, let down our guard, and find ourselves in the gravest danger.

After that call with my mom, I started writing and interviewing again, waking early before work and setting aside at least one weekend day for a deep dive. I launched a blog. I published a few articles online. And then, a funny thing happened. My mom read them and it made her feel . . . better. Whatever she imagined I might have to say, it was far worse than what I actually said.

Today, it's my mom sending me daily text messages saying, "You can do it!" "Keep writing honey!" And my dad who tells me, "Don't worry if people are mad at you for what you have to say; you are a truth-teller."

I think often about the fears my family and community expressed the first time I tried to write this book, but these thoughts no longer immobilize me. I am careful with people's stories. I don't ever want to be in a position of shaming the evangelical community for having shamed me. The point is that we must *all* move past shaming. But today, I know that telling my story and the stories of those who have trusted me to tell theirs is about more than answering a call to help others. It is the only way to the other side of the granite block of shame that is still within me. Every time I tell my story—come what may—I am closer to free.

*   *   *

The thing about a wound is that, when treated, it heals. A light wound disappears altogether and a deep wound develops into a scar—that thick, dark fabric, raised and stronger than the skin around it, as Jane Hirshfield describes in her poem "For What Binds Us."

Today, I have a scar as strong as the literal scars that hold my insides together, as concrete as the black tar road that led me away and then home again. It has become a bond between me and the religion I grew up in that keeps me coming back. A bond between me and my family forged by having faced that which might have broken us, and not having been broken.

This is not just a book about wounds.

It is a book about scars.

I can't imagine what it must have been like for my mother, who once felt so blessed to be able to give to me the greatest gift that she had ever received—evangelical Christianity—to see me walk away from it. I can't imagine how it must have felt for her to watch me deconstruct the values of the religion around which she had shaped her entire mothering of me. But I will never forget that every morning in the months I lived at home at the age of thirty—whether or not she or my dad and I had argued the night before—we ate breakfast together. Dad and I shared a pot of coffee. Mom gave me a hug. Then I walked down the hallway to the guest bedroom, closed the door, and did the thing that made us all most afraid.

And afterward, we ate lunch.

15

The No Shame Movement

"Some people write in and say I'm shaming people who choose abstinence before marriage," said Laura P., an anthropologist and founder
of the No Shame Movement,* a website that shares people's stories of
leaving behind conservative Christian beliefs about sexuality. "Which
is funny," she laughed into the phone. "Because in my personal life, I'm
actually *practicing* abstinence. I turned thirty-eight yesterday, and I've
really only ever had two physical encounters and have never had penis-
in-vagina sex. But I used to be abstinent because I thought I *had* to be
based on what I learned in the church. Now I'm abstinent by *choice*. I
want to wait and have it with the right person and I just haven't found
them. Which used to make me feel really bad, but now I understand
why that is."

"Why?" I asked her.

"Purity culture messaging . . . internalizing that men are predators . . .
I'm recognizing it all now. One thing I appreciate about the No Shame
Movement community is there are so many people in it who are in the
same boat as me. That's helped."

---

* Laura asked me to add that she created the #noshamemov hashtag that led to the
creation of the No Shame Movement website with friends, and that a number of
friends and collaborators have been involved in the No Shame Movement's work over
the years.

Like me, Laura was part of the first generation of adolescents to be raised in the era of the purity industry. But Laura didn't grow up in the white evangelical church like I did. Laura is African American and was raised in a variety of churches, including a predominantly African American church. Still, the same white evangelical purity messages that shaped my life, shaped hers. Our parents watched the same TV shows on the Christian Broadcasting Network. Our moms listened to the same nationally syndicated programs on our local Christian radio stations. And we got many of the same messages about sexuality.

But things changed for Laura when her family moved to Ghana while she was in high school. "In Ghana," she explained, "the conservative Christian adults around me were *convinced* dating was a sin, whereas the adults in the United States were *convinced* dating wasn't a sin. My fifteen-year-old brain had trouble reconciling these two conflicting views. I remember thinking to myself 'Somebody's lying.' And then you would see other things in Ghana."

"Like what?" I asked.

"Like public breastfeeding. Or, in the rural north, women who went topless because breasts weren't necessarily seen as sexual, so it was no big deal."

The discord Laura saw among the values she learned in US churches, the values she saw in Ghanaian churches, and the values held in other parts of Ghanaian culture made Laura question the claim that religious purity teachings were noncultural—that is to say, that they had nothing to do with race, ethnicity, region, et cetera. In time, Laura began to see religious purity teachings as *distinctly* cultural, and to recognize how the white American evangelical church had exported these teachings across the country and the world. The history of US-based purity purveyor True Love Waits alone offers an illustration: In 1995, they displayed 220,000 purity pledges from thirteen countries in Argentina; in 2004, they displayed over 460,000 pledges from twenty countries in Athens,

Greece; in 2007, they hosted an international summit in South Africa and announced a $950,000 expansion of its abstinence-only-until-marriage programs in South Africa, Botswana, Lesotho, Swaziland, Tanzania, and Zambia. . . .[1]

In her late twenties, Laura began engaging with people critiquing purity culture online, most of whom were, or had been, part of the white American evangelical Christian subculture. The conversations were helpful, but "as a black woman, I wanted to see *myself*," she insisted. "I thought, 'What if we had a tag for the rest of us? Black women—as purity culture is very much ingrained in black church culture as well—people who are queer, or plus-sized, or disabled, or don't feel seen in the existing spaces for some other reason?'"

Laura launched the No Shame Movement in 2013 with precisely this purpose in mind.

"I don't write a lot of original content," she told me. "I'm very intentional about inclusivity and trying to find other voices to put up on the site. It's tedious, and slow, but I do the work: I make Twitter lists, bookmark things, form authentic relationships with people in groups that are underrepresented on the site. For example, when I knew the site needed more queer representation, I went to a group in DC called Many Voices," a black church movement for gay and transgender justice. "That group led me to another group; I read the things they wrote; I followed their voices; some of those people pointed me to other people." Today, the No Shame Movement represents a diversity of identities and experiences.

I first learned about the No Shame Movement in the summer of 2016 when I came across an online roundtable discussion in which Laura participated.[2] The discussion circled around the book *I Kissed Dating Goodbye: A New Attitude Toward Romance and Relationships*, which argues that the secret to maintaining your sexual purity is not to date. *Ever.*

This book came up a lot in my interviews.

"That stupid, stupid, stupid book," my interviewee Meagan railed from across my couch, for example. "What was it?"

"*I Kissed Dating Goodbye*?" I asked, having had so many interviewees talk about it that it seemed a viable guess.

"Yes!" she exclaimed. "If I ever meet that guy, I'm going to punch him in the face."

"Who wrote it, again?" I asked her. "Joshua Harris?"

"Yes," Meagan answered. "Have you met him?"

"No."

"I'm going to punch him." Meagan lifted her fists preparing for a mock fight, "Right! In! The! Face!" Then her fists fell onto the pillow on her lap and she collapsed back onto the arm of my couch. "I don't know," she said, looking up at the ceiling. "I just took it very seriously. I wanted to be good and get into Heaven. And I didn't have any sense of—I hadn't learned to read things critically yet, right? So I was like, 'Here's this thing recommended to me by people I trust who are good. I should read it, and I should do it.' I just took it in. I was like, 'This must be true . . .'"

Before *I Kissed Dating Goodbye*, there were other books. Every good girl in my youth group, for instance, had to read Elisabeth Elliot's *Passion & Purity: Learning to Bring Your Love Life Under Christ's Control*. But from what I can see, *I Kissed Dating Goodbye* blew those books right out of the water. It was so popular, in fact, that, like New Kids on the Block (NKOTB) and Justin Timberlake (JT), the book went by an acronym: *IKDG*.

The author was just twenty-one years old when he wrote it— handsome, single, sexually abstinent, and even more conservative in his understanding of sexual propriety than most conservative Christian parents were. Josh's parents were pioneers of the Christian home-schooling movement and when he was in high school, Josh founded a magazine for fellow homeschooled teenagers. But it was *IKDG* that launched him into evangelical stardom. In the book, he suggests that in order to avoid physical intimacy before marriage Christians should refrain from dating. Instead, he suggests his readers select their "intended" and engage in a period of courtship with the involvement of both sets of parents. He further suggests that Christians manage even their "guy-girl friendships" carefully, avoiding physical, and even too much *emotional* intimacy before marriage.

Josh was *just* what the purity industry had been waiting for.

IKDG quickly became required reading for white,* American evangelical adolescents, teenagers, and young adults who were serious about their faith, selling over one million copies.† Josh, meanwhile, became one of the bestselling evangelical authors of all time. He wrote many more purity culture favorites and eventually became the head pastor of a megachurch.

I knew *IKDG* was huge among people who looked like me, but when reading the transcript of the roundtable in which Laura had participated, it hit home for me just how many more people were impacted by this book in particular, and by white American evangelical purity culture in general, than I had previously understood.

Another one of the roundtable's participants, Rev. Verdell A. Wright, is a preacher, teacher, and scholar working in the American black church. Verdell assured me that, whether or not the churches he works with are considered "evangelical," many of them teach evangelicalism's purity message and push books like *IKDG* as must-reads.

"There are definite distinctions between American evangelical communities segregated by race and ethnicity," he explained. "A professor of mine once said, 'Whenever you talk about Christianity, it's incorrect. *Whose* Christianity? Which one? It's always Christiani*ties*.' But the body

---

* Josh Harris is himself biracial—his mother is Japanese—but he rose to the most fame in the white evangelical Christian subculture.

† *I Kissed Dating Goodbye* received the Evangelical Christian Publishing Association's Platinum Award for selling over one million copies in May 2005.[3]

theology in black and white churches is similar, and there is a *reason* why that is." In short, white supremacy. Verdell explained how people of color have historically had to adopt white values and affects in order to assimilate and survive within the dominant white culture. "So everything starts to taste like vanilla ice cream," he summarized. "The ice cream comes in different colors, but the flavor is the same."

Another of the roundtable's panelists, Dr. Keisha McKenzie, grew up in a Seventh-day Adventist Caribbean immigrant church in London before moving back to her family's homeland of Jamaica. In both of these environments, she told me in an interview, the white American evangelical purity message came in loud and clear. "The sad thing about religious colonialism, which I see *IKDG* as part of, is that it doesn't respect borders well," she said in the roundtable. "I would never have known Joshua Harris's name was it not for this book and his elevation based on it. Even though I didn't see myself as his primary audience, I and others like me reaped the consequences of his work. The US church was afraid of sex and sin, and so we became afraid too. That didn't serve us well."

In an interview, Keisha further explained: "The Christian church is rendered as a trans-national movement—beyond your race, ethnicity, gender. You're suddenly 'in-Christ,' which supposedly subsumes your ethnic/racial/gendered experience. Even in the United States, instead of being a black Christian, you become *a* Christian—which is defined with white, male, straight assumptions, including those about sexuality and the body. And internationally, whatever the indigenous, often majority, experience is, it's overridden, including the indigenous approach to the body.

"Access to the Internet saved me in so many ways," Keisha continued. "Web forums, reading things on the general Web, and social media where I meet people who I would never meet in person. There are people I talk to weekly, but have never met face-to-face. And there is an expression of concern among us. If any of us is having a rough day, we can come to one another and be received and seen. We didn't all grow up within American evangelical purity culture, but religious patriarchy is a common language that has affected us all. Our alliances do not have to be drawn by race or subculture anymore. They can be drawn by shared pain. Shared rage. Shared hurt. Shared healing experiences. And a shared desire and actions taken to heal others."

If the purity movement places stumbling blocks before us, coming together—as those in the roundtable did, and as those on the No Shame Movement website continue to do every day—is what helps us hurdle them. It allows us to point the stumbling blocks out to one another—to say, "Hey, watch out for that one, it's a doozy"; to help each other back up when we fall; to catch one another; and to be caught—sometimes by someone across an ocean from us.

It isn't simple. It isn't easy. The virus of religious sexual shaming does not affect us all in the same way. White women, for example, experience gender-based subjugation, but enjoy racial privilege and will never *really* understand the way in which racism and sexism interact and impact women of color in this country. Straight women enjoy many privileges queer people do not. Cisgender women enjoy many privileges trans people do not. Those who have never been raped or assaulted enjoy many privileges that those who have been do not. And so on.

Yet we come together.

Some, to heal the church.

More, to heal ourselves.

And whether or not our conversations are intended for the church's ears, some in it are listening.

Including Josh Harris.

The roundtable discussion on *IKDG* I mentioned earlier? It didn't come out of nowhere. In the early 2010s, Josh Harris's megachurch, Covenant

Life, was named in a sexual assault case. A woman who attended Covenant Life as a toddler said she was molested by a male babysitter from the church. When her mom told their pastor, she reports that the pastor advised her not to call the police. Instead, the alleged victim was required to meet with her babysitter and forgive him. Years later, the now-grown child and her mother found others sharing stories of similar experiences on a blog called Sovereign Grace Ministries. Together, some of these individuals filed a class-action civil lawsuit. Civil lawsuit attorney Susan Burke told WJLA, the ABC affiliate in Washington, DC: "We are alleging that a group of men, pastors, conspired together to cover up ongoing sexual abuse of children." The suit was later dismissed, in large part because a judge ruled that the alleged victims had to sue within three years of turning eighteen and many were older than this.[4]

But in an interesting turn of events, in January 2015—five years after Covenant Life was named in the case, and a year and a half after Josh revealed to his church that he himself had been a childhood victim of sexual abuse perpetrated by someone in the church—Josh announced that he would be leaving his pastoral post to attend seminary.[5] He said he made the move because he wanted to learn how other religious leaders handled complex issues like child sexual abuse, admitting that the decision not to go to the police may have been a mistake.[6]

In other words, after twenty years of having people listen to him, Josh was ready to listen to others for a little while. And some of the voices he heard when he did that were those from the online anti-purity movement.

"I never went to prom. #BecauseFundamentalism," tweeted Elizabeth Esther, author of the memoir *Girl at the End of the World: My Escape from Fundamentalism in Search of Faith with a Future*, in May 2016.[7]

"@elizabethesther my school wasn't allowed to have a prom. Because @HarrisJosh lol," one of Esther's followers tweeted back to her.[8]

And then, Josh stepped in: ". . . Sorry about that, Jess," he tweeted.[9]

From there, a group discussion began:

"Honestly, your book was used against me like a weapon. But now, I just feel compassion for the kid you were when you wrote it."[10]

"I'm sorry. And I'm planning to dig into that in the next year or two. Again, I'd love to chat."[11]

"Add me to ur IKDG victims. 37, never married, now infertile . . . Many regrets!"[12]

"Kristine, I don't know what to say. I'm sorry for the loss you've experienced and ways my book contributed."[13]

"This tweet made me cry. Had to see if I read that right. Thank you."[14]

"I gotta say, fella, you don't get off the hook for the enormous damage you caused by just saying 'oops, sorry.' Unbelievable."[15]

And on and on and on.

That Twitter conversation catalyzed the online roundtable I mentioned earlier, and inspired the hashtags #KissShameBye, #IKDGStories, and #LifeAfterIKDG. Josh began soliciting stories about the impact of *IKDG* on his readers via his website, and another story collection site* launched in response, targeted at people who wanted to tell their stories but did not want to agree to Josh's terms.

A few weeks after the story collection page on Josh Harris's website went live, I copied the stories featured on the site into a Word doc.[16] The document was 162 pages long. It included stories from the United States, the United Kingdom, Indonesia, South Africa, China, New Zealand, Australia, Brazil, France, Singapore, Mauritius, Canada, Wales, and the Philippines.

From my count, about a quarter of the reviews were positive with people writing things like: "This book helped shape my standards on building godly relationships and friendships," and "I believe by the grace

---

* www.LifeAfterIKDG

of God, and the help of your book, I was spared from YEARS of heart-ache and chasing the dating game." Another quarter of the reviews were what I categorize as "it's complicated." Most of these reviews included both positive and negative commentary.

Half of the reviews on Josh's site, meanwhile, were negative (to say nothing of those who posted on the alternate site created for those who didn't trust Josh with their story). Some focused on *IKDG*, saying things like "If there could be one book that I could unread it would be this one," and "This book was easily the worst thing to happen during my four years of high school." But many spoke about purity culture in general, naming *IKDG* as just part of the damage the larger culture had done to them: "I found myself deep in a pit of self-loathing and fear. I became a fearful and untrusting person. I struggle to this day with the damage I caused myself in my formative years from adhering so precisely to the ideals set in the book. I regret putting myself in chains. I mourn the untapped freedom of learning to love, to forgive, to trust, and to care."

In August 2017, Josh Harris and a fellow seminary student completed a Kickstarter campaign to create a documentary that promises to tell us where he landed at the end of his listening tour. I hope Josh has meaningfully grappled with the stories of those who have been hurt by his work and that this will be reflected in the film. But whatever conclusion this one author reaches about whether this one book (he does not appear to be questioning any of his *other* books on the importance of purity) was more helpful or harmful, it doesn't change what those of us who shared our stories know to be our truth.

And the fact that a major evangelical thinker even publicly *considered* that perhaps some part of the purity message may not be so great for people is illustrative of what I believe is a shift in evangelical culture that activists like Laura, Keisha, and Verdell can take a lot of credit for. As Laura said: "I've seen an increasing number of conservatives who are still shaming but saying, 'Maybe we shouldn't be shaming *so much.*' Even five or ten years ago, you didn't see that in the same way. *We* did that."

The root meaning of the English word *text* is "to weave"—to wind one perspective, one interpretation, one context around another. I like this idea, as even the most tightly woven tapestry is invariably full of holes. It is the holes in the tapestry—the space between the thread—that make it a living thing, able to be undone and done again.

The tapestry I was presented by the evangelical Christian church included only one color of threads—the stories of those who thrived in purity culture, women who found bliss with their husbands for whom they had "saved" themselves, men who would never leave or hurt their wives whose supportive, feminine submission made them feel strong, masculine, and protective of them. In this book, I offer threads of another color—stories from those who did not, or who *are* not, flourish(ing) in purity culture.

Yet this text too has holes.

As this chapter illustrates, the purity message cuts across racial, ethnic, gender, sexual, national, and even religious borders, intersecting with a range of cultures and identities. And so the tapestry must be unwoven and woven again, as the multicolored stories of individual experiences from across multiple spectrums are told. Until, one day, perhaps we will see the loose end of shame's thread appear, and know, the spool is empty.

16

Sanctuary

Pastor Rachael McClair grew up in an evangelical megachurch in Albuquerque, New Mexico. She remembers smoke machines, rock music, and kids getting saved every week. And shame. She remembers shame.

"It was always this war," she told me, propped up by pillows on her bed, her computer on her lap as we spoke over Skype. "I really wanted to be a good Christian; I wanted to be a pure person; I wanted a relationship with a guy who was going to be the head of my household. Or, I was trying to want those things. But I always felt like I was just on the verge of getting called into the principal's office. I'm vocal. I'm loud. It's how I'm made. We would do these women's Bible studies on being a woman of a gentle and quiet spirit and I'd be like, 'Oh shit.'"

Rachael loved her church in New Mexico, but it was beginning to make her hate herself. When a couple of friends said they were driving to Denver for a concert, she decided this might be her chance to start over. Rachael drove out with them, and stayed.

In Denver, Rachael began attending, and then working at, a church called Pathways, which was part of evangelicalism's emergent church movement, popular in the nineties and early 2000s.

"Which—just to be sure I understand," I interrupted Rachael's story, "means that its rules around sexuality and gender would have been the same as a traditional evangelical church's rules, but it being 'emergent' means there would have been some real intentionality around being loving and nonjudgmental toward anyone who were to break those rules, rather than going down the shaming route with them."

"Yes," Rachael confirmed. "I was on staff at Pathways for about seven years. And at one point, I heard God's voice."

"What did God say to you?"

"He said, 'We're going to go somewhere new. But I can't take you there if you keep looking behind you wishing that things were like they used to be.'"

"I don't understand."

"Wishing it was like when I was in my Bible study in New Mexico, for example. God was like, 'I'm not there anymore. You have to follow me into this new frontier.'"

Rachael was later approached by a fellow Pathways staff member named Mark Tidd. Mark had been an evangelical pastor for twenty-five years but had recently taken on a more supportive staff role at Pathways in preparation for planting a new Pathways Church. When Mark confided in Rachael that he wanted this new church to be inclusive, she wondered if this might be the new frontier God was talking about.

"You mean LGBTQ+ inclusive?" I interrupted Rachael again.

"Yes," she replied.

"Okay, go on."

Rachael was one of the first people at the church Mark talked to, but eventually, his intentions became more widely known. Not everyone was as interested in Mark's plans as Rachael had been. Many, in fact, were so upset that they left the church, and Mark himself was defrocked.

So there they were, eight people sitting around a table—Rachael, Mark, and six others asking one another: "Should we make a go of this?" The collective launched Highlands, an independent, inclusive evangelical church, in 2009. Less than a year later, Rev. Dr. Jenny Morgan—a newly ordained United Church of Christ minister who was in a long-term relationship with a woman (both Mark and Rachael, who were co-pastoring Highlands at this point, are straight)—completed what is now the church's improvisational three-pastor team. At the start of each service—which averages around 400 attendees but can draw up to 1,000—Highland's ethos is read aloud:

> *Married, divorced and single here, it's one family that mingles here.*
> *Conservative and liberal here, we've all gotta give a little here.*
> *Big and small here, there's room for us all here.*
> *Doubt and believe here, we all can receive here.*
> *Gay and straight here, there's no hate here.*
> *Woman and man here, everyone can here.*
> *Whatever your race here, for all of us grace here.*
> *In imitation of the ridiculous love Almighty God has for each of us and*
>   *all of us,*
> *let us live and love without labels!**

"But how did your church go from LGBTQ+ inclusive to rethinking the whole sexual ethic?" I asked Rachael.

"It's been an ongoing conversation," she answered, adjusting the pillows behind her. "As soon as you become inclusive, you have to face all kinds of things. Right when we first started the church, for instance, we had a straight married couple that was very frustrated that we were okay letting an unmarried straight couple who were living together host a small church group. They felt that was inappropriate. But they were okay on the inclusive thing. As soon as you open the door, you begin to recognize all your biases and other stuff.

"So it was like, 'We have to talk about this or it's going to become a problem.'" As the years went on, Rachael told me, more and more

---

* The use of this ethos has since spread to several other churches.

complex questions arose. Whether the pastors were approached with questions about polyamory or about sadomasochism, she told me, they guided parishioners to reach their own morally rooted conclusions rather than telling them what was "right" and what was "wrong."

"Our role as pastors is simply to ask the right questions in order to help people find the answers themselves. And that's what I'm hoping the sexuality sermon series we are doing now will accomplish: that it will give people some questions that they can ask themselves that will help guide their decisions around sexual behavior."

To give you a taste of what the sermons in the series Rachael referred to are like, I've included an excerpt from one below. This sermon just so happened to have been given by a trans woman parishioner who is herself a reverend and had been the CEO of a large evangelical church planting company before she was forced to resign upon announcing her intention to transition.

The Bible has very few rules and regulations about sexuality. The church didn't develop its fixation with sexuality until 400 years after Jesus. That was Augustine's fault and he had issues. But that's not to say the Bible does not give us a touchstone for our sexual experience, a place from which to begin to understand a healthy expression of our sexuality, and I believe it happens in the twenty-second chapter of the Gospel of Matthew.

It's Jesus' last public day with crowds at large. After this he's only going to meet with a smaller group of followers, particularly his disciples. So it kind of has a press conference kind of feel. . . . The last question of the last press conference . . . is "Which of the laws is the greatest?"

There were 613 of them.

Jesus answers: "Love the Lord your God with all your heart,

soul and mind." There's a second one: "Love your neighbor as yourself."

Now, it's important to note there was zero surprise in his answer. That's exactly what they expected him to answer. In fact, they began all their religious services quoting those laws. It's what Jesus said next that bothered them so much. He said, "On this, are all the laws and the prophets based." . . . Jesus comes along and says, Yeah . . . no, it's not about 613 laws; it's about three things: Loving God, loving neighbor, loving self.

The forty-sixth verse of Matthew says, "There was dead silence." This was a press conference! They could have enough questions to take until next Tuesday, but they are stunned into silence. And he says, "From that day on, no one dared to ask him any more questions." . . . It was devastatingly simple: Love God, love neighbor, love self. Simple. Not easy. But in that instruction, we have a touchstone for our sexuality. . . . Does our sexual expression show love for God? Does our sexual expression show love for our neighbor? And does it show love toward self?"[1]

When Rachael and I ended our Skype call, I knew: I needed to go out to Denver and see this church for myself.

Susan Camp, a midcareer seminary student interning at Highlands Church, pulled up to the airport pickup in a black Jeep. She leaned across the passenger seat and pushed the Jeep's door open for me. "Linda!" she called my name—her short hair and wide smile visible through the open door. I raised my hand and hurried across the drive toward her. As Susan drove, I asked her to tell me her story.

"I ended up at a Texas Southern Baptist Church revival in the seventh grade because I had a crush on my basketball coach," she laughed as we drove down the highway. "She invited me to go. I was like, 'Yes! We can go *anywhere*! Let's *go*! Let's *do it*!' Little did I know, the joke was on me. Because there was a moment there at that revival when I intersected with God for the first time, and something changed. Something ontologically changed in me. I'm not the same person that I was before, even though I was just a kid."

But the spiritual change Susan experienced wasn't enough for the evangelical community she joined after her conversion. They wanted her to change in *other* ways too.

"I think what fascinates me about being a gay person is that from the minute that that part of me comes out, that's all I am, right?" Susan said. "As a heterosexual person, can you imagine that that is all the identity you get? When you walk in the room, that's what people see? It's who you are?" Susan turned to me for a moment. I shook my head. No, I couldn't imagine it. She turned back to the road.

"It wasn't that I expected they were going to be okay with it. But what I couldn't see was that they were going to completely reject all the rest of me because of it. I was very active in the church; every time the church doors were open I was there. And I knew I had a calling in my life to be a pastor even then. But when they find out you are gay, that's that. My sexuality became my entire identity. So I kept myself out of this transformational spiritual thing that had happened in my life because of the shame that I was carrying about my sexual orientation.

"What Highlands has done for me is help me to understand that the transformational power of the Gospel, it's for me too. It includes me as a gay person. And not only *includes* me, but because each of us are created in the image of God, each of us brings some part of that image that only *we* can carry. So we're not done until we've opened this thing up to *everyone*."

Pastor Jeana Pynes, Highland's pastor of family and children's soul care, was waiting for Susan and me at the restaurant when we arrived. We all ordered lunch and when Susan also ordered a beer, Jeana teased her for drinking midday, and Susan teased Jeana right back for ordering decaf, which "everyone knows is not real coffee." This warm, playful teasing—characteristic of the evangelical subculture—was present in just about every group interaction I had with Highlands folks. And it was little things like this—a particular style of teasing familiar from my childhood, the passion with which people spoke about their beliefs, even the rock-and-roll band and the karaoke-style praise and worship service—that made Highlands *feel* evangelical to me, even though their positions on many issues countered most of their peers'.

Over lunch, Susan and Jeana told me about Highlands's adolescent sexuality education pilot, which they'd just completed. The curriculum they used is called Our Whole Lives (OWL): Lifespan Education Curriculum.* OWL was developed by the United Church of Christ (UCC) and the Unitarian Universalist Association. A secular model with religious supplements, OWL is used in a wide range of churches, schools, nonprofits, and community centers, though Highlands is the only evangelical church the curriculum's UCC coordinator was aware of having tried it when I spoke with her. On its website, OWL is described as a "holistic program that moves beyond the intellect to address the attitudes, values, and feelings that youth have about themselves and the world."[2]

While Susan and her co-facilitator met with the adolescents, Jeana met with their parents to discuss what the young people were learn-

---

* OWL is abstinence-based, and is further based on the value that it is healthier for younger teens to wait to have sex, but it is not an abstinence-*only* educational model. OWL discusses many forms of contraception and disease-prevention, and aims to create safe, shame-free environments for all participants. It also actively incorporates the perspectives and experiences of those who may not see themselves in other sexuality curricula—such as people across the gender and sexuality spectrums, people with physical and mental challenges, and so on.

ing that day, answer any questions parents might have, and recommend how they could engage with their kids about what they were learning.

"One of the parents said, 'I'm not sure I can put my kid through this,'" they told me. "She said, 'My kid isn't even *thinking* about this stuff, and I'm afraid this is going to *get* them thinking about it.'"

In conversation with sexuality educators, I've learned this is a common concern. Parents often want to limit their kids' access to information about sex in hopes that it will delay their interest and involvement. But life gives kids its own sexuality education, and its lessons—learned from friends or on TV, engaged with on the Internet,* or experienced firsthand are rarely what parents want for their kids.

But there's something even more frightening for many parents than their kids having sexual information, and that's their kids having sexual autonomy. Trusting young people to make their own safe, developmentally appropriate† decisions is really scary. But whether we're looking at school performance, healthcare maintenance, political activity, physical exercise, environmental activism, intimate relationships, or even religion, research continuously shows that external rewards and punishments (like "I do this because my parents will be proud of me" or "I don't do this because my peers will judge me") are less likely to support lasting healthy decision-making than *internalized* motivations (like "I do this because it's important to me" or

---

* Studies have found that children start seeing online pornography as young as the age of six and that by the age of eighteen most kids have seen it.[3]
† There are OWL curricula available for groups of almost every age—from kindergarteners to adults—each of which focuses on topics that are developmentally appropriate for that age group. For instance, the seventh–ninth grade curricula that Highlands is using focuses on topics like body image, social media/Internet, bullying/bystander responsibilities, and consent education.

"I don't do this because it makes me feel bad")." Supporting people's internal motivations requires supporting their autonomy, walking alongside them and helping them identify their own values (which may, for some, be religiously inspired) and how they can choose to act on them, rather than dictating to them what's right and what's wrong in every instance.

As I shared earlier in this book, people who receive abstinence-only education, which tends to use external motivations, start to have sex around the same time as their peers and have around the same number of sexual partners overall.[5] Meanwhile, people who receive comprehensive sexuality education, which focuses on giving people a broader range on information (including information on abstinence, condoms, and contraception) in hopes that they will use this education to make their own internally motivated decisions, report delayed or reduced sexual activity (not to mention an increased use of contraceptives when they *do* have sex).[†6]

The more parents at Highlands Church understood this, the more comfortable they became with their children receiving a different tool to help them make sexual decisions than the one most of them had grown

---

* When researchers R. M. Ryan and J. P. Connell studied schoolchildren's achievement behaviors, for instance, they found "the more students were externally regulated the less they showed interest, value, and effort toward achievement and the more they tended to disown responsibility for negative outcomes." In contrast, more internally regulated motivations were "associated with more interest and enjoyment of school and with more positive coping styles, as well as with expending more effort." The findings were essentially the same when studies were performed by other researchers in education and in other fields. In healthcare, for example, internalized motivations have been found to improve people's likelihood to take their medications, maintain their weight loss, and attend treatment for addictions.[4]

† "Two-thirds of the 48 comprehensive programs that supported both abstinence and the use of condoms and contraceptives for sexually active teens had positive behavioral effects. Specifically, over 40 percent of the programs delayed the initiation of sex, reduced the number of sexual partners, and increased condom or contraceptive use; almost 30 percent reduced the frequency of sex (including a return to abstinence); and more than 60 percent reduced unprotected sex."

up with. Rather than receiving a metaphorical ruler by which to assess whether or not they have gone "too far," their kids were getting a kind of Swiss Army Knife, with tools like self-worth, sexual health, responsibility, justice, and inclusivity all at the ready.

Susan and her co-facilitator (a straight male) began each workshop with the adolescents by answering anonymous questions that had been placed in a question box at the end of the previous workshop. "We would bring the questions back to the kids," Susan explained to me over lunch. " 'Okay, let's think about this question through the lens of the values that we talked about,' " she illustrated. "Let's start with self-worth, for example. 'Through the lens of self-worth, how might we answer this question?' " Susan and her co-facilitator were shocked by how quickly the adolescents progressed from asking what they were supposed to think to thinking *themselves*.

"We would just read the question and watch them go! For example, a member of the church was talking with the kids about how sex is powerful, like dynamite, and one of the kids—he's a first year in high school— he raised his hand and said, 'No, I don't agree with that. Because that's like saying sex is dangerous and bad.'

"And I said, 'Well, what would you say then? What's the metaphor you would use?'

"And he said: 'I would use the sun.'

"I said, 'Say more about that.'

"And he goes: 'Well, if you spend too much time in the sun, you're going to get burned. And if you get too close to it, you're going to die. But yeah, if you don't get any sun, you die too. It's like, you have to have a healthy sun exposure.' We're going to steal that metaphor from him for next time we teach OWL," Susan laughed.

Highlands parents and other parishioners I spoke with often expressed a kind of generous jealousy over the programming adolescents were receiving. "A piece of me wants to go to the youth sexuality class that is being offered," one parishioner told me in an interview. "I'm so grateful they're getting that experience. And so sad that I didn't. I spent so much of my adult life being ashamed of being a woman, and ashamed of being a sexual being. I'm thrilled to have a partner who is sitting beside me here talking about this," she said, gesturing to her boyfriend, "but I'm also sad for what I didn't have."

Meanwhile, adult parishioners are finding healing through the sexuality sermon series mentioned earlier. "At first I had this anxiety about 'What are we getting into?'" a male parishioner confessed. "It was a similar anxiety to the kind I felt when I was part of evangelical communities where talking about sex meant having to lay out all the things I'd done wrong. There would be an altar call and you would say all your sins to the minister, and then in some cases get up onstage and tell everybody else everything you'd done wrong. Every week during this series at Highlands, I've thought, 'This is going to be the week it happens. It's going to be this week.' And it hasn't been! Instead, the series has made my sexuality feel *less* life-defining. There's a certain amount of weight to it, but it was *so big* before, whereas now it's just a part of who I am. And that gives me hope that the five-year-old me, and the thirteen-year-old me, might have some chance at healing."

Though a growing number of evangelical churches are opening their doors to the LGBTQ+ community, only a few are teaching the values-based sexual ethic Highlands is (though it is more common in some other denominations). Another evangelical church teaching a values-based sexual ethic is LifeJourney in Indianapolis. Here, adults go through an interactive workshop similar to the one adolescents go through at Highlands—identifying and exploring religiously rooted personal values for sexual and other decision-making in a safe, spiritual space.

Rev. Jeff Miner, the head pastor of the church, went to college at Bob Jones University,* one of the most conservative evangelical colleges in the country. "I began to put two and two together in college, and realized I was what people would call 'homosexual,'" Jeff told me, leaning across the large desk in his office, his hands folded in front of him. "This was '76 to '80, before information on homosexuality was out there. I saw it as a problem that could be solved through prayer. And I felt I had to put my ministry on hold to give God time to fix it. But I didn't want to tell people that was what was happening. So instead, I told them God had called me to change my major to pre-law," he smiled, adjusting his glasses.

After he graduated from Bob Jones, Jeff attended Harvard Law. And, because "God still hadn't answered my prayer that I wouldn't be gay anymore," went on to become a lawyer working out of Washington, DC. But just about every weekend, Jeff was buried in one of the city's theological libraries where he continued to wrestle with the rift between the theology he loved and the lived experience he couldn't refute.

"Actually," he smiled, leaning back in his desk chair, "theologians and lawyers use very similar methods. In the law, every time a court addresses a subject area, you get a fuller and more thoughtful and well-rounded picture of how we as a culture are going to approach that issue. So when you've got ten decisions on a subject area, you have a much more well-developed understanding than when you've got one. The same thing happens with the Scriptures as they build over time.

"I began to study how Jesus dealt with ethical questions, which wasn't something that I learned about growing up," Jeff told me. "I

---

* Bob Jones is probably best-known by much of the non-evangelical world for its ban on interracial dating, which was not broken until 2000 when it became a topic of national conversation after George W. Bush campaigned at the school.

looked at every instance where Jesus was asked to make an ethical decision and asked myself, 'How is Jesus doing this?' And then, 'How can I apply Jesus's approach to ethical decision-making to my own ethical decisions?'

"Jesus will often start with relating a spiritual question to Scripture," he explained. "But he's referring to it in order to go beyond it—to refine it, to enhance it, and sometimes, to put it aside and say, 'We need to go in a new direction.' And then in John 16:12, Jesus says near the end of his ministry: 'I still have many things to say to you, but you cannot bear them now. When the Spirit of truth comes, he will guide you into all truth.' That's Jesus saying, even after he's finished, there's a whole lot *more* that the Spirit of God needs to teach us. So you can't freeze this in time at any point. Even now, we have to remain open to the idea that God is still teaching us things we weren't even ready to receive in Jesus's time."

Using Jesus' approach for making ethical decisions, Jeff reached the conclusion that when it came to sexuality, this was one of those times that the church needed to go in a new direction.

Today, Jeff is ordained through the Metropolitan Community Churches (MCC), a church of refuge for the LGBTQ+ community. In 1997, he moved back to Indiana, where he grew up, and took over a small MCC church of forty people. Many of the church's congregants had been raised fundamentalist or evangelical and, under Jeff's leadership—a man who was trained at one of the most conservative Christian colleges in the country and ordained in one of the most progressive denominations—LifeJourney truly became a "progressive evangelical" community. Jeff tells me that both of these two descriptors are equally important, and that he would never use one without the other.

Like the pastors at Highlands, Jeff is regularly approached by congregants—whose numbers have grown to 350—asking, "'If it's okay to be LGBTQ+, then what about the rest of our sexual ethics? What rules do we carry forward for sexuality from traditional Christianity and what do we reinvent?'" For the first eight years of his ministry, Jeff spent many a one-on-one counseling session walking congregants through Jesus's approach to ethical decision-making so they could emulate it, as he himself had done. Finally, in 2005, Jeff developed an eight-week course so groups of congregants could learn the approach together.

In class, Jeff leads the group through discussions around various sexual issues using this approach. "For example, if a key biblical value is populating the earth, how do we look at birth control now that the world is changing and there is overpopulation? What about sex before marriage now that we no longer live in a lawfully based patriarchal world?" Discussions always start with Scripture, modeling Jesus's approach, but the group is also urged to consider reason, science, experience, tradition, and the individuals' own intuition or sense of the Spirit.*

"I love the verse where Jesus says that a theologian† is like the master of a household who brings out of his treasure what is new and what is old," Jeff said.[7] "There is this dynamic tension between progressive and conservative that I see in Jesus and that I would advocate is a balance we need to carry forward if we want to be authentic Jesus followers—blending the old with the new and living in that dynamic balance. Sometimes saying, 'We've got to stick with this old because it's so wise,' and other times saying, 'No, the Spirit of God has shown us something new, and we have the liberty to move a step forward.'"

Jeff estimates that over a quarter of his church has gone through the course, which they have been hosting every two years since 2005. "People are desperate for this kind of thing, something that creates a safe space in which you can really explore questions," he said. "You can just feel the—relief isn't the right word. You can feel the thank-God-there's-

---

* Here, Jeff is using a modified version of the Wesleyan Quadrilateral.
† "He says 'scribe' but a 'scribe' means a 'theologian,'" Jeff clarified.

a-space-where-we-can-have-these-conversations feeling. After people have taken the course, I see more confidence in people. For example, someone may say, 'Maybe it's normative in the LGBTQ+ community to be sexually intimate early in the dating process with someone, but if that's not what I feel called to, I have confidence that I can say, "No I want to wait."' I see more thoughtfulness. I see more peace of mind."

"Have you ever had people from outside the church join the class?" I asked.

Jeff began to laugh. "We've never *dared* to advertise outside the church!" he bellowed.

The leaders at Highlands and LifeJourney churches had to overcome the stumbling blocks that being raised in the purity movement *themselves* had placed in front of them before they were able to do their healing work on behalf of others. Today, they are dedicated to creating a smoother terrain for those under their religious care. At a time when most churches (evangelical and otherwise) struggle to own their complicity in sexual shaming—be it through the sin of commission or the sin of omission—Highlands and LifeJourney prove it is possible to disrupt the status quo.

I am still a Christian, but I don't go to church much anymore. Maybe if I lived in Denver or Indianapolis, I would. But I can't bring myself to attend a church that teaches purity culture and other things that I know hurt people as deeply as they do, and when I attend progressive churches I sometimes find myself thinking I may as well be at home watching a TED Talk. It's just not my kind of church. When I go to church, I want to throw my hands up in the air! I want to sing at the top of my lungs! I suppose in some ways I am still an evangelical after all.

And so, these days I mostly do "church" at home: Praying, meditating, journaling, reading, and sometimes throwing my hands up and singing praises or laments to God at the top of my lungs in the privacy of my apartment where only my neighbors—who can undoubtedly hear me through my thin New York City walls—are invited to join in. I know my teenage self, rulebook in hand, would have certainly been wary of my salvation. My faith looks very different than what I was taught it must. More private. More quiet (if you're not my neighbor, that is). More my own.

The closest I've ever come to finding a church home as an adult wasn't a church at all; it was a choir. We sang gospel music together. And at the end of every rehearsal, we stood in a circle and shared the most painful and beautiful things happening in our lives, and then, we prayed for one another. That was it. And it was everything. Enough to inspire us to visit one another in the hospital; to sing at one another's weddings and funerals; to attend each other's celebrations; to help one another move or paint our living rooms; and much more. There was no sermon; there were no teachings; but *we* had *church*.

I crossed Broadway and walked down Twenty-Ninth Street—past my favorite restaurant where they roast whole pigs, past the Pakistani place where they always give me extras when packing up my leftovers, past the basement mosque, the street salesmen whose incense you smell before you see him, the sari shop, and the cheap perfumery before turning the corner onto Fifth Avenue. As the front door of the mainline Protestant church where my gospel choir was performing that day came into view, I stopped in my tracks. A huge gay pride flag, larger than any I've ever seen, engulfed the grand entrance of the church with its bright welcome. I knew our choir was going to be singing on the steps of the church for the lesbian Pride parade that day, but somehow, seeing the church take such a public stand still shocked me.

Church volunteers held out trays with cups of water and the paraders

stopped and listened to us sing. I'll never forget the image of the paraders dancing and crying in one another's arms as they looked up at us, or
the image of the woman who mouthed "thank you," her hand over her
heart, tears pouring down her cheeks. I'll never forget seeing them receive what I had needed growing up—the promise that God loved them,
and that some in God's community would stand by them and their sisters no matter *what* they had been told by others.

And then, I heard in the distance the dark, husky boos. The rumble
of two angry men walking quickly while carrying huge signs that told
those marching in the parade they were going to Hell. As they neared
us, the men directed their boos and hisses at our choir. They booed our
claim to be Christians. They booed our saying there was more than one
conclusion Scripture could lead you to. They booed our insistence that
God loved and accepted those marching in the parade that day just as
they were.

I remember how small the men looked. In a sea of celebratory dancing and singing, how dark and shriveled they seemed. They looked up
at us with disdain, and yet, I noticed, they also quickened their pace, as
though afraid. As they moved past us, we sang louder. I smiled bigger,
brighter. I tried to shine God's love out from my body toward them.
Smiling through the tears that were now streaming down *my* face, I
made eye contact with one of the men, and he quickly looked away.

As I sang, I thought about how powerful it was to be standing on the
steps of the church that day. I have had a very hard time going back to
the church after so many years of disappointment and broken trust. But
in that moment, I wouldn't have wanted to be anywhere else. If I had not
been on the steps of the church, I would have been Linda Kay Klein—
a straight ally who just so happened to have a rich spiritual life. My
voice would have been important, but only one voice. But *here*, here on
the steps of the church with my beloved community singing, my voice
meant so much more. From here, my choir mates and I said we believed

God had something different to say than those men with their hateful signs would have us all believe. And *that* is the message those standing before us crying needed to hear.

Remember the old nursery rhyme? The one that you would always do with your hands? *Here is the church; here is the steeple; open the doors, and see all the people?* I've come to believe that this is just how it is. The church is made up of us. Our hands. We are the church. We are the steeple. We are the doors and we are the people. No company, no institution, no pastor can tell us whether we're in or out because it *is* us. You can choose the church or not—that's up to you—but no one can choose *for* you. Because if you choose it, it already *is* you.

Today, when my apartment is still and I am alone, I sometimes sit in the center of a room. I cross my legs, close my eyes, take a moment, and then, I open my mouth and I sing. I start low, where I've come to know my true voice resides. And then, I let the music wander—searching the space around me, telling God the things that I am sometimes too distracted to uncover until the music helps me find them. It is a kind of meditation, a kind of prayer. I allow words or phrases to repeat— praying anger, sadness, joy, and longing into them until the words get worn out and lie down raggedly, panting on the hardwood floor, and I can move past them. And sometimes, when I am very lucky, I sing my way not only through questions but into answers. They show up in my mouth, coming right off my tongue, and I have no idea how they got there except to say that for one brief moment I could hear the voice of the divine in my own.

"Oh!" I exclaim. "Hi, God."

A Message for Readers
from the Interviewees

"What message," I asked most of my interviewees, "do you have for readers who might be seeking healing?" Among their answers, three categories emerged.

1. Know you are not alone.
My message for readers is: You're not alone. You're not alone, and you're not crazy. (Katie)

This journey has certainly been a lonely one in many ways, and just knowing that I'm not alone makes me feel 1,000 times better. (Holly)

2. Know yourself.
Learn who you are. Be okay to get on a bus, or get on a train, or get on a plane by yourself. Go somewhere new, take a deep breath, and find a place for yourself. (Piper)

I wrote this embodiment gratitude practice for those who have internalized body shame: Find a quiet, comfortable place to sit. Beginning with your feet, name why you are grateful for them. How do they enable you throughout the day? Move on to your legs. Move all the way to the top of your body, and include as many parts as you need to. It might help you to gently touch each part as you name your gratitude. If you are able, include your genitals. Re-membering is a process of integrating all of you and understanding that your bodies are here for you, not others. Gratitude helps us to reframe the stories we've been told about our bodies. (Rachael)

3. Trust yourself.

Don't doubt yourself, thinking you're a mess. Accept what's uncomfortable and trust yourself. Trust your own instincts, your own feelings of what's right and wrong, safe and unsafe, because they are not from nowhere. We have deep memories. (Jo)

You have to trust what's in you, which has been really hard for me to learn. I want to say to people: "Trust yourself and believe in yourself." And I just really want to affirm that they're good: "You're good." I just want to say that over and over again: "You're good; you're good; you're good." (Meagan)

About the Interviewees

When I began writing this book—ten years after my first interview—my first task was to connect with the twenty or so individuals I had interviewed in the first three years of my journey. Though I'd had several hundred conversations with people raised as girls in the evangelical church in the years that followed, and drew heavily on those conversations when developing this book, it was the people with whom I'd had my first eye-opening conversations over days, weeks, and months that I knew I needed to talk with most.

And so, I wrote to all those I could find and did calls with as many as would let me. I invited people to be re-interviewed, to comment on what they had told me in the past and to update their story. All but four of my original interviewees who agreed to be featured in the book took me up on this offer, sitting down with me for second, third, and sometimes fourth interviews.

Among those I originally interviewed, the most difficult to connect with were those I originally spoke with who did *not* talk to me about suffering from sexual shame. Most of these individuals did not respond to my most recent outreach. Those who did respond declined being featured or shared so little of their stories that it was impossible to feature them. Though I would have liked to represent the voices of those who felt positively about their experience with the purity movement, perhaps the hesitancy these women had about speaking with me and/or having their stories in this book tells its own story.

While in the midst of re-interviewing people, a number of others contacted me asking if they could also be interviewed. Some I knew well; others I had never met. Trusting the process, I formally interviewed over eighty individuals for this book. Interviewees had either experienced evangelicalism's adolescent sexuality education firsthand and/or are experts on this, or a closely related, topic. These interviews ranged from an hour to several days long. The stories of those I have chosen to include in this book represent themes I have heard from multiple people in interviews and/or conversations.

My interviewees who grew up in the evangelical purity movement ranged in age from their early twenties to their early forties. Unless otherwise identified, they are white. The majority grew up middle class. They were raised across the country and (in a few cases) the world. The communities they grew up in generally fall somewhere in the middle of the spectrum of religious extremity, though they were personally devout in their adolescent years.

I put a great deal of effort into upholding the integrity of each interviewee's story, message, and spirit as it was told to me. I did, however, sometimes make interpretive changes to clarify content and improve narrative flow. For instance, in one chapter I might rearrange the order of a single conversation, whereas in another, I might adjust the timeline more dramatically (for instance, combining several conversations with the same person into one). I sometimes modify my interviewees' and my language with careful attention to upholding the intended message. Scene descriptions, physical descriptions (i.e. interviewee mannerisms while speaking, such as when or how someone sighed or picked up their cup of coffee), and opening/closing/transitional dialogue were sometimes recreated after the interview based on memory. All interviewees were offered the opportunity to see their sections of the book in advance and asked to verify the content to ensure that none of these changes resulted in factual inaccuracies or altered their intended message in any way. The vast majority took me up on this offer, suggesting changes they deemed necessary, which I made.

None of my interviewee "characters" are composites. They are all real people and their stories are true as told to me; in other words, what I have written here is what they said to me. Most are using pseudonyms, and I sometimes change or omit personal and/or physical details to further hide people's identity. Some, however, prefer to use their real names and personal descriptions. This is generally noted in the text.

Acknowledgments

In the twelve years that I spent exploring the purity movement's impact on girls as they grow up, I was never alone. Holy warriors walked alongside me.

I am grateful to be able to acknowledge some of those warriors here, though the truth is that this project has been so much a part of me for so long that nearly every person in my life has in some way touched it. And so, to all of you—including the many unnamed—*thank you.*

To Mom and Dad, you raised me on a theology of kindness. You taught me to be on the lookout for those getting a raw deal, and when I found them, to love them up. I know you never thought that teaching would translate into my writing a book about sex and religion. *Thank you* for rolling with it when it did.

To Jimmie, you once bought me a cherrywood desk crafted out of an organ. "This is where you will write your book," you told me. It is the greatest gift I have ever received. These pages were written on the solidity of your belief in me, and in the importance of my voice in the world. *Thank you.*

To Mariela, you model what it means to be mighty. I wish I could have known you when I was your age. If I had, I think I would have moved through some of the challenges I write about here a whole lot faster. *Thank you.*

To my talented literary agent, Jane von Mehren, and the entire team at Aevitas Creative Management, including Jacob Moore who has since gone west, your wisdom, insight, and guidance on this book was nothing short of catalytic. *Thank you.*

To my expert editor Trish Todd, and the team at Touchstone and Simon & Schuster, your trust in and tremendous support of me—an unknown writer with an aversion to social media—has floored me from the very beginning. *Thank you.*

To my mentors and friends who have offered me insights on early drafts, writing retreats at their homes, and countless other forms of support for this book, *thank you.* I am especially grateful to Cameron Kane; JB; Dev Aujla; Kelly Sheahen Gerner; Owen Campbell; Brian McLaren; Jamia Wilson; Patricia de Jong; Alice Hunt; Carolyn Custis James; Pamela Rossi-Keen; Amy Johnson; Philip Church; Valarie Kaur; Teresa Vazquez; Bonnie Friel; Scott Sherman; De-Andrea Blaylock-Johnson; Kaji Dousa; Madhu Ramachandran; Kate Scelsa; Emma Zyriek; Isabella Johnson; Karen Beale; Michael Kimmel; Curt Thompson; Tama Lane; Rebecca Krauss; Thomas Jay Oord; Karen Strand Winslow; Sarah Derck; Cassandra Farrin; Gabriel B. Grant; Chitra Panjabi; Martha Kempner; Sam Clover; Fiona Maazel; Gary Matthews; Andrew Keltz; Fozzie Nelson; Kevin Childress; Kent M. K. Haina Jr.; Cheryl Klein Bowman; Gary Klein; my writing professors at NYU, Sarah Lawrence College, and the University of Montana-Missoula; The Righting Klub; The Red Ladies Writing Collective; Carol, Kathy, and Jonathan's writing group; Simone Sneed and Mimi McGurl, founders of the UUAX Woodswoman Residency; NYU Reynolds; The Sister Fund; Echoing Green; the Forum for Theological Exploration; and the Marble Collegiate Church Community Gospel Choir.

Most importantly, *thank you* to my interviewees. I am humbled by your courage and your trust. My healing was made possible by your healing, my strength by seeing you so strong. I will never be able to say thank you enough for that.

Notes

Introduction

1 Matthew 5:27–29 New American Standard Bible (NAS).

2 Sigmund Freud, *Totem and Taboo: Resemblances Between the Psychic Lives of Savages and Neurotics*, trans. A. A. Brill (New York: Moffat, Yard and Company, 1918).

3 Curt Thompson, *The Soul of Shame: Retelling the Stories We Believe About Ourselves* (Downers Grove, IL: InterVarsity Press, 2015), 48.

4 Thompson, *The Soul of Shame*, 66.

5 Brené Brown, *I Thought It Was Just Me (But It Isn't): Making the Journey from "What Will People Think" to "I Am Enough"* (New York: Gotham Books, 2007), 89.

6 Frances Fitzgerald, *The Evangelicals: The Struggle to Shape America* (New York: Simon & Schuster, 2017), 5.

7 Barbara G. Wheeler, "You Who Were Far Off: Religious Divisions and the Role of Religious Research," *Review of Religious Research* 37, no. 4 (1996): 289–301, doi:10.2307/3512010.

8 "Religious Landscape Study," Pew Research Center's Religion & Public Life Project, May 11, 2015, http://www.pewforum.org/religious-landscape-study/; Christian Smith and Lisa Pearce, *National Study of Youth and Religion, 2002–2003* (Chapel Hill, NC: University of North Carolina at Chapel Hill, 2003), quoted in Mark Regnerus,

Forbidden Fruit: Sex & Religion in the Lives of American Teenagers (Oxford: Oxford University Press, 2007), 12.

9 Donna Freitas, *Sex and the Soul: Juggling Sexuality, Spirituality, Romance, and Religion on America's College Campuses* (New York: Oxford University Press, 2008), 80.

10 Rachel Hooker (@tangleknits), "Pastor to husband: 'May I give her a hug?,'" Twitter, April 20, 2017, https://twitter.com /tangleknits/status/855114214742020096?ref_src=twsrc%5Etfw &ref_url=https%3A%2F%2Fwww.huffingtonpost.com%2Fentry %2Fchristian-women-on-twitter-unload-about-misogyny-in-the -church_us_58f8f71ce4b018a9ce592e05, quoted in Antonia Blumberg, "Christian Women on Twitter Unload About Misogyny in the Church." *The Huffington Post,* April 20, 2017, https://www.huff ingtonpost.com/entry/christian-women-on-twitter-unload-about -misogyny-in-the-church_us_58f8f71ce4b018a9ce592e05?ncid =tweetlnkushpmg00000050.

11 Reagan: "Dedicated Federal Abstinence-Only-Until-Marriage Pro- grams," Sexuality Information and Education Council of the United States, May 2017, accessed August 5, 2017, http://www.siecus.org /index.cfm?fuseaction=document.viewDocument&documentid= 663&documentFormatId=772&vDocLinkOrigin=1&CFID= 12509806&CFTOKEN=4418cba96dc27fc-FE7F5F9E-1C23-C8EB -80A628AD05F95DE2; Clinton: "A History of Federal Funding for Abstinence-Only-Until-Marriage Funding FY 10," Sexuality Infor- mation and Education Council of the United States, accessed Au- gust 5, 2017, http://www.siecus.org/index.cfm?fuseaction=page .viewpage&pageid=1340&nodeid=1; Bush: "Dedicated Federal Ab- stinence-Only-Until-Marriage Programs," Sexuality Information and Education Council of the United States, May 2017 (as above).

12 "Dedicated Federal Abstinence-Only-Until-Marriage Programs," Sexuality Information and Education Council of the United States.

13 "A History of Federal Funding for Abstinence-Only-Until-Marriage Funding FY10," Sexuality Information and Education Council of the United States.

14 Interview with Doug Pagitt, June 21, 2016.

15 Sara Moslener, *Virgin Nation: Sexual Purity and American Adolescence* (New York: Oxford University Press, 2015), 126, 149.

16 Moslener, *Virgin Nation*, 112.

17 Sara Moslener, "Don't Act Now! Selling Christian Abstinence in the Religion Marketplace," in *God in the Details: American Religion in Popular Culture, Second Edition*, ed. Eric Michael Mazur and Kate McCarthy (London: Routledge, 2011), 200–201.

18 Interview with Sara Moslener, August 25, 2017.

19 "Silver Ring Thing," Silver Ring Thing, accessed August 4, 2017, https://www.silverringthing.com.

20 "Choosing the Best," Choosing the Best, accessed August 5, 2017, http://www.choosingthebest.com.

21 US Census Bureau, *Annual Estimates of the Resident Population for Selected Age Groups by Sex for the United States, States, Counties, and Puerto Rico Commonwealth and Municipios: April 1, 2010 to July 1, 2015*, retrieved October 26, 2017, factfinder.census.gov/bkmk/table /1.0/en/PEP/2015/PEPAGESEX?slice=GEO~0100000US.

22 Christopher Trenholm, *Impacts of Four Title V, Section 510 Abstinence Education Programs: Final Report* (Princeton, NJ: Mathematica Policy Research, 2007).

23 "Dedicated Federal Abstinence-Only-Until-Marriage Programs," Sexuality Information and Education Council of the United States.

24 Interview with Doug Pagitt, June 21, 2016.

25 Thompson, *The Soul of Shame*, 92–93.

26 Mark Regnerus, *Forbidden Fruit: Sex & Religion in the Lives of American Teenagers* (Oxford: Oxford University Press, 2007), 104–105.

27 Regnerus, *Forbidden Fruit*, 106.

28 Regnerus, *Forbidden Fruit*, 107.

29 K. S. Beale, E. Maynard, and M. O. Bigler, "The Intersection of Religion and Sex: Sex Guilt Resiliency among Baptists, Catholics, and Latter-day Saints" (Presentation at the Society for the Scientific Study of Sexuality: Phoenix, AZ, November 2016).

30 Romans 14:19–22 New Revised Standard Version (NRSV).

31 Romans 14:3–6 NRSV.

32 Romans 14:10 NRSV.

33 Romans 14:12–13 NRSV.

34 Zahara Hill, "A Black Woman Created the 'Me Too' Campaign Against Sexual Assault 10 Years Ago," *Ebony*, October 18, 2017, http://www .ebony.com/news-views/black-woman-me-too-movement-tarana -burke-alyssa-milano#axzz53R5Ng574; Stephanie Zacharek, Eliana Dockterman, and Haley Sweetland Edwards, "2017 Person of the Year: The Silence Breakers," *Time Magazine*, December 18, 2017, http://time.com/time-person-of-the-year-2017-silence-breakers/.

35 Hayley Gleeson, "#ChurchToo: Christian Victims of Abuse Join Social Media Outpouring," *Australian Broadcasting Corporation News*, November 23, 2017, http://www.abc.net.au/news/2017-11-24/church-too-chris tian-victims-of-abuse-join-social-media-twitter/9188666?pfmredir=sm.

Chapter 1

1 Rachel Held Evans, *A Year of Biblical Womanhood: How a Liberated Woman Found Herself Sitting on Her Roof, Covering Her Head, and Calling Her Husband "Master"* (Nashville, TN: Thomas Nelson, 2012), 179.

2 "Youth Minister Charged with Child Enticement," *Milwaukee Journal Sentinel*, June 10, 1997; John Lee, "Minister Allegedly Enticed Child, 12," *Post Crescent*, June 9, 1997.

3 David Chidester, *Authentic Fakes: Religion and American Popular Culture* (Oakland, CA: University of California Press, 2005).

4 Rudolph Otto, *The Idea of the Holy*, trans. John W. Harvey (London: Oxford University Press, 1923), 23–24, quoted in David Chidester, *Authentic Fakes*, 78.

5 Rebecca Ann Parker, "Prelude," in *Proverbs of Ashes: Violence, Redemptive Suffering, and the Search for What Saves Us*, Rita Nakashima Brock and Rebecca Ann Parker (Boston, MA: Beacon Press, 2001), 3.

Chapter 2

1 Choosing the Best, *Choosing the Best SOUL MATE: Leader Guide* (Atlanta, GA: Choosing the Best Publishing, 2008), 51, quoted in "Curriculum Review: *Choosing the Best SOUL MATE*," Sexuality Information and Education Council of the United States, 2008, http://www.communityactionkit.org/index.cfm?fuseaction=Page.ViewPage&PageID=1184&stopRedirect=1.

2 N. Giesbrecht and I. Sevcik, "The Process of Recovery and Rebuilding among Abused Women in the Conservative Evangelical Subculture," *Journal of Family Violence* 15, no. 3 (2000): 234–235, https://doi.org/10.1023/A:1007549401830.

3 Giesbrecht and Sevcik, "The Process of Recovery and Rebuilding among Abused Women in the Conservative Evangelical Subculture," 236.

4 Giesbrecht and Sevcik, "The Process of Recovery and Rebuilding among Abused Women in the Conservative Evangelical Subculture," 241.

5 Giesbrecht and Sevcik, "The Process of Recovery and Rebuilding among Abused Women in the Conservative Evangelical Subculture," 229.

Chapter 3

1 Jessica Valenti, *The Purity Myth: How America's Obsession with Virginity Is Hurting Young Women* (Berkeley, CA: Seal Press, 2009), 10.

2 Valenti, *The Purity Myth*, 14, 9.

3 Donna Freitas, *Sex and the Soul: Juggling Sexuality, Spirituality, Romance, and Religion on America's College Campuses* (New York: Oxford University Press, 2008), 84.

4 Mark Regnerus, *Forbidden Fruit: Sex & Religion in the Lives of American Teenagers* (Oxford: Oxford University Press, 2007), 57.

5 "About," Add Health: The National Longitudinal Study of Adolescent to Adult Health, accessed October 29, 2017, http://www.cpc.unc.edu/projects/addhealth/about.

6 Regnerus, *Forbidden Fruit*, 73.

7 Phil Rich, "Recognizing Healthy & Unhealthy Sexual Development in Children," MN Adopt, accessed October 29, 2017, https://www.mnadopt.org/wp-content/uploads/2014/03/Recognizing-Healthy-Unhealthy-Sexual-Development-in-Children.pdf.

Chapter 4

1 Nina Burleigh, "Confronting Campus Rape," *Rolling Stone*, June 19, 2014, http://www.rollingstone.com/politics/news/confronting-campus-rape-20140604.

2 Sarah Larson, "'Spotlight' and Its Revelations," *The New Yorker*, December 8, 2015, http://www.newyorker.com/culture/sarah-larson/spotlight-and-its-revelations.

3 Azmat Kahn, "What's Behind 'Rape Culture' on Campus?," *Al Jazeera*, October 30, 2013, http://america.aljazeera.com/watch/shows/america-tonight/america-tonight-blog/2013/10/30/what-will-change-therapecultureoncampuses.html/; Burleigh, "Confronting Campus Rape."

4 Steve Clapp, Kristin Leverton Helbert, and Angela Zizak, *Faith Matters: Teenagers, Religion, & Sexuality* (Fort Wayne, IN: LifeQuest, 2003), 9, quoted in Debra W. Haffner and Kate M. Ott, *A Time to Speak: Faith Communities and Sexuality Education, Third Edition* (Bridgeport, CT: Religious Institute, 2011).

5 The Catholic University of America, Dean of Students, "Code of Student Conduct," press release, October 29, 2014.

Chapter 5

1 Jennette Lybeck and Cynthia J. Neal, "Do Religious Institutions Resist or Support Women's 'Lost Voice?,'" *Youth & Society* 27, no. 1 (September 1995): 13.

2 Lybeck and Neal, "Do Religious Institutions Resist or Support Women's 'Lost Voice?,'" 21.

3 "Two Sexes 'Sin in Different Ways,'" *BBC News*, February 18, 2009, http://news.bbc.co.uk/2/hi/europe/7897034.stm.

4 Valerie Saiving Goldstein, "The Human Situation: A Feminine View," *The Journal of Religion* 40, no. 2 (1960): 100–112, http://www.jstor.org/stable/1200194.

Chapter 6

1 Joshua Harris, *Sex Is Not the Problem (Lust Is): Sexual Purity in a Lust-Saturated World* (Sisters, OR: Multnomah Publishers, 2003), 111–112.

2 Kristin Aune, *Single Women: Challenge to the Church?* (Carlisle; Waynesboro, PA: Paternoster Press, 2002), 19.

3 Aune, *Single Women*, 23.

4 Aune, *Single Women*, 24–25.

5 Rebecca Traister, "The Single American Woman," *New York* magazine, February 2016, http://nymag.com/thecut/2016/02/political-power-single-women-c-v-r.html#.

6 Robert Wuthnow, *After the Baby Boomers: How Twenty- and Thirty-Somethings Are Shaping the Future of American Religion* (Princeton, NJ: Princeton University Press, 2007), 55.

7 Agnieszka Tennant, "Dating Jesus: When 'Lover of My Soul' Language Goes Too Far," *Christianity Today*, December 6, 2006, http://www.christianitytoday.com/ct/2006/december/17.56.html.

8 Stephen Arterburn, Fred Stoeker, and Mike Yorkey, *Every Young Man's Battle: Strategies for Victory in the Real World of Sexual Temptation* (Colorado Springs, CO: WaterBrook Press, 2002), 113.

9 Stephen Arterburn and Shannon Ethridge, *Every Young Woman's Battle: Guarding Your Mind, Heart, and Body in a Sex-Saturated World* (Colorado Springs, CO: WaterBrook Press, 2004), 50.

10 Jessica Valenti, *The Purity Myth: How America's Obsession with Virginity Is Hurting Young Women* (Berkeley, CA: Seal Press, 2009), 24–25.

Chapter 7

1 James Dobson, *Life on the Edge: The Next Generation's Guide to a Meaningful Future* (Carol Stream, IL: Tyndale House Publishers, 1995), 89–93.

2 Tim and Beverly LaHaye, *The Act of Marriage: A Christian Guide to Sexual Love* (Grand Rapids, MI: Zondervan, 1976), 9–10.

3 LaHaye, *The Act of Marriage*, 10.

4 Interview with Dr. Marlene Winell, November 10, 2015.

5 Luke Malone, "Virginity's Unwitting Casualties," *The Sydney Morning Herald*, May 25, 2012, http://www.smh.com.au/lifestyle/life/virginitys-unwitting-casualties-20120525-1z8ti.html.

Chapter 8

1 Mark Regnerus, *Forbidden Fruit: Sex & Religion in the Lives of American Teenagers* (Oxford: Oxford University Press, 2007), 60.

2 Regnerus, *Forbidden Fruit*, 67, 63.

Chapter 9

1 Julie Ingersoll, *Evangelical Christian Women: War Stories in the Gender Battles* (New York: New York University Press, 2003), 58.

2 Ingersoll, *Evangelical Christian Women*, 53.

3 Ingersoll, *Evangelical Christian Women*, 57.

4 Ingersoll, *Evangelical Christian Women*, 54–55.

5 Layton E. Williams, "Who Owns a Pastor's Body: The Roots of Inappropriate Comments and Congregational Entitlement," Sojourners Online, May 3, 2016, accessed October 29, 2017, https://sojo.net/articles/who-owns-pastor-s-body.

6 Ingersoll, *Evangelical Christian Women*, 15.

7 Ingersoll, *Evangelical Christian Women*, 1.

8 "Religious Trauma Syndrome," Journey Free, accessed January 11, 2018, http://journeyfree.org/rts/.

9 Tina Schermer Sellers, "A Biblical Scholar and Clinical Sexologist Debate Christian Sexual Purity," June 22, 2012, accessed October 31, 2017, http://tinaschermersellers.com/2012/06/22/a-biblical-scholar-and-clinical-sexologist-debate-christian-sexual-purity/.

10 Interview with Dr. Tina Schermer Sellers, August 10, 2016.

11 "About the Flawless Project," The Flawless Project, accessed October 29, 2017, http://theflawlessproject.org/about/.

Chapter 10

1 Norman Doidge, *The Brain That Changes Itself: Stories of Personal Triumph from the Frontiers of Brain Science* (New York: Penguin, 2007), 122–123.

2 Mark Regnerus, *Forbidden Fruit: Sex & Religion in the Lives of American Teenagers* (Oxford: Oxford University Press, 2007), 104–105.

3 Regnerus, *Forbidden Fruit*, 153.

4 US House of Representatives, Committee on Government Reform, Minority Staff Special Investigations Division, *The Content of Federally Funded Abstinence Education Programs: Prepared for Rep. Henry A Waxman*, December 2004, http://spot.colorado.edu/~tooley/Henry Waxman.pdf.

Chapter 11

1 Brené Brown, *I Thought It Was Just Me (But It Isn't): Making the Journey from "What Will People Think" to "I Am Enough"* (New York: Gotham Books, 2007), 29.

2 Curt Thompson, *The Soul of Shame: Retelling the Stories We Believe About Ourselves* (Downers Grove, IL: InterVarsity Press, 2015), 68.

Chapter 13

1 US Department of Justice, Office of Justice Programs, Bureau of Justice Statistics, *National Crime Victimization Survey: 2010–2014* (2015), quoted in "Perpetrators of Sexual Violence: Statistics," RAINN, accessed October 26, 2017, https://www.rainn.org/statistics/perpetrators-sexual-violence; US Department of Justice, Office of Justice Programs, Bureau of Justice Statistics, *Sexual Assault of Young Children as Reported to Law Enforcement* (2000), quoted in "Perpetrators of Sexual Violence: Statistics," RAINN, accessed October 26, 2017, https://www.rainn.org/statistics/perpetrators-sexual-violence; US Department of Justice, Office of Justice Programs, Bureau of Justice Statistics, *Female Victims of Sexual Violence, 1994–2010* (2013), quoted in "Scope of the Problem: Statistics," RAINN, accessed October 26, 2017, https://www.rainn.org/statistics/scope-problem.

2 David Ellis Dickerson, "The Ten Commandments," *This American Life*, podcast audio, May 4, 2007, https://www.thisamericanlife.org/radio-archives/episode/332/the-ten-commandments?act=5.

3 Lilit Marcus, "Josh Duggar and the Sexual Abuse Allegations Rocking *19 Kids and Counting*," *The Guardian*, May 22, 2015, https://www.theguardian.com/tv-and-radio/2015/may/22/josh-duggar-sexual-abuse-19-kids-counting-tlc.

4 Elizabeth Smart, "Child Trafficking Symposium: Elizabeth Smart," Johns Hopkins Bloomberg School of Public Health video, 13:26,

September, 10, 2014, https://www.jhsph.edu/research/centers-and
-institutes/moore-center-for-the-prevention-of-child-sexual-abuse
/news/symposium-on-meeting-needs-of-child-trafficking-survi-
vors/child-trafficking-symposium-elizabeth-smart1.

5 J. K. Rowling, *Harry Potter and the Goblet of Fire* (New York: Scholastic, 2000), 217.

Chapter 15

1 "History of True Love Waits," LifeWay, accessed August 4, 2017,
http://www.lifeway.com/History/True-Love-Waits/c/N-1z0zq7rZ1z13wiu
?intcmp=TLWMain-Hero-History-20131216; Don Beehler, "True
Love Waits to Expand Anti-AIDS Initiative," *Baptist Press*, April 12,
2007, http://www.bpnews.net/25373/true-love-waits-to-expand-anti
aids-initiative-in-africa.

2 Lyz Lenz, "Recovering from *I Kissed Dating Goodbye*: A Roundtable,"
The Toast, June 8, 2016, http://the-toast.net/2016/06/08/recovering
-from-i-kissed-dating-goodbye-a-roundtable/.

3 "Gold/Platinum/Diamond Awards Winners," Christian Book Expo,
accessed October 29, 2017, http://christianbookexpo.com/sales
awards/.

4 Greta Kreuz, "Sovereign Grace Ministries, Class-Action Civil Lawsuit Involving Child Sex Abuse," WJLA News, July 10, 2015, http://
wjla.com/news/crime/sovereign-grace-ministries-class-action
-civil-lawsuit-involving-child-sex-abuse-88894.

5 Suzanne Calulu, "Josh Harris Reveals Childhood Abuse," *Patheos*,
May 26, 2013, accessed October 29, 2017, http://www.patheos.com
/blogs/nolongerquivering/2013/05/josh-harris-reveals-childhood
-abuse/.

6 Michelle Boorstein, "Pastor Joshua Harris, an evangelical outlier,
heads to mainstream seminary," *The Washington Post*, January 30,
2015, https://www.washingtonpost.com/local/long-an-outsider

-popular-evangelical-pastor-heads-for-the-mainstream/2015/01/30
/31827364-a881-11e4-a7c2-03d37af98440_story.html.

7 Elizabeth Esther (@elizabethesther), "I never went to prom. #Be
causeFundamentalism," Twitter, May 10, 2016, https://twitter.com
/search?f=tweets&q=I%20never%20went%20to%20prom%20
%23becausefundamentalism%20elizabeth%20esther&src=typd.

8 Jessica (@jessicakathryn), "@elizabethesther my school wasn't allowed to have prom. Because @HarrisJosh lol," Twitter, May 10, 2016,
https://twitter.com/search?f=tweets&q=%40jessicakathryn%20Be
cause%20%40HarrisJosh&src=typd.

9 Joshua Harris (@HarrisJosh), "@jessicakathryn @elizabethesther
Sorry about that, Jess," Twitter, May 10, 2016, https://twitter.com
/search?f=tweets&q=%40HarrisJosh%20Sorry%20about%20
that%2C%20Jess&src=typd.

10 Elizabeth Esther (@elizabethesther), "@HarrisJosh honestly, your book
was used against me like a weapon. But now, I just feel compassion for
the kid you were when you wrote it," Twitter, May 10, 2016, https://
twitter.com/search?f=tweets&q=honestly%2C%20your%20book%20
was%20used%20against%20me%20like%20a%20weapon&src=typd.

11 Joshua Harris (@HarrisJosh), "@elizabethesther I'm sorry. And I'm
planning to dig into that in the next year or two. Again, I'd love to
chat," Twitter, May 10, 2016, https://twitter.com/search?f=tweets&q=
I'm%20sorry.%20And%20I'm%20planning%20to%20dig%20
into%20that%20in%20the%20next%20year%20or%20two.%20
Again%2C%20I'd%20love%20to%20chat&src=typd.

12 Kristine Kruszelnicki (@kruszer), "Add me to ur IKDG victims. 37,
never married, now infertile. Set bar too high cause of ur book. Many
regrets! @elizabethesther," Twitter, May 17, 2016, https://twitter
.com/search?f=tweets&q=Add%20me%20to%20ur%20IKDG%20
victims.%2037%2C%20never%20married%2C%20now%20
infertile&src=typd.

13 Joshua Harris (@HarrisJosh), "Kristine, I don't know what to say. I'm sorry for the loss you've experienced and ways my book contributed," Twitter, May 17, 2016, https://twitter.com/search?f=tweets&q= Kristine%2C%20I%20don't%20know%20what%20to%20say.%20 I'm%20sorry%20for%20the%20loss%20you've%20experienced%20 and%20ways%20my%20book%20contributed&src=typd.

14 Lana Hope (@wideopenground), "@HarrisJosh @jessicakathryn @elizabethesther This tweet made me cry. Had to see if I read that right. Thank you," Twitter, May 11, 2016, https://twitter.com/search ?f=tweets&q=This%20tweet%20made%20me%20cry.%20Had%20 to%20see%20if%20I%20read%20that%20right.%20Thank%20 you&src=typd.

15 Paul Cottingham (@pcottingham), "I gotta say, fella, you don't get off the hook for the enormous damage you caused by just saying 'oops, sorry.' Unbelievable," Twitter, May 11, 2016, https://twitter .com/search?f=tweets&q=I%20gotta%20say%2C%20fella%2C%20 you%20don%27t%20get%20off%20the%20hook%20for%20the%20 enormous%20damage%20you%20caused%20by%20just%20 saying%20%22oops%2C%20sorry.%22%20Unbelievable&src=typd.

16 Joshua Harris, "Feedback List," accessed July 27, 2016, http://joshharris .com/feedback-list/?pagenum=11&sort=date_created&dir=DESC.

Chapter 16

1 Paula S. Williams, "A Touchstone for Sexual Health," Highlands Church Denver, recording audio, April 17, 2016, http://highlands churchdenver.org/audio-items/a-touchstone-for-sexual-health -paula-s-williams/.

2 Pamela M. Wilson, *Our Whole Lives, Grades 7–9, 2nd Edition* (Boston, MA: UUA, 2014).

3 Nancy Jo Sales, *American Girls: Social Media and the Secret Lives of Teenagers* (New York: Alfred A. Knopf, 2016), 14.

4 Richard M. Ryan and Edward L. Deci, "Self-Determination Theory and the Facilitation of Intrinsic Motivation, Social Development, and Well-Being," *American Psychologist* 55, no.1 (January 2000): 73.

5 US Department of Health and Human Services, *Impacts of Four Title V, Section 510 Abstinence Education Programs*, April 2007.

6 Douglas Kirby, *Emerging Answers 2007: Research Findings on Programs to Reduce Teen Pregnancy and Sexually Transmitted Diseases* (Washington, DC: The National Campaign to Prevent Teen Pregnancy, 2007).

7 Matthew 13:52 NRSV.

Bibliography

Add Health: The National Longitudinal Study of Adolescent to Adult Health. "About." Accessed October 29, 2017. http://www.cpc.unc.edu/projects/addhealth/about.

Arterburn, Stephen, and Shannon Ethridge. *Every Young Woman's Battle: Guarding Your Mind, Heart, and Body in a Sex-Saturated World.* Colorado Springs, CO: WaterBrook Press, 2004.

Arterburn, Stephen, Fred Stoeker, and Mike Yorkey. *Every Young Man's Battle: Strategies for Victory in the Real World of Sexual Temptation.* Colorado Springs, CO: WaterBrook Press, 2002.

Aune, Kristin. *Single Women: Challenge to the Church?* Carlisle; Waynesboro, PA: Paternoster Press, 2002.

BBC News. "Two Sexes 'Sin in Different Ways.'" February 18, 2009. http://news.bbc.co.uk/2/hi/europe/7897034.stm.

Beale, K. S., E. Maynard, and M. O. Bigler. "The Intersection of Religion and Sex: Sex Guilt Resiliency among Baptists, Catholics, and Latter-day Saints." Presentation at the Society for the Scientific Study of Sexuality: Phoenix, AZ, November 2016.

Beehler, Don. "True Love Waits to Expand Anti-AIDS Initiative." *Baptist Press*, April 12, 2007. http://www.bpnews.net/25373/true-love-waits-to-expand-antiaids-initiative-in-africa.

Blumberg, Antonia. "Christian Women on Twitter Unload About Misogyny in the Church." *The Huffington Post*, April 20, 2017. https://www.huffingtonpost.com/entry/christian-women-on-twitter-unload-about-misogynyinthechurch_us_58f8f71ce4b018a9ce592e05?ncid=tweetlnkushpmg00000050.

Boorstein, Michelle. "Pastor Joshua Harris, an Evangelical Outlier, Heads to Mainstream Seminary." *The Washington Post*, January 30, 2015. https://www.washingtonpost.com/local/long-an-outsider-popular-evangelical-pastor-heads-for-the-mainstream/2015/01/30/31827364-a881-11e4-a7c2-03d37af98440_story.html.

Brown, Brené. *I Thought It Was Just Me (But It Isn't): Making the Journey from "What Will People Think?" to "I am Enough."* New York: Gotham Books, 2007.

Burleigh, Nina. "Confronting Campus Rape." *Rolling Stone*, June 19, 2014. http://www.rollingstone.com/politics/news/confronting-campus-rape-20140604.

Calulu, Suzanne. "Josh Harris Reveals Childhood Abuse." *Patheos*, May 26, 2013. Accessed October 29, 2017. http://www.patheos.com/blogs/nolongerquivering/2013/05/josh-harris-reveals-childhood-abuse/.

The Catholic University of America. Dean of Students. "Code of Student Conduct." Press release, October 29, 2014.

Chidester, David. *Authentic Fakes: Religion and American Popular Culture*. Oakland, CA: University of California Press, 2005.

Choosing the Best. "Choosing the Best." Accessed August 5, 2017. http://www.choosingthebest.com.

———. *Choosing the Best SOUL MATE: Leader Guide*. Atlanta, GA: Choosing the Best Publishing, 2008.

Christian Book Expo. "Gold/Platinum/Diamond Awards Winners." Accessed October 29, 2017. http://christianbookexpo.com/salesawards/.

Clapp, Steve, Kristin Leverton Helbert, and Angela Zizak. *Faith Matters: Teenagers, Religion, & Sexuality.* Fort Wayne, IN: LifeQuest, 2003.

Cottingham, Paul (@pcottingham). "I gotta say, fella, you don't get off the hook for the enormous damage you caused by just saying 'oops, sorry.' Unbelievable." Twitter, May 11, 2016. https://twitter.com/search?f=tweets&q=I%20gotta%20say%2C%20fella%2C%20you%20don%27t%20get%20off%20the%20hook%20for%20the%20enormous%20damage%20you%20caused%20by%20just%20saying%20%22oops%2C%20sorry.%22%20Unbelievable&src=typd.

Dickerson, David Ellis. "The Ten Commandments." *This American Life.* Podcast audio. May 4, 2007. https://www.thisamericanlife.org/radio-archives/episode/332/the-ten-commandments?act=5.

Dobson, James. *Life on the Edge: The Next Generation's Guide to a Meaningful Future.* Carol Stream, IL: Tyndale House Publishers, 1995.

Doidge, Norman. *The Brain That Changes Itself: Stories of Personal Triumph from the Frontiers of Brain Science.* New York: Penguin, 2007.

Esther, Elizabeth (@elizabethesther). "@HarrisJosh honestly, your book was used against me like a weapon. But now, I just feel compassion for the kid you were when you wrote it." Twitter, May 10, 2016. https://twitter.com/search?f=tweets&q=honestly%2C%20your%20book%20was%20used%20against%20me%20like%20a%20weapon&src=typd.

———. "I never went to prom. #BecauseFundamentalism." Twitter, May 10, 2016. https://twitter.com/search?f=tweets&q=I%20never%20went%20to%20prom%20%23becausefundamentalism%20elizabeth%20esther&src=typd.

Evans, Rachel Held. *A Year of Biblical Womanhood: How a Liberated Woman Found Herself Sitting on Her Roof, Covering Her Head, and Calling Her Husband "Master."* Nashville, TN: Thomas Nelson, 2012.

Fitzgerald, Francis. *The Evangelicals: The Struggle to Shape America.* New York: Simon & Schuster, 2017.

France, R. T. *The Gospel of Matthew*, NICNT. Grand Rapids, MI: Eerdmans, 2007.

Freitas, Donna. *Sex and the Soul: Juggling Sexuality, Spirituality, Romance, and Religion on America's College Campuses*. New York: Oxford University Press, 2008.

Freud, Sigmund. *Totem and Taboo: Resemblances Between the Psychic Lives of Savages and Neurotics*. Translated by A. A. Brill. New York: Moffat, Yard and Company, 1918.

Giesbrecht, N., and I. Sevcik. "The Process of Recovery and Rebuilding Among Abused Women in the Conservative Evangelical Subculture." *Springer Journal of Family Violence* 15, no. 3 (2000): 229–241. https://doi.org/10.1023/A:1007549401830.

Gleeson, Hayley. "#ChurchToo: Christian Victims of Abuse Join Social Media Outpouring." *Australian Broadcasting Corporation News*, November 23, 2017. http://www.abc.net.au/news/2017-11-24/church-too-chris tian-victims-of-abuse-join-social-media-twitter/9188666?pfmredir=sm.

Goldstein, Valerie Saiving. "The Human Situation: A Feminine View." *The Journal of Religion* 40, no. 2 (1960): 100–112. http://www.jstor .org/stable/1200194.

Haffner, Debra W., and Kate M. Ott. *A Time to Speak: Faith Communities and Sexuality Education, Third Edition*. Bridgeport, CT: Religious Institute, 2011.

Harris, Joshua (@HarrisJosh). "@elizabethesther I'm sorry. And I'm planning to dig into that in the next year or two. Again, I'd love to chat." Twitter, May 10, 2016. https://twitter.com/search?f=tweets &q=I'm%20sorry.%20And%20I'm%20planning%20to%20dig%20 into%20that%20in%20the%20next%20year%20or%20two.%20 Again%2C%20I'd%20love%20to%20chat&src=typd.

———. "@jessicakathryn @elizabethesther Sorry about that, Jess." Twitter, May 10, 2016. https://twitter.com/search?f=tweets&q=%40 HarrisJosh%20Sorry%20about%20that%2C%20Jess&src=typd.

————. "Kristine, I don't know what to say. I'm sorry for the loss you've experienced and ways my book contributed." Twitter, May 17, 2016. https://twitter.com/search?f=tweets&q=Kristine%2C%20I%20don't%20know%20what%20to%20say.%20I'm%20sorry%20for%20the%20loss%20you've%20experienced%20and%20ways%20my%20book%20contributed&src=typd.

Harris, Joshua. "Feedback List." Accessed July 27, 2016. http://josh harris.com/feedback-list/?pagenum=11&sort=date_created&dir =DESC.

————. Sex Is Not the Problem (Lust Is): Sexual Purity in a Lust-Saturated World. Sisters, OR: Multnomah Publishers, 2003.

Hill, Zahara. "A Black Woman Created the 'Me Too' Campaign Against Sexual Assault 10 Years Ago." Ebony, October 18, 2017. http://www .ebony.com/news-views/black-woman-me-too-movement-tarana -burke-alyssa-milano#axzz53R5Ng574.

Hooker, Rachel (@tangleknits). "Pastor to husband: 'May I give her a hug?'" Twitter, April 20, 2017. https://twitter.com /tangleknits/status/855114214742020096?ref_src=twsrc %5Etfw&ref_url=https%3A%2F%2Fwww.huffingtonpost .com%2Fentry%2Fchristian-women-on-twitter-unload-about -misogyny-in-the-church_us_58f8f71ce4b018a9ce592e05.

Hope, Lana (@wideopenground). "@HarrisJosh @jessicakathryn @elizabethesther This tweet made me cry. Had to see if I read that right. Thank you." Twitter, May 11, 2016. https://twitter.com /search?f=tweets&q=This%20tweet%20made%20me%20cry.%20 Had%20to%20see%20if%20I%20read%20that%20right.%20 Thank%20you&src=typd.

Ingersoll, Julie. Evangelical Christian Women: War Stories in the Gender Battles. New York: New York University Press, 2003.

Jessica (@jessicakathryn). "@elizabethesther my school wasn't allowed to have prom. Because @HarrisJosh lol." Twitter, May 10, 2016.

https://twitter.com/search?f=tweets&q=%40jessicakathryn%20Be
cause%20%40HarrisJosh&src=typd.

Journey Free. "Religious Trauma Syndrome." Accessed January 11, 2018.
http://journeyfree.org/rts/.

Kahn, Azmat. "What's Behind 'Rape Culture' on Campus?" *Al Jazeera*,
October 30 2013. http://america.aljazeera.com/watch/shows/amer
ica-tonight/america-tonight-blog/2013/10/30/what-will-changethe
rapecultureoncampuses.html/.

Kirby, Douglas. *Emerging Answers 2007: Research Findings on Programs
to Reduce Teen Pregnancy and Sexually Transmitted Diseases.* Washington, DC: The National Campaign to Prevent Teen Pregnancy, 2007.

Kreuz, Greta. "Sovereign Grace Ministries, Class-Action Civil Lawsuit
Involving Child Sex Abuse." *WJLA News*, July 10, 2015. http://wjla
.com/news/crime/sovereign-grace-ministries-class-action-civil
-lawsuit-involving-child-sex-abuse-88894.

Kruszelnicki, Kristine (@kruszer). "Add me to ur IKDG victims. 37,
never married, now infertile. Set bar too high cause of ur book. Many
regrets! @elizabethesther." Twitter, May 17, 2016. https://twitter
.com/search?f=tweets&q=Add%20me%20to%20ur%20IKDG%20
victims.%2037%2C%20never%20married%2C%20now%20
infertile&src=typd.

LaHaye, Tim and Beverly LaHaye. *The Act of Marriage: A Christian
Guide to Sexual Love.* Grand Rapids, MI: Zondervan, 1976.

Larson, Sarah. "'Spotlight' and Its Revelations." *The New Yorker*, December 8, 2015. http://www.newyorker.com/culture/sarah-larson
/spotlight-and-its-revelations.

Lee, John. "Minister Allegedly Enticed Child, 12." *Post Crescent*, June 9,
1997.

Lenz, Lyz. "Recovering From *I Kissed Dating Goodbye*: A Roundtable."
The Toast, June 8, 2016. http://the-toast.net/2016/06/08/recovering
-from-i-kissed-dating-goodbye-a-roundtable/.

LifeWay. "History of True Love Waits." Accessed August 4, 2017. http://www.lifeway.com/History/True-Love-Waits/c/N-1z0z q7rZ1z13wiu?intcmp=TLWMain-Hero-History-20131216.

Lybeck, Jennette, and Cynthia J. Neal. "Do Religious Institutions Resist or Support Women's 'Lost Voice?'" *Youth & Society* 27, no. 1 (September 1995): 13–21.

Malone, Luke. "Virginity's Unwitting Casualties." *The Sydney Morning Herald*, May 25, 2012. http://www.smh.com.au/lifestyle/life/virgini tys-unwitting-casualties-20120525-1z8ti.html.

Marcus, Lilit. "Josh Duggar and the Sexual Abuse Allegations Rocking *19 Kids and Counting*." *The Guardian*, May 22, 2015. https://www .theguardian.com/tv-and-radio/2015/may/22/josh-duggar-sexual -abuse-19-kids-counting-tlc.

Milwaukee Journal Sentinel. "Youth Minister Charged with Child Enticement." June 10, 1997.

Moslener, Sara. "Don't Act Now! Selling Christian Abstinence in the Religious Marketplace." In *God in the Details: American Religion in Popular Culture, Second Edition*. Edited by Eric Michael Mazur and Kate McCarthy. London: Routledge, 2011.

———. Personal Interview. Conducted August 25, 2017.

———. *Virgin Nation: Sexual Purity and American Adolescence*. New York: Oxford University Press, 2015.

Otto, Rudolph. *The Idea of the Holy*. Translated by John W. Harvey. London: Oxford University Press, 1923.

Pagitt, Doug. Personal Interview. Conducted June 21, 2016.

Parker, Rebecca Ann. "Prelude." In *Proverbs of Ashes: Violence, Redemptive Suffering, and the Search for What Saves Us*. Rita Nakashima Brock and Rebecca Ann Parker. Boston, MA: Beacon Press, 2001.

Pew Research Center's Religion & Public Life Project. "Religious Landscape Study." May 11, 2015. http://www.pewforum.org/religious -landscape-study/.

RAINN. "Perpetrators of Sexual Violence: Statistics." Accessed October 26, 2017. https://www.rainn.org/statistics/perpetrators-sexual-violence.

———. "Scope of the Problem: Statistics." Accessed October 26, 2017. https://www.rainn.org/statistics/scope-problem.

Regnerus, Mark. *Forbidden Fruit: Sex & Religion in the Lives of American Teenagers.* Oxford: Oxford University Press, 2007.

Rich, Phil. "Recognizing Healthy & Unhealthy Sexual Development in Children." MN Adopt. Accessed October 29, 2017. https://www.mnadopt.org/wp-content/uploads/2014/03/Recognizing-Healthy-Unhealthy-Sexual-Development-in-Children.pdf.

Rowling, J. K. *Harry Potter and the Goblet of Fire.* New York: Scholastic, 2000.

Ryan, Richard M., and Edward L. Deci. "Self-Determination Theory and the Facilitation of Intrinsic Motivation, Social Development, and Well-Being." *American Psychologist* 55, no.1 (January 2000): 73.

Sales, Nancy Jo. *American Girls: Social Media and the Secret Lives of Teenagers.* New York: Alfred A. Knopf, 2016.

Schermer Sellers, Tina. "A Biblical Scholar and Clinical Sexologist Debate Christian Sexual Purity." June 22, 2012. Accessed October 31, 2017. http://tinaschermersellers.com/2012/06/22/a-biblical-scholar-and-clinical-sexologist-debate-christian-sexual-purity/.

———. Personal Interview. Conducted August 10, 2016.

Sexuality Information and Education Council of the United States. "A History of Federal Funding for Abstinence-Only-Until-Marriage Funding FY 10." Accessed August 5, 2017. http://www.siecus.org/index.cfm?fuseaction=page.viewpage&pageid=1340&nodeid=1.

———. "Curriculum Review: *Choosing the Best SOUL MATE.*" 2008. http://www.communityactionkit.org/index.cfm?fuseaction=Page.ViewPage&PageID=1184&stopRedirect=1.

———. "Dedicated Federal Abstinence-Only-Until-Marriage Programs." May 2017. Accessed August 5, 2017. http://www.siecus.org/index.cfm?fuseaction=document.viewDocument&documentid=663&documentFormatId=772&vDocLinkOrigin=1&CFID=12509806&CFTOKEN=4418cba96dc27fc-FE7F5F9E-1C23-C8EB-80A628AD05F95DE2.

Silver Ring Thing. "Silver Ring Thing." Accessed August 4, 2017. https://www.silverringthing.com.

Smart, Elizabeth. "Child Trafficking Symposium: Elizabeth Smart." Johns Hopkins Bloomberg School of Public Health video, 13:26, September 10, 2014. https://www.jhsph.edu/research/centers-and-institutes/moore-center-for-the-prevention-of-child-sexual-abuse/news/symposium-on-meeting-needs-of-child-trafficking-survivors/child-trafficking-symposium-elizabeth-smart1.

Smith, Christian, and Lisa Pearce. *National Study of Youth and Religion, 2002–2003.* Chapel Hill, NC: University of North Carolina at Chapel Hill, 2003.

Tennant, Agnieszka. "Dating Jesus: When 'Lover of My Soul' Language Goes Too Far." *Christianity Today,* December 6, 2006. http://www.christianitytoday.com/ct/2006/december/17.56.html.

The Flawless Project. "About the Flawless Project." Accessed October 29, 2017. http://theflawlessproject.org/about/.

Thompson, Curt. *The Soul of Shame: Retelling the Stories We Believe About Ourselves.* Downers Grove, IL: InterVarsity Press, 2015.

Traister, Rebecca. "The Single American Woman." *New York Magazine,* February 2016. http://nymag.com/thecut/2016/02/political-power-single-women-c-v-r.html#.

Trenholm, Christopher. *Impacts of Four Title V, Section 510 Abstinence Education Programs: Final Report.* Princeton, NJ: Mathematica Policy Research, 2007.

US Census Bureau. *Annual Estimates of the Resident Population for Se-*

lected Age Groups by Sex for the United States, States, Counties, and Puerto Rico Commonwealth and Municipios: April 1, 2010 to July 1, 2015. Retrieved October 26, 2017. factfinder.census.gov/bkmk /table/1.0/en/PEP/2015/PEPAGESEX?slice=GEO~0100000US.

US Department of Health and Human Services. *Impacts of Four Title V, Section 510 Abstinence Education Programs*, April 2007.

US Department of Justice, Office of Justice Programs, Bureau of Justice Statistics. *Female Victims of Sexual Violence, 1994–2010*, 2013.

———. *National Crime Victimization Survey: 2010–2014*, 2015.

———. *Sexual Assault of Young Children as Reported to Law Enforcement*, 2000.

US House of Representatives, Committee on Government Reform, Minority Staff Special Investigations Division. *The Content of Federally Funded Abstinence Education Programs: Prepared for Rep. Henry A Waxman*, December 2004. http://spot.colorado.edu/~tooley/Henry Waxman.pdf.

Valenti, Jessica. *The Purity Myth: How America's Obsession with Virginity Is Hurting Young Women*. Berkeley, CA: Seal Press, 2009.

Wheeler, Barbara G. "You Who Were Far Off: Religious Divisions and the Role of Religious Research." *Review of Religious Research* 37, no. 4 (1996): 289–301. doi:10.2307/3512010.

Williams, Layton E. "Who Owns a Pastor's Body: The Roots of Inappropriate Comments and Congregational Entitlement." Sojourners Online, May 3, 2016. Accessed October 29, 2017. https://sojo.net /articles/who-owns-pastor-s-body.

Williams, Paula S. "A Touchstone for Sexual Health." Highlands Church Denver. Recording audio. April 17, 2016. http://highlandschurchden ver.org/audio-items/a-touchstone-for-sexual-health-paula-s-williams/.

Wilson, Pamela M. *Our Whole Lives, Grades 7–9, 2nd Edition*. Boston, MA: UUA, 2014.

Winell, Marlene. Personal Interview. Conducted November 10, 2015.

Wuthnow, Robert. *After the Baby Boomers: How Twenty- and Thirty-Somethings Are Shaping the Future of American Religion.* Princeton, NJ: Princeton University Press, 2007.

Zacharek, Stephanie, Eliana Dockterman, and Haley Sweetland Edwards. "2017 Person of the Year: The Silence Breakers." *Time Magazine,* December 18, 2017. http://time.com/time-person-of-the-year-2017-silence-breakers/.

Permissions

publication, is prohibited. Interested parties must apply directly to Penguin Random House LLC for permission.

Excerpts from *Sex and the Soul: Juggling Sexuality, Spirituality, Romance, and Religion on America's College Campuses* by Donna Freitas (2008) 200w from pp. 80, 84. By permission of Oxford University Press, USA.

Excerpts from "The Process of Recovery and Rebuilding Among Abused Women in the Conservative Evangelical Subculture" by N. Giesbrecht and I. Sevcik. Copyright © 2000 by Plenum Publishing Corporation. Used by permission of Springer Nature.

Excerpts from *Evangelical Christian Women: War Stories in the Gender Battles* by Julie Ingersoll. Copyright © 2003 by NYU Press. Used by permission.

Excerpts from *The Act of Marriage: A Christian Guide to Sexual Love* by Tim and Beverly LaHaye. Copyright © 1976. Used by permission of Zondervan. www.zondervan.com.

Excerpt from " 'Spotlight' and Its Revelations" by Sarah Larson. *The New Yorker* Copyright © Condé Nast. Used by permission.

Excerpts from *Forbidden Fruit: Sex & Religion in the Lives of American Teenagers* by Mark Regnerus (2007) 588w from pp. 12, 57, 63, 73, 107, 153. Copyright © 2006, Oxford University Press, Inc. Used by permission of Oxford University Press, USA.

Excerpt from *Harry Potter and the Goblet of Fire* by J. K. Rowling. Copyright © 2000 by J. K. Rowling. Used by permission.

Index

INDEX

Highlands Church, Denver, Colo.,
    271–80
  adolescent sexuality education,
    276–79
  inclusive ethos of, 272, 272n
  sermon excerpt, 273–74
Hirshfield, Jane
  "For What Binds Us," 258
Holiness groups, 19
homeschooling, 80, 81, 82, 154, 231,
    262
"Human Situation, The: A Feminine
  View" (Goldstein), 109

I

I Kissed Dating Goodbye (IKDG)
    (Harris), 261–62, 263, 263n, 264,
    265, 266–68, 267n
Ingersoll, Julie, 162, 167
  Evangelical Christian Women, 162
interviewees, 69n, 150, 150n, 251n
  about, 31, 31n, 291–93
  message for readers from, 289–90
  pseudonyms, 31, 150n, 293
Intimate Behaviour (Morris), 134–35
I Thought It Was Just Me (But It Isn't)
    (Brown), 15–16

J

John *16:12*, 282
Jones, Blue, 101–3, 104, 109
Joy, Emily, 31n

K

kissing, 2, 5, 11, 13, 119
  as being impure and, 12
  first kiss, ideally from husband, 8,
    13, 24, 77, 135–36
  "half-kiss," 13, 13n, 70

"kissginity," 175
  lack of, woman in late twenties, 121
  purity and, rules for, 77–78
  shame and, 6
Klein, Linda Kay, 244–45
  adolescent sexuality of, 2–3, 3n, 4,
    39–40
  approval sought by, 54–55
  in Australia, study abroad
    program, 42–44, 104
  born again, 38, 56, 58
  breaking free and, 33–34, 198,
    252–53, 257
  "church" at home and, 284–85, 287
  denial of pain, 48, 49
  denial of sexual passion and, 4–6
  desire to be pure and breakup with
    boyfriend, 2–3, 4–6, 39–40, 156,
    156n
  diagnosis of IBS then Crohn's
    disease, 44, 48, 49–50, 55
  eczema and, 183–84, 187
  evangelical church left by, 7, 192,
    256, 284
  family joins evangelical church, 38
  fear of pregnancy (without having
    sex), 7, 183–84, 188, 189–90,
    191, 195
  fears and anxiety, linked to
    church's messages, 7, 33, 183–84,
    186, 187–88, 191–92
  gender and sexuality expectations
    and, 109, 110–11
  as "good girl," 107–8, 110
  identity as Christian/evangelical,
    38, 56–58
  investigation of impact of purity
    movement on women, 7–8,
    31–32, 31n, 193

332

INDEX

Reading Group Guide
Pure: Inside the Evangelical

PURE

LINDA KAY KLEIN

This reading group guide for Pure includes an introduction, discussion questions, ideas for enhancing your book club, and a Q&A with author Linda Kay Klein. The suggested questions are intended to help your reading group find new and interesting angles and topics for your discussion. We hope that these ideas will enrich your conversation and increase your enjoyment of the book.

Introduction

In this fascinating look inside white evangelical Christian culture, Linda Kay Klein explores the purity movement that defined her coming of age in the 1990s. Frustrated by her own shame about sex and intimacy, Klein began a twelve-year journey that took her across the country to speak with countless other young women raised in purity culture—women who, like her, were implicitly and explicitly taught that their bodies were dangerous and posed a threat to themselves and others. *Pure* is the result of her extensive research—part history, part journalism, part memoir—and stands as both a chronicle of pain and a testament to what the human spirit can endure. Through it all, Klein's faith in God remained steady and led her to seek new churches and communities that might better exemplify her understanding of love, God, and fellowship.

Topics & Questions for Discussion

1. In chapter 1, Linda Kay Klein recalls how, at sixteen, she yearned to prove to herself, her God, and her church that "I was good despite my developing body" (page 39). Why does the separation of the spirit from the body come up again and again in *Pure*? Does this imposed separation feel particular to the church, or do you think secular culture also promotes a separation between the spirit and the body?

2. Klein was taught to cover herself so as not to threaten the men in the community with sexual temptation. In this regard, she suggests that women are made to bear the burden of responsibility for ensuring sexual propriety. Discuss this phenomenon from your own experience inside and/or outside a church community.

3. On page 14 Klein concludes that "the purity message is not about sex. Rather, it is about *us*: who we are, who we are expected to be, and who it is said we will become if we fail. . . . This is the language of shame." Consider how the words (i.e., "pure") used in purity culture contribute to the sense of shame that Klein and so many others have felt. What word or words stood out to you as you read?

4. Consider the structure of *Pure*: four sections documenting what purity culture is; challenges faced by girls and women in the church as a result of this culture; challenges girls and women face outside of the church as a result of this culture; and how many individuals and even church communities are finding ways to overcome the damage done by purity culture. Why do you think the author structured the book in this way? If you were to add a fifth section, what would it be, and why?

5. When Chloe confides in Klein that she experimented with oral sex (with girls) as an eight-year-old, she tells Klein she was shamed by her parents, and, at the same time, her parents were shamed by the larger church community. Do you believe that shame can be passed on from one generation to the next? Have you ever seen this happen?

6. "You can't win," one interviewee laments (page 99). Have you ever felt this way when it comes to women and sexuality?

7. Share a time in your life when you questioned an important aspect of your upbringing, whether it was a religious belief or a family tradition or lifestyle.

8. In Muriel's narrative, she shares that she feels God "in her greatest moments of suffering" (page 148), though the experience is different than she had been taught it would be when she was young. Why do you think Muriel feels this way? What experiences have you had as an adult that looked or felt different than you had thought they would feel when you were young?

9. On pages 178–79, Klein presents the idea of "the gap." How did Klein overcome the gap in her own life? Could the image of the gap serve as a metaphor for the entire book?

10. Discuss the irony in the conclusion Eli draws about the evangelical community: that the "ideology is more important . . . than people" (page 201). In your experience, do churches and/or other institutionalized cultural communities sometimes sacrifice people for ideology (or the individual for "the greater good")? If this is the case, can such institutions really be considered *communities*? Why or why not?

11. In your experience, have you found, like the interviewee Jo, that "women are taught their bodies are evil; men are taught their minds are" (page 235)? If so, why do you think it is that church and society place so much more attention on women's bodies than on men's, and on men's minds than on women's?

12. Although *Pure* is a critique of the evangelical purity movement, the author highlights other, positive aspects of the evangelical subculture. On page 276, for example, she describes the "warm, playful teasing" that is typical in the evangelical community. Do you read *Pure* as a criticism of evangelical Christian culture, or as something else?

13. Discuss the ending of the book. Did it surprise you to learn that Klein's faith is still strong, if different than before? How did she manage to take ownership of her faith, from your point of view? Have you ever had a similar experience, either of taking ownership of your faith or of something else that you first learned about from others?

Enhance Your
Book Club

1. Linda Kay Klein invites us into her personal life—even her bedroom—in *Pure,* and readers come to form an intimate relationship with the author. Spend more time with Klein's candor and honesty. With your book club, watch Klein's TEDx Talk (https://www.youtube.com/watch?v=bB99HIBT9b4). Afterward, compare how it felt listening to her voice and watching her speak to reading her words on the page.

2. *Pure* joins the conversation of the #MeToo movement, a conversation that has been long overdue and that is gaining momentum in nearly every industry in the U.S. and abroad. Klein highlights the ways in which evangelical Christianity's purity movement contributes to larger cultural problems, such as silencing and excusing sexual and gender-based violence. Look into the #MeToo and #ChurchToo hashtags on Twitter with your book club. Review the ways in which the narratives feel similar to or different from the narrative that Klein shares in *Pure.* Why do you think this movement is happening at this particular cultural moment?

3. *Pure* offers an ethnographic study of several female experiences in

the purity movement. Ethnography, or the "study and systematic recording of human cultures" (*Merriam-Webster*), can be a fun and hands-on way to conduct research about a subculture. Consider all the subcultures you are a part of, whether they are religious groups, community organizations, or enthusiast groups, and conduct your own informal research into one subculture. Talk to friends and family, take pictures, and offer your own creative reflection on what makes the subculture unique. Share with your book club the results of your efforts. You might be surprised to learn something new about your book club members and perhaps even yourself.

A Conversation with
Linda Kay Klein

Q: *Pure* refers to an extraordinary number of books on shame, religion, and sexuality. If you were to offer one book club suggestion for further reading, which book would it be and why?

A: *Pure* is about the ways the purity movement shames white evangelical girls, but we are by no means the only ones suffering because of it. Recently I've been learning more about the role that white patriarchal hegemony plays in the purity movement and how this undergirding impacts other communities. Right now I'm reading *Sexuality and the Black Church: A Womanist Perspective* by the Rev. Dr. Kelly Brown Douglas. I highly recommend it for book clubs interested in broadening their understanding of how these teachings impact various communities, starting with the black church.

Q: What prompted you to begin thinking deeply about the evangelical subculture? Can you pinpoint a specific moment when you felt called to reconsider your relationship to the evangelical church?

A: If I had to choose just one moment, it would be the moment I write about in the book, when I was sitting on the rocky beach on the edge of the Indian Ocean in Australia and reading those newspaper articles about my youth pastor having attempted to sexually entice a twelve-year-old child under his professional care.

But there's more to that story than I share in the book. The part about my having been in Australia—an ocean away from my religious community—is important. I was too far away to be told how I was "supposed" to feel about what my youth pastor had done when I learned about it; too far away to listen to the sermon I learned about later in which my congregation was instructed never to talk about what happened because that would be gossip, and gossip was a sin; too far away to be pulled aside and informed I shouldn't be angry, but should forgive my youth pastor, and learn to let go of the whole horrible situation.

And so, I *did* talk about what happened.

And I *was* angry.

And I *didn't* let go.

Instead, I wrestled with what happened and how the evangelical church had handled it. And in the midst of that wrestling, I first felt called to reconsider my relationship to the church.

Q: **Do you agree with the interviewee Piper that a real danger of the purity movement is the "hatred of self that comes from that lack of place in the community" (page 66)? How have you dealt with your own "lack of place" after leaving the evangelical community in which you were raised?**

A: To be honest, I experienced a lack of place *inside* the evangelical community more than I ever experienced one outside of it. I first began to feel I didn't belong in the church when I was in my midteens. After all, it's hard to feel like you belong when you are constantly being pulled aside and told about all of the ways in which you don't.

After I left, I leaned into a community of creatives. I found my place as a creator—a music-maker, a puppeteer, a performance artist, a visual artist, a writer. I processed the loss of place I had felt in my religious community by writing music, plays, performance pieces, and so on in a creative community.

Q: **Who is your target audience for *Pure*? What message do you hope this audience will receive after reading your book?**

A: This book is written for everyone who has experienced sexual shame.

I hope readers will have new questions to ask themselves, and new conversations that they want to have with others. I hope they will feel less alone. I hope they will feel less hope*less*, and just a little more ready to break free.

Q: **Describe the research that went into writing this book. What was the process like? Did you uncover any facts that were particularly surprising?**

A: I've spent the past twelve years reading, writing, interviewing, investigating, going to courthouses and public libraries across the country, whatever it took to get to the next answer, which inevitably led me to the next question.

During some of this time, I earned an interdisciplinary master's degree from NYU for which I wrote a thesis focused on white American evangelicalism's gender and sexuality messaging for girls. I also had the privilege of working alongside gender justice activists to create change within the world's major religions, from whom I learned a tremendous amount.

What surprised me most were the egregious forms of sexism and abuse I found among some evangelical leaders and institutions in the process. This book is about how everyday purity culture impacts people, not about extremes, so I chose not to refer to these more heinous ideas and actions, but they still haunt me.

Q: **Your discussion of the experiences of single people in the evangelical culture mirrors our larger cultural bias; that is, bachelorhood is exciting, cool, sexy. For a woman to be single, however, is to be odd, a spinster, or even dangerous. That's the message we're given. From your research and writing, what conclusions can you draw about this?**

A: I believe the legacy of wives being owned by their husbands in this country still haunts us today, emerging in assumptions like it's not okay for a woman to be single too long, though a man has more freedom and flexibility. Rebecca Traister's book *All the Single Ladies: Unmarried Women and the Rise of an Independent Nation* is an awesome resource on single womanhood in America that goes much deeper than I can take readers.

Q: **Do you hope to break any stereotypes with this book? What is the most important stereotype you'd like to shatter?**

A: I think it's fair to say this entire book is about shattering stereotypes—gender stereotypes, sexual stereotypes, religious stereotypes: they all distance us from our whole selves (and from the whole selves of others). In fact, you might even say that the way we sum one another up using stereotypes is what makes shaming possible. We all know what the stereotype of a "bad girl" is, for example. Our cultural agreement around the definition of that term is what gives it its shaming punch for a young woman who is called one or who fears being thought of as one.

Q: **Do you agree that in the end *Pure* is ultimately about *how* you wrote as much as what you wrote—a book about writing a book on a difficult, personal topic? Why did you decide to take this meta-approach to telling this story?**

A: A huge part of my healing journey was performing interviews for this book. Essentially, I put myself through narrative therapy—telling my story over and over again and hearing shades of my story told back to me in the stories of others. And, as it turns out, the interviews did the same for many of my interviewees.

There was a seven-to-ten-year gap between my first and last interviews with many people. In our last interviews, I was surprised by how many people told me our first interviews had changed their lives. They said they had never been asked questions like the ones I had asked them before. For many, it was the first time they had reflected on the messages they had been raised with and how they had impacted them. They added that they felt less alone after our interview. Hearing that there were others around the country struggling in the same way they were allowed them to stop simply blaming themselves for their shame.

In order for readers to understand how my interviewees and I are healing, it was important to show this process.

Finally, publishing this work—telling the world what, at one point, I couldn't even tell myself—is yet another step in my own healing journey. Overcoming my fears around the inevitable shaming that I will receive as a result of publishing my story—a shaming not too dissimilar from that which, at one time, controlled my life though it was only my immediate community shaming me then—is huge for me. And I wanted to share that with readers as well. Because if any of this is ever going to change, more and more of us have to do just that.

Q: Although you are an insider in the evangelical movement, certainly some of what you heard over the last twelve years must have come as a surprise. What was the most shocking thing you learned in the course of your interviews and research?

A: Perhaps the thing that surprised me most in my research was the number of times I heard someone tell me they didn't feel like a person. Many of my interviewees described trying so hard to be who they were "supposed to be" that eventually it became difficult for them to access their true selves, which made them feel like less of a person.

> "I thought, 'I'm going to take it all on, because that's how you show people you love them.' But meanwhile, I just wasn't a person. I had no self. So much of myself was underground."

> "It's hard for me to say 'No, I'm not in the mood,' or 'No, I'm tired,' or 'It's been a hard day at work.' Which are valid reasons not to do something. But for some reason, they're not valid for me. Then, a couple of months ago, I had this thought. I was like, 'I'm a person, actually. I'm a person.'"

It wasn't until people stopped hiding their true feelings, thoughts, desires, beliefs, and experiences, both from themselves and others, that their language changed. For example:

> "I really feel like I became fully myself," one woman—who had previously told me it was difficult to be both a woman and a person in evangelicalism—said of the period of time after she began telling people about the sexual abuse she had suffered.

"The more I had the space to keep becoming a person, the more confident in the goodness of God I was," another woman told me about the years she spent in seminary, after having long denied herself the right to attend seminary, in part because she was raised to believe women can't become preachers.

Q: What advice can you offer someone who feels shamed by their religious or cultural community?

A: I have to go with my interviewees' advice here:

1: Know you are not alone. Not by a long shot.

2: Know yourself. Observe your feelings, your thoughts, your beliefs, your experiences. Don't judge them as good or bad, just simply observe them. And when you are ready, wonder, perhaps, about them. Why you said one thing though you thought another. Or why you feel so much shame after doing something you don't actually think was very shameful.

3: Trust yourself. You know in your gut that the shaming you are experiencing is wrong. But it can be hard to remember that when shame does its work—trying to convince you that your feelings or your experiences are somehow your fault. Hold on to that gut knowledge. Write down what you know. I mean what you *know*. Remember it. And remind yourself of it, pulling that little piece of paper or section of your journal out, whenever you forget: It *is* wrong.

About the Author

Linda Kay Klein is the founder of Break Free Together. She has spent over a decade working at the intersection of faith, gender, sexuality, and social change, and earned an interdisciplinary master's degree from New York University focusing on American evangelical Christian gender and sexuality messaging for girls. Linda lives in New York City with her family.